SHAPED BY SILENCE

SHAPED BY SILENCE

Stories from Inmates of the Good Shepherd Laundries and Reformatories

RIE CROLL

ISER Books

A CIP catalogue record for this book is available from Library and Archives Canada.

ISBN 978-1-894725-53-8
Social and Economic Studies: 83

Cover image: *Silent Scream*, crayon and ink wash, Rachael Romero, 1973
Cover design: Alison Carr
Page design and typesetting: Alison Carr
Copy editing: Iona Bulgin

Published by ISER Books
Institute of Social and Economic Research
Memorial University of Newfoundland
PO Box 4200
St. John's, NL A1C 5S7
www.hss.mun.ca/iserbooks/

Printed in Canada
25 24 23 22 21 20 19 1 2 3 4 5 6 7 8

This book has been published with the help of a grant from the Federation for the Humanities and Social Sciences, through the Awards to Scholarly Publications Program, using funds provided by the Social Sciences and Humanities Research Council of Canada; and by the Memorial University Publications Subvention Program.

To the survivors of the Good Shepherd laundries and "reformatories," and to all who still bear the painful legacy of these and similar institutions.

CONTENTS

ACKNOWLEDGEMENTS

Thank you to Rachael Romero, Janice Konstantinidis, Maureen Sullivan, Chaparral Bowman, and Autumn for your trust in me and for your courage in dredging up many disturbing memories. Thank you for your countless insights and your patience over the long haul.

Thank you to Karen Riggs and Clara for adding your invaluable intergenerational perspectives to this work.

Thank you to Kate Reid for bringing your New Zealand experience with the Good Shepherds forward.

Thank you to Claire McGettrick for taking the time to speak with me about your vital work with Justice for Magdalenes. Thank you too for the connections you created for me and for the many insights you offered.

Thank you to Patrick Galvin and Mary Johnson for hosting me with open arms in Ireland. The outrage that you carried over Patrick's—and others'—brutal childhood experiences of institutionalization as a Raggy Boy and your unrelenting work toward politicizing such conditions, brought me to attention. Although departed, you are both unforgettable to me.

Thank you to Kristin Harris Walsh for your eyes, your ears, your optimism, and for your editorial expertise.

Thank you to the ISER Books team who so attentively helped me to bring this sensitive material to light. Thank you especially to Alison Carr, Fiona Polack, and Iona Bulgin.

Thank you to Brian Titley for your interest in this project and for your generously detailed answers to my questions.

Thank you to James Croll and Karon Croll for your ongoing and genuine interest in this work.

Thank you to Marta Croll-Baehre and Emma Croll-Baehre, two ideologically untamed beings who in another time or place might well have found yourselves inside one of these institutions.

Thank you to Patrick Monaghan and Caroline Sawyer for continuing to ask how it was going, long after most had stopped.

Thank you to Ann Millar for your untiring reinforcement.

Thank you to Rainer Baehre for your patience, your practical and emotional support, your enduring belief in the importance of this research, and for your sage advice.

INTRODUCTION

> *My mother was sent to the Monastery of the Good Shepherd in Halifax [Nova Scotia], somewhere around 1930 … for what she was told was an infinite sentence. Can you believe that? There was no end date on it ... She was renamed Cecilia by the nuns and forced to work in the laundry, in silence…. When she arrived, she was still so small that they had to give her something to stand on so that she could reach the laundry equipment.*
>
> (Clara, interview, 2016)

Shaped by Silence brings together five stories of women from Ireland, Canada, and Australia whose lives were shaped by forced confinement in Magdalene laundries and related reform "schools" operated by the Roman Catholic Order of Sisters of the Good Shepherd. Their narratives include one teen's experience in a Good Shepherd training school in Toronto, Canada; one story of a child born into a Canadian Good Shepherd laundry; and three accounts of adolescent girls who were incarcerated in Good Shepherd Magdalene laundries in Ireland and Australia. In the following pages, I provide a general context[1] for these stories of twentieth-century female confinement, a starting point for understanding the complex and conflicted purpose of these institutions and the Roman Catholic Church's immense influence in defining the character of the girls and women who were committed to them. My introduction briefly traces as well how these institutions moved from relative obscurity to become a ripe political issue in Ireland and, increasingly, elsewhere. As a result, some of the surviving former inmates have come forward to protest the Church's unjust characterization of them and to document the harsh and sometimes brutal conditions of their confinement. These women—generally referred to as "penitents" by the nuns and "inmates" by the state—provide insight into these conditions.

All the women who agreed to speak with me about their incarceration experiences had been Good Shepherd inmates.[2] The Good Shepherds are a French[3] Order founded by Saint Mary Euphrasia Pelletier in 1835.[4] One of the Order's websites tells us that the Good Shepherds moved beyond France and established themselves in Canada in 1844, in Ireland in 1848, and in Australia, via Ireland, in 1863. Directives established for the Good Shepherds in 1890 confirm that the congregation was founded "only to receive

---

1 Some excellent histories and analyses of the Magdalene laundries include James Smith's *Ireland's Magdalen Laundries and the Nation's Architecture of Containment*, Frances Finnegan's *Do Penance or Perish*, Rebecca McCarthy's *Origins of the Magdalene Laundries: An Analytical History*, and Maria Luddy's *Prostitution and Irish Society 1800–1940.*

2 The Good Shepherds are but one of several Catholic orders that ran Magdalene laundries—including the Sisters of Mercy and the Sisters of Charity (Luddy 2007, 77).

3 Although many Magdalene institutions used the Anglicized spelling, Magdalen, I use the French spelling Magdalene, in keeping with the Good Shepherds' origins.

4 The Congregation of the Sisters of the Good Shepherd began as a branch of the Order of Our Lady of Charity (founded in Caen, France, by Saint John Eudes). Each convent of the Order of Our Lady of Charity was independent and operated autonomously. With the Good Shepherds, Sister Mary Euphrasia Pelletier created a new governing structure that permitted nuns and other resources to be transferred between convents as needed. The new congregation received the name Our Lady of Charity of the Good Shepherd of Angers, better known as Sisters of the Good Shepherd.

girls and women, who, have fallen into licentiousness" (Sisters 1890, 60). In the Good Shepherd reform institutions, supposedly convertible souls became a coerced workforce, performing hard, unpaid, and relentless physical toil. Physical labour, isolation from unseemly forces, and prayer were a large part of the nuns' strategy for converting their charges into the Christian image of pure womanhood. This is an objective that Good Shepherd nuns were plainly reminded of by their founder in her instructions: "On your part, you pledged yourself to labour in a special manner for the conversion of sinners, and the salvation of those poor sinful Magdalens who, under you, become penitent Magdalens" (*Conference* 1907, 10). The nuns of this Order, committed to a mission of religious conversion, regarded their all-female inmates as sinful, incorrigible, and in need of moral protection and reform. As we will see, these directives were repeatedly emphasized to the penitents. Moral protection involved the strict regulation and restriction of their sexuality. Therein, it was the nuns' duty to bring their penitents "from the most shameful disorders to a chaste life" (Sisters 1890, 60).

The women who shared their experiences with me were inmates between the 1930s and the late 1960s in institutions that were variously designated as reformatories, laundries, homes, asylums, training schools, convents, refuges, and monasteries. These institutions acquired different names, forms, and purposes, depending on when and where they were located. In England, for example, they were initially sustained mostly as privately funded halfway houses, but in former British colonies, where women's rights were more limited, they became places of forced labour (McCarthy 2010, 2–3). By the twentieth century, they had become part of what James Smith (2007a, 46) dubbed an "architecture of containment," a network of reform that rendered invisible the "women and children who fell afoul of society's moral proscriptions." In Ireland, as well as in Canada and Australia, the Church assumed responsibility for a variety of these institutions, thereby bringing "many aspects of social life under clerical surveillance and a disciplinary regime that emphasised spirituality, frugality and sexual restraint" (Titley 2006, 2). These laundry reformatories flourished throughout Europe, Britain, Ireland, New Zealand, Canada, Australia, and the United States before the last laundry closed in Dublin in 1996.

While historians have yet no evidence to say with certainty that in the nineteenth century women's stays in these asylums were anything but voluntary, the twentieth-century accounts that follow attest to forced confinement under punitive conditions (Smith 2007a, 42–43). O'Sullivan and O'Donnell (2007, 44) further observe that, while in twentieth-century Ireland the stated emphasis was on reform as opposed to punishment, "the regime in some of the industrial or reformatory schools, district mental hospitals, county homes and Magdalen homes in the middle of the 20th century was more austere than many prisons of the 21st century." With enforced stays and unpaid labour, the laundry operations in these longer-term Catholic reformatories also became more profitable.[5]

The Magdalene homes are widely believed by the public to have only housed unwed mothers and so-called incorrigible girls, or any females who transgressed or threatened the Church's moral authority (McCarthy 2010, 8); however, the term "incorrigible" was often carelessly applied. Inmates' alleged wrongdoings also included being unwanted, stolen,[6] socially inconvenient, mislabelled, and disregarded and/or neglected. Therefore, despite their commonly assumed purpose as refuges for pregnant girls and women, the accounts of the women I interviewed demonstrate

5 Luddy (2007, 116) tells us, for instance, that in the twentieth century the Good Shepherds "advertised their laundry services with brochures and price lists." And, according to Clear (1987, 162), "Nuns did not cost very much, in proportion to the amount of work which they performed; they worked until they dropped; and they did not disturb the status quo." The unpaid labour of inmates and nuns in these institutions rendered the laundries lucrative.

6 A reference to Australia's "stolen generation." It is estimated that between one in three and one in ten Indigenous and Torres Strait Islander children were forcibly removed from their families and communities from approximately 1910 to 1970, and some of that population became Magdalene inmates. https://www.humanrights.gov.au/sites/default/files/content/pdf/social_justice/submissions_un_hr_committee/6_stolen_generations.pdf.

that this is simply not the case. It was not uncommon for unmarried mothers to be relocated to Magdalene asylums following their confinement in mother and baby homes, but these institutions were not one and the same (Titley 2006, 10). In Canada, for example, Magdalene homes are thought to have been the forerunner of mother and baby homes (Splane 1965, 248). Similarly, in Ireland Good Shepherd homes had a distinct purpose apart from mother and baby homes, although they sometimes operated in tandem, as part of a "network of communication which facilitated the movement of inmates from one place to another when circumstances warranted" (Titley 2006, 10).[7]

In 1830s Ireland, Magdalene homes, according to Caitriona Clear (1987, 106–7), "ran in tandem with the development of the prison system, the setting up of the work houses ... and the expanding network of lunatic asylums"; "the tendency to 'gather in' certain sections of the poor, to separate them into groups according to need and to control and manage them in a formalized setting took root in many religious congregations at this time." The Good Shepherds' "civilizing" agenda was one significant arm of this control and management system, one which specialized in the shaping and moral regulation of female inmates in all countries where these institutions

7 In 1920s Ireland, mother and baby homes, managed by female religious congregations, operated as a system of services for different categories of unmarried mothers (Luddy 2001, 804). According to Luddy, some homes contained only first offenders, or first-time unwed mothers. These homes supposedly sheltered those sent there from social stigmatization while simultaneously rescuing them from the potential of falling into prostitution (804). "The exclusions enforced by these homes" promised "respectable" society "freedom from contamination" (804). But those who had given birth outside of marriage on more than one occasion—the "less hopeful cases" or the "intractable" girls—were those "whose sexuality had to be managed and contained" and they could be retained for two or more years depending on their number of previous admissions (805–6). Luddy found that, although the duration of women's stays was difficult to calculate, many women spent considerable periods of time in these homes after giving birth, on the basis that they were "weak willed" and required protection against a "second lapse" (804). "What appears to have happened" is that some of these "repeat offenders" were admitted to Magdalene asylums, "which proved difficult to leave" (806).

existed.[8] What is more, where approaches to overseeing women's sexual purity was concerned, state and religious forces worked in tandem. They shared a belief in the rightness and righteousness of "Rescue Work" of the late nineteenth century, when most Magdalene asylums were set up (Finnegan 2004, 227). Their common agenda is a significant factor in understanding why societies did not resist the Church's internment of hundreds of thousands of their female citizens and why investigations into the laundries came historically so late.

As Frances Finnegan explains, concerns about prostitution in the nineteenth century drew politicians, intellectuals, and even royalty into the work of rescuing "fallen women" (7). By mid-century, poetry, religious tracts, and other "Rescue literature" had picked up the rescue theme and played a role in shaping thinking on this subject (15). With this came a growing appreciation for the Church's reform missions as a necessary social safety net and a strengthening of its capacity to operate its institutions with little state intervention or public scrutiny (O'Sullivan and O'Donnell 2007, 11). James Smith (2007a, xiv) maintains that in "a society where even the faintest whiff of scandal threatened the respectability of the normative Irish family, the Magdalen asylum existed as a place to contain and punish the threatening embodiment of instability." Clear (1987, 162) demonstrates that the nuns upheld that mandate so faithfully that, as the twentieth century approached, many of the poor perceived them as an arm of state authority. In Ireland, the Catholic Church's power was so entwined with the state's (161) that inmates' families, in many cases, were reluctant to question the necessity of having their loved ones incarcerated or to examine the conditions of these

8 For a concise and readable overview of Roman Catholic nuns' monasticism, including the context for their social isolation and their rejection of worldliness, as well as a sketch of the rules and practices by which they operated and the stated purpose of various orders, see chapter 1 of Brian Titley's 2017 work, *Into Silence and Servitude: How American Girls Became Nuns, 1945–1965*. For a more comprehensive historical overview of the establishment and development of the Magdalene laundries and reformatories, from a structural and institutional perspective, see Jacinta Prunty's 2017 work, *The Monasteries, Magdalen Asylums and Reformatory Schools of Our Lady of Charity in Ireland, 1853–1973*.

reformatories. Under such cultural pressure, many families co-operated with the Church in these legally sanctioned involuntary incarcerations (Smith 2007b, 453). Further, as the following stories indicate, in families' efforts to evade community perception of moral nonconformity, judgment, and possible retribution, many refused to visit their sisters, aunts, lovers, mothers, and daughters during their internment. Even into twentieth-century Ireland, "No one sought to understand how these institutions actually operated; that religious congregations were in control was enough to excuse official inquiry, inspection, or regulation" (Smith 2007a, 47).

Further confirmation of the Church's power was in its ability to circumvent common legal practice. The Magdalene asylums were not only resistant to "all forms of state inspection and regulation" (Smith 2007a, 78), but the following stories consistently reveal how, in the twentieth century, nuns could and did extend, at will, the sentences of girls assigned to them. Supposedly fixed sentences of say, six months, were almost always protracted to a year. These indefinite sentences left inmates feeling insecure, for any misstep was greeted with the threat of an even longer sentence or confinement in isolation rooms. In this regard, Titley notes that the independent functioning of these institutions in Ireland (and, based on the following stories, in other countries also) often left girls and women without due process. The quotation from the daughter of a Magdalene laundry survivor at the beginning of this introduction attests to the fact that for many there was no "fixed sentence," since these institutions operated outside the justice system (Titley 2006, 12). This point was noted by the Kennedy Commission in its 1970 report on Irish industrial and reformatory schools; it characterized the Magdalene reformatories as "a haphazard system" of dubious legal validity. The commission contended further that the girls incarcerated "in this irregular way" were not aware of their rights and could remain for extended periods without due process, to the point of social reintegration becoming problematic. Of particular note, "In the past, many girls had been taken into these convents and remained there all their lives" (12).

Despite this damning evaluation, the Kennedy Commission posed no serious challenge to the use of Magdalene asylums as a control of female sexual activity in Ireland at the time. For still another decade or more, Ireland was unprepared to challenge "clerical moral authority in such a sensitive matter" (Titley 2006, 12). According to Titley, this nation's "age-old deference to men and women of the cloth" began to diminish only in the 1980s, as evidenced "in declining religious vocations, and campaigns, ultimately successful, for the right to birth control and civil divorce" (12). O'Sullivan and O'Donnell (2007, 31) characterize this shift as Ireland's becoming a more secular and "self-confident" society in the throes of change. Under a variety of fluctuating social conditions, including expanding in-migration, "deeply rooted deference for traditional forms of authority came under profound and sustained attack" (31).

Toward the mid-1990s, the Irish Catholic Church was challenged further, by a series of sexual abuse scandals. Notably, in June 1994, an Irish Catholic priest in Belfast, Brendan Smyth, pleaded guilty to seventeen counts of child sexual assault. As a result, Irish Taoiseach (prime minister) Albert Reynolds resigned, and his government crumpled under assertions that his attorney general had conspired with Church authorities to delay a British extradition order for Smyth. Through the mid-to-late 1990s these and other prominent scandals involving abuses of children by priests, some resulting in lawsuits, surfaced in a number of countries and further eroded public confidence in the Catholic Church. The year 1999 proved to be pivotal in this regard when Rev. Sean Fortune (Ferns diocese) took his life in prison while awaiting trial on sixty-six charges of sexual molestation of boys. Later that year, Mary Raftery's television documentary series "States of Fear" exposed the abuse of children in Irish Church-operated industrial schools, reformatories, and orphanages. Together, these events and others prompted the May 1999 apology to all those abused in Church-run institutions, from the then-prime minister Bertie Ahern. By December 2002 Ireland had established a reparation board to address those abused in Church-run institutions. In order to receive compensation, however, claimants had to renounce their right to sue. By December 2005 the Redress Board maintained that more than 14,000 people filed claims for restitution for reported childhood abuse in Church-run institutions ("Timeline" 2009). As a result of these and other scandals and developments, the Roman Catholic Church and the state were "severely bruised and had lost much of the control and obedience that had for so long characterized their operations" (O'Sullivan and O'Donnell 2007, 31).

In Australia and Canada, the re-examination of these and other powerful structures began earlier. For example, the post-war period, from 1945 to the 1970s, was a time for re-evaluating the usefulness of imprisonment, resulting in the last laundries closing in these countries by the 1970s. Alternatives to incarceration were already being sought in the 1950s and 1960s, but efforts in this direction were energized by the penal reform debates of the 1970s (McMahon 1992, 4). Leading up to the 1970s in Ontario, Canada, for example, a rehabilitative attitude prevailed (xvii). With "the coming of age of rehabilitation" in the 1960s, reform activity accelerated. Maeve McMahon found two interesting features of this shift: "first, that people were sent to correctional institutions as, and not for, punishment; and second, that promotion of self-respect is a key to rehabilitation" (85). It was at this point that new community programmes came on stream in earnest, with a view to "destructuring," deinstitutionalizing, and reducing the arbitrary and excessive application of state power (21).[9] Those I interviewed

9 It was for these reasons and others, such as changing public perceptions of women, and perhaps as Finnegan (2004, 242) asserts, with the advent of domestic technologies such as washing machines, that convent laundries eventually grew to be no longer profitable, and therefore no longer viable as a form of detainment. According to Brian Titley, Vatican II also contributed to making the laundries unprofitable, albeit in an indirect way. He argues that "the liberalization of convent life that emerged from the renewal proposed by Vatican II undermined the foundations of monasticism and probably contributed to the mass desertions that affected most congregations after 1965" (email to author, January 1, 2018). These desertions, in tandem with "the simultaneous collapse of recruitment to religious life," meant that congregations no longer had the supports to operate the network of institutions, such as laundries and reformatories, they had in the past. If institutions closed following Vatican II, said Titley, it was due to lack of resources/personnel rather than to directives from Rome. This rationale is in agreement with Clear's (see n.5).

knew nothing of these wider discussions or of the changes to come; both the conditions and the antiquated reform practices they describe were based on rules established a century earlier and remained largely unchanged through the course of their confinements.[10]

In both Canada and Australia in this era, the criminal justice system was influenced by feminist and Marxist challenges (among others) to the concept of the individual deviant (Sangster 2001, 200; Bessant 2013, 311). Experts were beginning to understand that deviance was informed by a tangle of social conditions. "The word 'promiscuous,'" for example, "used repeatedly in legal judgements to categorize and punish" girls and women (and consistently aimed at those girls confined to Good Shepherd laundries and reformatories), came to be understood as a concept that reinforced class divisions as well as "colonialism and the social construction of 'race.' It also reproduced inequalities between men and women, and separated well-placed middle-class experts from those with marginal social status who were being judged" (Sangster 2001, 200).

Joan Sangster (2001) characterizes the 1920s to the 1960s as "optimistically modernist" in that there existed a strong confidence in the "power of medical and social science experts, to study, treat, and alter criminal behaviour and the suffering associated with it." She further remarks that those advocating for the Juvenile Delinquents Act at this time "believed they were creating a more humane and reformative youth justice system by stressing the alteration of girls' inner character rather than simply punitive incarceration." Such transformations, however, expanded the delinquency classifications and "wove a wider net of informal forms of surveillance." Even within this expanded scrutiny, Sangster found, the need for punishment, for the sake of punishment, was never entirely eradicated. This was especially the case in penal institutions. Even when the workers within these institutions avowed to be operating within a culture of "maternal rehabilitation," the "threat of

10 Janice (chapter 3) is perhaps an exception, since based on an external intervention in the form of psychological testing, it was recommended, toward the end of her confinement in 1965, that she be permitted to attend an external school.

reformatory or training school never disappeared from the legal arsenal" (199). Moreover, this threat was most commonly used "against poor, working class, and racialized women and girls, precisely because the dominant definitions of immorality were associated with class and race" (199–200).[11]

In recent years, growing demands for accountability from the Roman Catholic Church began with legal and scholarly inquiries in Ireland into their various reform institutions. For example, a state interdepartmental committee led by Senator Martin McAleese[12] was set up to probe the facts of state collusion in the Magdalene laundries and investigate the channels by which girls and women had entered these institutions. In 2013, the McAleese Report found that about 10,000 documented women had entered a Magdalene laundry "from the foundation of the State in 1922 until the closure of the last Laundry in 1996. Of the cases in which routes of entry are known, 26.5 per cent were referrals made or facilitated by the State" (i). This report then, importantly, established state involvement and its responsibility for protecting the inmates of these institutions. It also probed such questions as how many girls and women passed through the Magdalene laundries and how long they remained. Prior to this report, such basic details were unknown.

The McAleese Report found too that "the chronicle of the Magdalen Laundries was for many years characterised primarily by secrecy, silence and shame" (i–ii). Because of the Church's unwillingness to reveal its institutional records, as Rebecca McCarthy (2010, 3) points out, the Magdalene reformatory and laundry operations remained cloaked in secrecy, in part because

11 This finding aligns with Autumn's (chapter 5) experience in a Toronto training school in the early 1960s, in which she, as a child of a poor immigrant family, is plunged into a punitive institutional culture.

12 The McAleese Report has been criticized by historians, lawyers, Magdalene laundry survivors, and some of their advocates for numerous reasons, including what reporter Conall Ó Fátharta noted in his July 19, 2013, *Irish Examiner* article: the "vice chair of the UN Committee Against Torture, Felice Gaer, said the inquiry was not independent and failed adequately to examine allegations of physical abuse, forced labour, and arbitrary detention." Nevertheless, this report makes numerous significant revelations, several of which I touch upon in my introduction.

"[t]he convents (nineteenth and twentieth centuries) in England and Ireland were not legally bound to keep records of those entering the Magdalene convents, or of their financial transactions." Despite mounting public pressure and negative scrutiny into their operations, the Church continued exercising its legal right to place such records beyond the reach of anyone seeking information about these reformatories. For former inmates, this lack of access to the documented evidence of their lives in these institutions is symptomatic of the Church's continuing denial of their institutional identities.

Consequently, until relatively recently the "secrecy, silence and shame" mentioned by McAleese effectively served to conceal the experiences of girls and women who had been committed to these institutions. This is significant for multiple reasons. Their sense of disgrace from being repeatedly told that they were banished because of their own wrongdoing was successfully embedded in most of them. The inmates, for instance, were forced to function in almost complete silence. Speaking, except under specific circumstances, was forbidden. Once the girls and women became laundry inmates, sexual control broadened to include an absolute control of their bodies. Their stories reveal too that, upon release, many of them were warned by the nuns not to mention their incarceration. Shame and fear of re-incarceration compelled most to obey this order. For myriad reasons, therefore, a culture of silence surrounded them. It was only in the early 1990s, when investigations into the Magdalene laundries began in Ireland, where the institutions were most widespread, that this began to change. Yet, these laundries did not capture broader public attention until the early 2000s, and Ireland remained the primary focus.

The Morality of the Day

The Magdalene laundries were named after the biblical Mary Magdalene, who, until the mid-twentieth century, was commonly characterized as the converted prostitute who earned the compassion and love of Jesus Christ. While this representation has changed over time, Maria Luddy (2007, 82) notes, "The title 'Magdalen asylum,' used by many refuges, reveals the influence of religious symbolism using Mary Magdalen as the model of repentance and also of spiritual regeneration." This dual interpretation underscores the socially constructed nature of Mary Magdalene, whose "legacy has been transmuted, reinvented, and shaped throughout history to meet a society's particular needs" (Pickard 2011, 99–100). Mary Magdalene, Megan Pickard writes, "went from representing prostitutes and lepers in the medieval era, to representing prostitutes, fallen women and any other females who deviated from middle-class norms and ideologies of respectability in the nineteenth century" (99–100). Regardless of the actual circumstances which led to the incarceration of "fallen women ... [t]he washing of linens was an appropriate job for a reforming prostitute because it washed away her sins in the same manner Mary Magdalene washed away her sins when she anointed Christ's feet during her reformation" (80). Thus, the laundry inmates were called Magdalenes, or "Maggies," and long held this association with prostitution.

The laundries changed over time. They began primarily as short-term refuges for women, operated by a variety of Christian denominations and lay groups (Luddy 2007, 77) that provided a place for women who, like Mary, had committed moral transgressions. These refuges operated on the belief that temporarily isolating women who were "morally vulnerable" or, in other words, those who might give in to unseemly social influences, would ultimately steer them in a more honourable direction. Moreover, they would be provided with practical working skills, such as laundering. Initially, laundry stays were said to be voluntary. However, when the Catholic Church appropriated them as convent institutions, they held more inmates and kept them for longer periods of time (94).

Specifically, the Good Shepherd's belief that "wayward" women needed to be taken possession of and given protection helped to validate and legitimatize their "rescue" and reform approach. This belief, used to rationalize their control and subordination, is part of what Vivienne Jabri (2013, 134) calls a "protectionist discourse." Confinement in the name of protection, as Jabri suggests, "confers primacy to the dominant, but also impunity" (134).

The Roman Catholic Church's large scale and organized management of women's moral protection granted them licence to guard and reshape "incorrigible" females in any way they saw fit. To historians, says Sangster (2002, 3), the word *protection* "sends off alarm bells." In her work on delinquent girls in English Canada, she notes that this ethos has been and remains problematic: "Protection meant the increased moral surveillance of working-class and poor girls; protection meant incarcerating 'promiscuous' girls who had not broken the law but were deemed in need of moral re-education" (3). As Sangster (2001, 3) also notes, protection as judgmental surveillance "slid into stigmatization, marginalization, and incarceration." This general dynamic is reflected in the transnational stories that were shared with me.

The women I interviewed said that, once incarcerated, they were not only viewed as sinners but also objectified as delinquents, confined against their will, and dispossessed of personal rights and identities. The nuns, they told me, viewed them as unalterably deviant and regularly berated them through such messages as they "would never amount to anything" (Rachael Romero, interview, 2012). They were made to feel that their moral character was beyond redemption. Rachael Romero, a former Australian laundry inmate, viewed this objectification as "the most abusive thing of all.... that sense of condemnation of us." Beneath the nuns' project of gentle care and "doing good" lay instead what inmates experienced as a devastating judgment. This contradiction of purpose between hope and hopelessness had long-term destructive consequences for the girls and women whom the Church and the state targeted for "saving" but who were simultaneously treated as unsalvageable.

Rachael told me that she and others turned this harmful branding of their character inward, so that it became part of their self-identity, and they grew to identify with the labels used to justify their incarceration. For many inmates, this became a self-defeating cycle in a pattern which Michel Foucault (1997, 182) terms the "art of punishing." This indirect psychological approach to punishment carried the expectation that inmates would accept themselves as "deviant" by internalizing the external rationales for their incarceration. For those I interviewed, such labels became a reality both in the short and the long term. Upon their release, former inmates lived with an unrelenting sense of having done something wrong and an accompanying fear of re-incarceration. For many, the condemning judgments formally applied to them became a part of who they were. This sense of having personal moral responsibility for their incarceration, initially reinforced by family abandonment, community perception, and Church judgment, subsequently silenced them about their experiences in the laundries/reformatories. These institutions left a crushing legacy on such survivors in the form of life-long identity conflict resulting from a combination of forced confinement, stigmatization, and punishment. As the following stories reveal, the many forms of punishment left them with a lasting sense of exile from their communities, a sustained wariness of the Catholic Church, and loss of trust in other forms of authority.

Locks and Regimens: The Micromanagement of Morality

The 1890 Good Shepherd regulations had set the stage and made clear the conduct and practices that nuns and inmates alike were to follow—they provided an operational blueprint to completely standardize such reformatories from country to country. Early guidebooks outlined times and locations for speaking, topics of conversation, and even the language that nuns used to address inmates, practices that remained strictly regulated as late as the 1950s and 1960s, and in some cases beyond. For example, one such rule book stated that "[t]he penitents are always called by the sweet name of 'children' and in respect for her feelings each one is given a different name from that which she bore in the world" (Sisters 1890, 9). Calling adult inmates "children" effectively infantilized and disempowered them, stripped them of their names, and robbed them of their identities. According to Claire McGettrick of Ireland's Justice for Magdalenes, the re-naming of the inmates upon incarceration had a dramatic impact on their identities: "One minute they were Jane Smith, the next they were Mary Murphy or worse still, a number." This was a focused and deliberate levelling of identity aimed at punishing non-conforming women (McGettrick, interview, 2009). Inmates were repeatedly told that their old identities were a source of shame and thus needed to be taken from them for their own good. Furthermore, along with changing their names, they were forbidden to mention the outside world: "They are never allowed to speak to one another of their relatives or of their past life" (Sisters 1890, 9). Former inmates say that the removal of their names and the enforced lack of reference to their previous lives left them deeply fragmented.

In addition to separating inmates from their pasts, they were strictly segregated from the nuns within these institutions. Rather than working closely with the girls and women in a mentoring and caregiving role, the nuns maintained a prisoner/guard relationship. Further, they made it clear that the inmates would never be fit to join their ranks. At best, they could aspire to become Magdalenes, those whose very name forever marked them as fallen women. This attitude and conduct were formally prescribed for the nuns:

> If any of them [inmates] wish to become a Religious, she shall be sent to the Monasteries destined for the reception of Penitents; for they shall never be received as Religious in this or in any other house of the same order, whatever qualifications or talents they may possess. But they may be admitted amongst the Magdalens, when they shall have been sufficiently tried, and that the Superioress considers them worthy and capable. (Sisters 1890, 61–62)

This separation between the "pure" nuns and the morally tainted, impure Others—the women and girls of the laundries—was not to be bridged.

Rachael recalled how stigmatizing and demoralizing this separation was to her, because the nuns taught the inmates to view themselves as impure and held this label over them as an unalterable personal flaw:

> The stigma thing, I was thinking about that and how the whole climate of the religious stigmata stuff played into it and how we were put down by the nuns as fallen. And I don't know if you realize this but there is a Magdalene order. And I remember at one point I was trying to escape so I spent a lot of time going to the chapel and going through the motions of prayer.... eyeing the only window that wasn't barred which was up high above the altar, something that I could kick in. Anyway, they came to me and said maybe I would be interested in converting to Catholicism and becoming a Magdalene nun. And I said, "why would I have to be a Magdalene? Why couldn't I be a Carmelite [laughter]?" And they said no way ... only a Magdalene because basically you are fallen, besmirched, soiled. And you can't, unless you're pure, be anything else. (Romero, interview, 2013)

Another Australian Good Shepherd laundry inmate, Janice Konstantinidis, also recalled this feeling of segregation. As a lonely and "terrified" child in a Good Shepherd home, she could not fathom why the nuns would not comfort her. "The girls were not allowed to touch the nuns," she told me, and the nuns showed them no affection (Konstantinidis, interview, 2014). Janice gradually learned that, in mind, body, and spirit, the nuns remained deliberately above and beyond inmate contact. This too was in keeping with their original rules of conduct:

> They [inmates] shall have their Refectory, Dormitory, Chapel, Garden, Courtyard, and the rest, entirely separated from the Religious by a wall, with a turn in it, by which all they require to eat or drink, or for any other purpose, shall be passed to them: so that although they be in the same Monastery, they shall have no communication with the Religious, excepting with those who govern them ... (Sisters 1890, 60)

In describing her experience in a Canadian Good Shepherd training school, Autumn[13] mentioned locked doorways that separated the nuns from the girls in their custody. The sound of the keys that signalled the arrival of a nun each morning to the inmates' quarters was a memory that stayed with her into adulthood. To be locked in her dormitory each night heightened Autumn's sense of alienation because it stressed her captive state. Again, like many other Good Shepherd practices, this prison-like strategy was outlined in an original Good Shepherd document:

> In this wall there shall be a door by which the Religious with the order of the Superioress, shall enter every morning the house of the Penitents, to remain with them during the day, in a room where they shall all assemble together, to watch over their conduct, cause them to pray to God, make spiritual lectures for them at the appointed hours, and oblige them to work the rest of the time. (Sisters 1890, 61–62)

Autumn recalled that most doors in the reformatory were always locked so that inmates could be effectively controlled. It was particularly memorable for her that the nuns' quarters "where they slept after they locked us up for the night" were inaccessible to the inmates (Autumn, interview, 2014). This strict separation emphasized for her the taintedness of the inmate population.

Autumn's memory is consistent with the original directives to which the nuns were expected to conform:

> After the prayers and examination, in the evening, the Penitents shall retire to their cells, and the Religious shall lock the door in the afore-said wall, and carry the key to the Superioress; they shall then withdraw to their own room, which ought to be contiguous to the apartment of the Penitents, and in

13 Autumn is a pseudonym.

> which there should be a door, of which the Religious shall keep the key, in order to be able to enter their dormitory in case of an accident. (Sisters 1890, 61)

Segregation was thus coupled with a strategy of surveillance. In her own archival research several years ago, Autumn found the original blueprints for the Good Shepherd reformatory in Toronto in which she had been held. The plans included a sketch of a two-way mirror linking the girls' dormitory to the nuns' room (Autumn, interview, 2014). From there, undetected, the nuns could watch the dormitories while remaining physically separate from the inmates.

Rachael too remembered the feeling of being chronically watched by the nuns; she described, for example, "an egress" in her dormitory where a nun could "hide and watch till lights out." In this small window, there was "a Madonna with a light." On her first night there, Rachael said, it "scared the bejesus out of [her]" (Romero, interview, 2016). Small details, such as this window, were purposeful, as outlined years earlier in the Good Shepherd guidebook:

> Further, there ought to be in the same room a little grated window, closing on the side of the Religious, and a lamp lighted opposite an image of the Blessed Virgin, which image shall be in the dormitory of the Penitents, opposite the window. (Sisters 1890, 61)

These excerpts from an early Good Shepherd guidebook cross-reference some of the practices and physical conditions, such as locked doors and inmate segregation, that remained consistent throughout the history of these institutions. The Order's original rules reinforce the legitimacy of inmates' accounts and their memories.

The Catholic Church in Ireland and elsewhere denied that inmate detentions were involuntary, except when girls and women were "condemned to seclusion by legitimate and competent authority" (Sisters 1890, 62). In those cases, the penitent was mandated to "submit to the penalty decreed and appointed by authority" (62). As indicated above, historians found little evidence to dispute that claim. However, inmates' testimonials from the twentieth century confirm a different picture. The women I spoke to recalled that, in order to be released, inmates had to go to extreme measures, such as self-injury or repeated runaway attempts. Even still, in the latter case, when runaways were caught, they were frequently returned to the Good Shepherds. The Order's original directives from 1890 demonstrate that nuns were expected to go to great lengths to keep inmates confined to their institutions, including the use of solitary confinement, when necessary:

> If any one of them be tempted to leave before being sufficiently instructed and solidly grounded in the fear of God, or who becomes obstinate and malicious, everything shall be done to retain her, first by way of gentleness and remonstrance; afterwards, if it be necessary, severity shall be employed, and some punishment, as confinement or some other penance. (62)

As this rule demonstrates, and the following stories corroborate, inmates were often powerless to resist their confinement.

According to the following accounts, girls who attempted to run away were hunted down and returned to the nuns by the police, often with the co-operation of Social Services.[14] This working relationship between the Church and the state appears to have been limited mainly to the business of ensuring that inmates remained incarcerated. Beyond this cursory and temporary contact, there is little to further suggest any state supervision of inmates. State intervention in Good Shepherd operations was something the former inmates whom I interviewed longed for. They often yearned for

14 See, for example, chapter 2, "Baptized in Disinfectant" (99) or chapter 3, "Behind the Clock" (148).

rescue from what they described as the cruel and unwarranted conditions of their incarceration, all the while doubting that Social-Services-related agencies were even aware of their situation. Aside from the tasks of returning runaways and performing annual inspections or ceremonial visits, state representatives rarely entered the reformatories. Their role in these places was at best ceremonial, with token appearances by visiting dignitaries in which inmates were paraded before them in fine outfits, sometimes performing skits.

Expunged Identities

Early Good Shepherd rule books directed the nuns to cut inmates off from the rest of society until they were "reborn." It was a rule that "[w]hilst in the house they shall keep the enclosure strictly. Nobody from without, who may be suspected, whether man or woman, shall be permitted to speak to them, not even their relations" (Sisters 1890, 61). This particular rule was adjusted over time, so that by the late 1950s and 1960s, some inmates were permitted a biweekly visitor for good behaviour, or, more rarely, an afternoon outside the institution. However, it was commonplace that many inmates never left the reformatory during their period of incarceration. This chronic confinement, as the women's stories demonstrate, was harmful.

Former inmates told me that their captivity constituted a deliberate breaking down of their formative identities. For them, Good Shepherd reformatories were spaces of abjection or spaces wherein "distressed, displaced, and dispossessed peoples are condemned to the status of strangers, outsiders, and aliens" and made "inexistent insofar as they become inaudible and invisible" (Isin and Rygiel 2007, 182–83). There, personal meaning collapsed under a series of losses—renaming, head shaving, silencing, and "spectacles of humiliation" (Konstantinidis, interview, 2012) designed to control them. While the nuns' intention may have been to remake these girls into "better" beings, they received nothing besides shaming, rote religion, and hard labour in a blank institutional world. Instead of growth, their lives were abruptly shattered because of their relocation to this artificial environment: they were taken away from their communities, schools, natural worlds, and significant family members—all that they knew—to be totally submerged in an alien and emotionally dissociated world. From their perspectives, instead of "rescue" Church and civil authorities had placed them into an even more adverse environment.[15]

Based on her Australian laundry experience, Rachael describes the nuns as particularly committed to expunging the identities of Indigenous girls and women. Similarly, Chaparral Bowman, a former Canadian laundry inmate of Indigenous descent, whose entire childhood was spent in a Home of the Good Shepherd, recalled that while all inmates were "scum," Indigenous inmates were even more so (see chapter 1). According to Shurlee Swain and Margot Hillel (2010, vi), who examine British colonial techniques for "rescuing" children, these techniques were applied "more brutally" to the rescue of Indigenous children in Australia and Canada. Drawing from survivors' narratives, they maintain that such institutions devoted to "Indigenous child removal policies were embedded in the psyches of both nations" (2). And as in the Good Shepherd laundries and reformatories, "training took precedence over education" in residential schools and residents came to view themselves as "slave labour" (169–70). Much like what former Good Shepherd inmates have told me, Swain and Hillel describe environments where cleanliness was stressed and where young residents saw themselves as "dirty" in comparison to the "pure and clean" nuns (167).

---

15 Given that the women I interviewed were children or young teens at the time of their incarcerations, the views that shaped the child welfare policy of the day also came to bear on their situations. According to Judith Bessant (2013, 311), until the late 1970s Australian social welfare policy-makers were predominantly viewed as "altruistic," and the "practices of welfare agencies were inherently philanthropic and beneficial." Since the late nineteenth century, the state had sanctioned the removal of children from their families who were deemed to be neglected, impoverished, abused, or, as they now say, at risk. Bessant says that the historians working from this child protectionist stance viewed state interventions as essential (311). That viewpoint, one which also prevailed in Canada, was ameliorated somewhat by revelations of widespread institutional abuse, particularly of Indigenous children, in these countries.

Nation-wide inquiries into the removal of Indigenous children from their homes[16] have produced notably consistent findings concerning supposedly "rescued" children exposed to harm within the institutions where they were held. According to Swain and Hillel, such inquiries "dismiss suggestions that abuse was consistent with disciplinary practices of the day, or the result of individual psychopathologies, and argue instead that it was systemic" (172). As with the laundries,[17] discoveries of various kinds of abuse, as well as exploitation and neglect, "stood in direct contradiction to the Christian ethos of the homes" (172).

In 2003, *The Irish Times* journalist and author Mary Raftery awakened the Irish public consciousness to some of what had gone on behind the walls of the Magdalene laundries. For her, the overwhelming symbol of the merciless conditions endured by the Magdalenes was their treatment after death. Her article described the 1993 unearthing of one of the oldest and largest Magdalene laundry burial sites, at Drumcondra, in Dublin. In this cemetery, the unaccounted bodies of at least 133 women and girls were discovered: unclaimed, forgotten, and hidden. The Roman Catholic Order responsible for their care, the Sisters of Our Lady of Charity, provided no remaining record of the birth names of some bodies, or even the cause of death. As Raftery further reported:

> Twenty-three of the women are listed under the heading "quasi-religious name"—the nuns admitted that they did not know their real names. They called them "Magdalen of St Cecilia, Magdalen of Lourdes, Magdalen of St Teresa," and so on. Another woman had only a first name.
>
> The nuns told the Department that as they had no names,

16 Notably, Canada's Truth and Reconciliation hearings (Truth and Reconciliation Commission of Canada 2015) and Australia's 1997 *Bringing Them Home: The Stolen Generation Report* (Human Rights 1997).

17 See testimonials from former inmates at http://www.magdaleneoralhistory.com/index.htm and https://www.waterfordmemories.com.

> death certificates for these 24 women could not be produced. The Department raised no objection, despite the fact that some of the women had died as recently as the late 1960s. The nuns also said that there were no death certs for a further 34 women. These women at least had names. But the cause and date of death for most of them are listed as "not known." Some of these women died as recently as the mid-1970s.

Raftery also discovered that many of this forgotten group had been buried in a common grave plot in Dublin's Glasnevin Cemetery, where the names on the gravestone did not accurately match those who were buried there. Her finding spoke compellingly to the Church's indifference to the fate of these girls and women. In awakening the Irish public to the previously hidden realities of the Magdalene laundries, Raftery unwittingly alerted other countries to the international existence of such institutions.

We now know that the secrecy surrounding the lives and deaths of former Magdalene laundry inmates in Ireland reflects a larger global picture of clerical abuses.[18] These nearly forgotten institutions in Ireland and elsewhere are but one lesser known model, in the Catholic Church's network of disciplinary institutions—residential schools, training schools, industrial schools, and reformatories—in which countless numbers of women, men,

---

18 Likewise, Australia conducted a five-year-long national inquiry into child sexual abuse, resulting in *The Final Report of the Royal Commission into Institutional Responses to Child Sexual Abuse*. This study, released in December 2017, consists of 17 volumes; it draws from 981 survivors of child sexual abuse in 8,013 private sessions, and an additional 25, 964 written testimonies. Commissioners found that the largest proportion of those who described sexual abuse within religious institutions had been in Catholic-run institutions. Of this group, they heard from 2,489 survivors, representing almost two-thirds (61.8 per cent) of survivors who told them about child sexual abuse in religious institutions and more than one-third (36.2 per cent) of all survivors they heard from in private sessions. Private sessions revealed that child sexual abuse occurred in 964 different Catholic institutions. Among the testimonials are numerous accounts from survivors of Good-Shepherd-operated laundries and reformatories. https://www.childabuseroyalcommission.gov.au.

and children suffered the private pain of institutional abuse and neglect, their treatment long left unchallenged.

This lack of public awareness changed relatively recently, when the past was catapulted front and centre into public consciousness with the disclosures of the Ryan Commission Report (2009), Ireland's decade-long investigation into institutional child abuse. Significantly, the Magdalene laundries were omitted from this report, in part because the Church continued to insist that young girls were not forced to work in the laundries while under its care. One group that made it its purpose to challenge the Ryan Commission's oversight, address the general widespread public silence about the laundries, and point out the Irish Catholic Church and the state's abuse of power was Justice for Magdalenes (JFM). This group, formed in 2009, offered support to former Magdalene inmates in Ireland and other countries where the laundries had existed. Claire McGettrick, a founding member, told me that the powerful symbol of the nameless, faceless, and undocumented burials revealed by Raftery precipitated the mobilization of JFM, and that her article had exposed how in life and once more in death these women were left utterly dehumanized by the Roman Catholic Church. The identities of the former Magdalenes, now cremated and buried at Glasnevin, remained forever buried, literally and figuratively. As such, the Glasnevin site has come to represent a vital symbol for former Magdalene survivors everywhere. Its distressingly anonymous mass burial markers confirm that, even in death, some identities were denied. Despite the powerful revelations of Raftery's inquiry, no official explanation for what took place at Drumcondra has been offered. JFM, along with the work of lawyers, reporters, and historians, has tirelessly pursued further inquiry into how this now recognized injustice could have occurred.

This advocacy on behalf of former Magdalenes has kept them in the spotlight in Ireland. Yet they remain less well known in Great Britain and Australia and even more marginally so in the United States. In New Zealand and Canada, the existence of such institutions is largely unheard of or forgotten. Yet the important perspectives and stories of those confined therein needed to be documented and shared before they are lost forever. The remaining generation of Good Shepherd Magdalene and reformatory survivors are few and aging, and so there is an urgency for their stories to be told. To punctuate this fact, just prior to my completing this book, one of my participants died and two others began to struggle with life-threatening illnesses.

Documenting and Remembering

> *Those fighting for justice naturally privilege the words of ordinary men and women, their own telling of their history rather than a version told by historians who almost always represent a dominant class and culture. It is often through these testimonies that we come to understand what really happened at a particular time, in a particular place.*
>
> (Randall 2015, 299)

Despite the many roadblocks to gathering evidence of what unfolded, a handful of scholars has provided important social and historical insights into the laundries, particularly in Ireland.[19] The Irish laundries have also been the subject of numerous documentaries and popular film dramas. *The Magdalene Sisters* (2002), *Sex in a Cold Climate* (1996), *The Forgotten Maggies* (2009), and, later, *Philomena* (2013) contributed to raising general public awareness about these institutions, and, in 2012, musician Sinead O'Connor joined the voices of other former inmates in decrying her treatment in a former Magdalene laundry (Agresta 2012). Each of these contributions has shed light on where and how such institutions operated, who was sent there and why, and how the Catholic Church was able to assume such complete authority over both individual lives and entire communities. Notably, most existing work—histories,

19 Mahood 1990, Finnegan 2004, Titley 2006, Smith 2007a and b, McCarthy 2010, O'Sullivan and O'Donnell 2007, and Luddy 2007, to name several significant contributions to the research in this area.

exposés, and lone voices—focuses on the Irish laundry experience, and we still have little sense of the experiences of laundry inmates elsewhere.[20]

A full disclosure of the Magdalene/reformatory experience has been globally evaded by Church and governments, although small inroads have been made toward acknowledging abuses that occurred in similar types of institutions. For example, in Australia, two formal apologies within two years were delivered by Prime Minister Kevin Rudd to those who had been forcefully removed from their families, as children, and who consequently suffered mistreatment. Rudd offered the government's first apology in February 2008 to the Indigenous Stolen Generations.[21] The second apology, in November 2009, was "to forced imperial child migrants, institutionalized children, and wards of the state, the so-called Lost Innocents and Forgotten Australians" (Cuthbert and Quartly 2013, 178). Also, in 2011–2012, the Australian government through the National Museum and the National Library launched a "Forgotten Australians" project, entitled *Inside: Life in Children's Homes and Institutions* (National Museum Australia 2011). This exhibit documented and commemorated oral histories of children in Australia's institutional care system; within that display, an installation represented experiences of the country's former inmates of Magdalene laundries and reformatories. This project came to fruition only after numerous hindered attempts by a few daring voices in public office to expose the institutional abuse of children in Australia's past. In her 2013 review of the *Inside* exhibit, Diana James (2013, 4) observed that "[t]he Australian nation had to grow up itself before it could face its own dark

20 And yet in Canada, a network of thirteen Good Shepherd "Homes" was devoted to the "rescue" of wayward/delinquent girls and women, and the Order supervised women's jails in Quebec and the Maritime provinces as well (Valin 1950, 20). In Australia there were nine such Good Shepherd establishments (James 2013, 20); in the US, fifty-six (Valin 1950, 20).

21 The "Forgotten Australians" is the name given to those who grew up in out-of-home care settings such as foster homes, orphanages, and other institutions throughout Australia. It has been estimated that 500,000 Australian children, both Indigenous and non-Indigenous, experienced out-of-home care in the twentieth century alone. See http://www.forgottenaustralians.com.

childhood and hidden histories. *Inside* is a stimulus for national rethinking of who we have been, who we are and what we aspire to be."

In Canada, some national reflection was likewise stirred by the Royal Commission on Aboriginal Peoples, which was established in 1991 in the wake of the Oka Crisis.[22] The report from this commission, the outcome of extensive research and consultation, was a broad review of historical and contemporary relations between Aboriginal and non-Aboriginal peoples in Canada. A still more recent impetus for national reconsideration has been the Truth and Reconciliation Commission (2015) in addressing the residential school experiences of Indigenous people. Provincial institutions, operating on principles similar to those of the laundries and the residential schools, have also received considerable public attention in this country. In 1989, for example, reports of widespread intergenerational abuse of boys in the Irish-Christian-Brother-run St. John's Newfoundland orphanage, Mount Cashel, led to the establishment of the Hughes Inquiry (Royal Commission 1991). In May 2013, a settlement was reached between the Catholic lay order and 160 male victims of sexual and physical abuse at the former orphanage (CBC News 2013). They received compensation of a $16.5 million payment for the 400 American and Canadian men and women who had filed claims for child molestation and physical abuse. Nevertheless, in this case, many claims were denied in the process of reaching this settlement, and many more are still being disputed. Investigations into Quebec's Duplessis Orphans (Les Orphelins de Duplessis), who were placed into Roman-Catholic-Church-run psychiatric institutions and gravely exploited, led eventually to some compensation (Campbell 2013). Similarly, in Nova Scotia, media attention on the so-called Butterbox Babies of the Ideal Maternity Home has produced significant recognition (Cahill 2006). At the federal level in Canada, formal inquiries into the residential school system for Indigenous children resulted in an apology from the Canadian prime minister in June 2008, and more

---

22 The Oka Crisis occurred between July 11 and September 26, 1990. It was a seventy-eight-day stand-off between police, army, and Mohawk protesters over the development of a golf course and condominiums on land that included a Mohawk burial ground.

recently in 2017. Some financial compensation for intergenerational abuses has been ordered as a result of an extensive investigation by the Truth and Reconciliation Commission of 2015. To date, however, neither the Church nor the government has yet acknowledged what happened to the former inmates of the Canadian Magdalene laundries.

Initially, in Ireland, both the government and the Church denied responsibility for the complex array of violations that occurred in the Irish laundries, but there have since been some important shifts at the state level. In 2013, the Irish prime minister issued an emotional apology which finally acknowledged the existence of Magdalenes as a distinct and wronged group. Prime Minister Kenny's apology on behalf of the state, the government, and Irish citizens expressed deep regret that Ireland had "swapped" its "public scruples for a solid public apparatus" ("In Full" 2013). By this comment, Kenny meant that the presentation of a sanitized and united front by the Irish justice system and the Church had been more important than upholding the well-being of its citizens.

Public apologies for past institutional abuses in Australia, Canada, and Ireland have received mixed reviews. Some say that such apologies have not been specific enough and that certain related issues have been glossed over. In their study of national apologies in Australian politics, Denise Cuthbert and Marian Quartly (2013, 197) call for "a mature politics of apology" which would address class, race, and gender as part of the equation. Such intersections, they maintain, have left some individuals more vulnerable to abuses of power than others, as was the case for the generally economically vulnerable and all-female inmates of the Magdalene laundries. Critics maintain that national apologies cannot present a generalized image of victimhood but must address difference without the claims of one group overriding or lessening the claims of others. That is, "it is not enough to say sorry without fully articulating the grounds on which the wrongs were done" (198).

The mistreatment of the girls and women who were relegated to the care of the Sisters of the Good Shepherd has never been fully acknowledged by the Roman Catholic Church in any of the countries in which it fostered, operated, and supported these institutions. Despite United Nations calls in 2014 for the Vatican to formally respond to the abuses in Magdalene laundries, the latter has remained silent on the subject (Agnew 2014). For survivors, this denial of any role and responsibility by the Church is deeply hurtful. For them, therefore, remembering,[23] documenting, and bringing their experiences into public view is an important step toward official accountability and helping them to restore their rightful identities.

Making Compliant Women

According to Mary Douglas (2002, 140), a pollutant, whether spiritual, physical, or moral, is always considered a social danger and "a polluting person is always in the wrong." This understanding of moral contagion clarifies the view of inmates as requiring isolation, for society's sake, to avoid the spread of their immorality. This view, according to the following interviews, was circumscribed by the nuns, who characterized inmates as impure pollutants. Because of their assumed sexual "nature," these girls had become a social danger as well as a danger to themselves.

In their work on Canadian reform schools for girls from 1930 to 1960 (the era in which those I interviewed were incarcerated), Tamara Myers and Joan Sangster (2001, 669) describe "the girl problem" as a construction by experts such as "psychologists, penal workers, administrators and nuns." They suggest that "the girl problem" was a social creation born of a desire to better control women. Franca Iacovetta probes this social creation further still in her 1999 examination of the plight of York, Ontario, suburban "bad"

23 Memory studies, say Maynes (an historian), Pierce, and Laslett (sociologists), have various disciplinary "genealogies" (2008, 40). Their cross-disciplinary exploration of memory in storytelling makes important mention of "history from below," an emphasis that grew out of 1960s historiography. It was then, they tell us, that historians in the West became interested in the memories of "the working class, women, and other marginalized historical actors." Their histories offered hope for rebutting "official histories" and for "uncovering and attesting to individual and group oppression."

girls from 1945 to 1960. Her particular interest is in the give and take between "confidential files, societal processes, and professional pronouncements" (592) and between caseworkers and clients. By choosing to concentrate on caseworkers, rather than legal experts, Iacovetta maintains that she is better equipped to expose the inner dynamics of "a hypocritical system" (623) of localized powers within "a highly bureaucratic system of justice" (592). This system, while professing to "reform wayward girls and restore harmonious family life ... operated in ways that permitted arbitrary experts armed with a vast repertoire of causes and cures, unsubstantiated claims, and tainted evidence, as well as patriarchal, class, and racial-ethnic biases, to impose oppressive rules" (623).

In this view, Good Shepherd nuns were considered an arm of such an "expert" machine, assembled to control the girl problem by expunging the "craving, instinctual body" (Bordo [1993] 2004, 165). Their enforcement of bodily discipline through endless work and silence can be understood in terms of the female body as a locus of social control. Such control is achieved in conventional ways "through table manners and toilet habits" and "through seemingly trivial routines, rules, and practices" (165). One poignant illustration of such corporeal disciplining was the nuns' practice of shaving inmates' heads. Their rationale was explained in an early Sisters of Mercy guidebook:

> It is very desirable to adhere to the rule, so generally established in asylums, of cutting closely the hair of each before admitting her amongst the other penitents.
>
> 1. As a means of bringing grace, which the willing sacrifice of their hair—on which they usually set such value—generally brings them.
> 2. As Magdalen began the evidence of her conversion by consecrating her hair to her Redeemer, so do they, and thus give reason to hope that they really intend to initiate her in her penance, as they have done in their sins.
> 3. As a check to the wild sallies of passion and temptation;

> under these violent impulses, some, who would not yield to better motives, have been known to defer leaving the Asylum until their hair should be sufficiently grown, in whom in the meantime grace grew and passion subsided, and they became good penitents. It is, therefore, very advisable to encourage them from time to time, during their fits of fervour, to make a renewed offering of their hair to God, in imitation of Magdalen. They should all be carefully prevented from oiling or greasing, or otherwise bestowing any unnecessary care on it, to which they are generally much inclined.
>
> 4. Cutting their hair is a test of their motive in entering, as often wicked ones have entered, merely to draw out with them others who had been doing well. (*Guide for the Religious* 1866, 59)

In this regard, Rachael described the forcible removal of body hair as part of a routine intake procedure. Having her armpit hair shaved by a nun as Rachael sat naked in a bathtub, she said, was a deep violation and "a corruption of her natural state" (Romero, interview, 2013). Likewise, Janice recalled the forcible shaving of inmates as a means of enforcing humility and, as the above guidelines called for, controlling "wild sallies of passion." In her reformatory, this happened as punishment for those who were caught in runaway attempts. She described one instance when the nuns shaved only half of the runaway's head—not to encourage spiritual growth but to disgrace and better control her. According to Janice, head shaving was one of a range of comparable practices, or "spectacles of humiliation" as she called them, meant to confirm the inmate's sense of powerlessness and lack of self-worth.

Another such practice of bodily regulation entailed the forcible wearing of the "punishment" dress. This burlap outfit was "a crude hapless frock that any girl who broke a rule was threatened with wearing" (Konstantinidis, interview, 2014). The mere threat of taking away any more of the little dignity that the inmates had left, be it their hair, their long fingernails, or exchanging their ugly standardized uniform for an even more hapless and unsightly one, was a powerful deterrent to resistance. Such practices were part of a coordinated series of disgraces to enforce modesty and impose a Christian female identity upon deviant bodies. Control through bodily discipline and routinization aptly describes how the nuns conducted themselves within the Good Shepherd Order, where they were strictly self-regimented in work and prayer routines. In turn, they effected a similar, albeit harsher, discipline on their charges with the goal of bringing sinful bodies closer to the Christian image of pure womanhood. In effect, girls and women were immersed in mundane and binding practices of cleaning and prayer as a means of regaining control of their sinful bodies.

As part of their role in the construction of pure womanhood, the Good Shepherd laundry/reformatories perpetuated the now widely recognized double standard of morality in committing "fallen" women, but not men, to the laundries (Finnegan 2004, 4). This represents a social contradiction "whereby women are deemed solely responsible for sexual transgression," while the Irish Catholic male avoids institutionalization and lives his life unconstrained (Smith 2007a, 41). Gender also played a role in who had the social authority to commit girls and women. Their incarceration, directed at controlling their bodies, was largely overseen by fathers, stepfathers, and/or priests. Those I interviewed were acutely aware of this double standard. For most, though, a recognition and resentment of the gendered power imbalance that so negatively shaped their lives came only later; as children, few questioned this prevailing cultural and patriarchal structure.

Sangster (2001), in reflecting on the double standard, has concluded that incarcerated girls in 1960s to 1970s Canada were generally branded as immoral, whereas incarcerated boys were characterized differently, as unfulfilled and destructive. The "problem" girl or woman—"the lonely nymphomaniac" (40)—was thus incarcerated in the name of social protection by containing and reforming her sexuality. The role of the nuns, as women, in this punitive and largely male-controlled process of moral reform was informed by a repressive patriarchy that offered them few options. It can hardly be disputed that the nuns inherited the religious institutional system that they then enacted. Within this system, they were largely left with little scope for self-definition, little-to-no agency, and next-to-no power to effect institutional change. Those who followed this life path, or calling, were expected to model what has been described as a certain species of womanhood, one rooted in "misogynistic notions of what women were like 'in essence'" (McKenna 2006, 48). Hence, within this methodically gendered construct, the nuns carried out their duties "by putting in place a system by which they controlled themselves" (48).

Questions of power, the perception of power, and the absence of power sit at the very heart of the often-ruthless treatment of the girls and women in the nuns' care. The disciplinary environment of the Good Shepherd reform institutions, as noted earlier, was modelled on a strict adherence to the early guidebooks, which the nuns were bound to follow.[24] Like the inmates, they too were cloistered in silence, their bodies always concealed, and with no formal power to alter the rules that defined them. Yet, to the girls and women incarcerated in their institutions, the nuns' power seemed unqualified. As Elizabeth Butler Cullingford (2006, 12) notes, "Nuns who ran laundries, asylums, and industrial schools wielded absolute authority over socially marginal people." The Order itself has made some apologies "but [has] not

24 With Vatican II came a decree called the Perfectae Caritatis, or the Decree on the Adaptation and Renewal of Religious Life. This 1965 decree aimed to change the relationship of the Church with the world, and it shifted the view of nuns toward what their roles as religious women ought to be. However, says Brian Titley, it effected little change "in the specifics of any of the diverse projects undertaken by nuns, including the operation of Magdalen asylums or reformatory schools." Perfectae Caritatis "was the only Council document that specifically addressed the work of nuns," said Titley, and it "principally suggested that communities of religious adapt their ways of living and working to modern times, but without any details on what that might look like" (email to author, January 1, 2018).

explained" the nuns' roles (14). Until they do, we cannot fully know how they perceived their power within this system.

While the nuns' perspectives on the operation and management of their institutions would likely provide a fuller picture, this information remains unavailable to researchers.[25] Catriona Crowe, head of special projects at the National Archives of Ireland, lamented this problem in her 2017 review of Jacinta Prunty's 2017 *The Monasteries, Magdalen Asylums and Reformatory Schools of Our Lady of Charity in Ireland, 1853–1973.* In her communication with the Catholic archives, Crowe discovered that the sources from which Prunty drew for her book are not available to other researchers. As a Holy Faith Sister, Prunty was permitted access to the archives, but Crowe was told that for others, including researchers, the congregation's archives are "private" and have "always been closed." This is something that Crowe characterizes as a "huge problem." For, as she points out, a significant principle of historical investigation is that "quoted sources can be inspected and interrogated by others, and assertions tested by access to the original material used to make them." This "serious matter," says Crowe, is rendered more serious still "since religious institutions played such a dominant part in the history of 19th and 20th Ireland, with the State's full blessing." Given the "harrowing testimonials" of those confined in Catholic-run institutions that have been brought forward over the last several decades, it is imperative that these institutions open their records for

25 According to James Franklin's 2013 article, the nuns have not yet provided a written perspective on the laundries, as insiders. Such accounts, he maintains, are rare, and what does exist does not deal with the Magdalene reformatories.

> The institutional histories of the orders, while informative, do not directly address the former inmates' allegations and say whether they believe them true or false. Requests to the Sisters of Charity and to the author of their institutional history for comment on that question for this article did not produce responses. The present-day Good Shepherd sisters have made an official statement (2013) that they are "deeply sorry for acts of verbal or physical cruelty that occurred," but do not expand on that. So it is necessary to make some tentative inferences from a small amount of evidence. (86)

scrutiny. Without access to these materials, "the full and complex story of what happened, both to the religious and to those who resided in their institutions," will remain unknown to us.

Defying Silence

In the name of performing a necessary social service, the Good Shepherds and related Orders caused generations of girls and women to disappear—while hidden in plain sight. Now, what we can learn about the Good Shepherd inmates is also disappearing. With the passing of time, fear of retribution, public denial of their truths, and difficulty speaking about their traumatic experiences, the forces that have induced their silence, remain compelling. However, a small group of former inmates, including those whose accounts appear here, have chosen to break their silence and make their past experiences public, despite potentially great personal risk. In offering a rendering of the internal workings of the Good Shepherd laundries and reformatories that contradicts official versions, their stories[26] are pioneering efforts and, as well, acts of resistance.

I first became aware of the laundries in the early 1990s while listening to Canadian singer and songwriter Joni Mitchell's "The Magdalene Laundries." Her haunting depiction of the girls and women who had been "cast in shame / Into the Magdalene Laundries" (*Turbulent Indigo*, Crazy Crow Music, 1994) stirred in me a combined sense of sadness and outrage. While Mitchell had never been incarcerated in a Magdalene laundry, she could identify with the

---

26 Numerous survivor accounts are being catalogued in the Irish *Magdalene Institutions: Recording an Oral and Archival History* project and the *Waterford Memories Project*. Accounts from former inmates are also being self-published and/or published through scholarly and non-scholarly facilitators and advocates. See, for example, O'Riordan et al. (2015). In addition, many testimonials from survivors have been picked up by journalists, transnationally, as with Johnston's 2013 coverage in the *Sydney Morning Herald*. Taken together these testimonials not only serve to cross-reference the conditions common to Magdalene laundries but they also strengthen and support the once-lone voices who initially broke the silence.

stigmatization of those who had. In a 1997 *Maclean's* interview with Brian Johnson she described being an unwed mother at the age of twenty-one and her decision to give her daughter up for adoption. At the time, she was "dirt poor and pregnant" and living in a Toronto rooming house. Her chief concern then was hiding her pregnancy from her parents. She described the "scandal" of being pregnant and unmarried as "so intense ... a daughter could do nothing more disgraceful. You have no idea what the stigma was," she told the reporter; "it was like you murdered somebody" (Johnson 1997, 51).

A short while after hearing Mitchell's song, while I was researching sexual abuse within Newfoundland's Mount Cashel orphanage, I again came across mention of the laundries. As I attempted to find out more about them, I learned that these lonely places were only sparsely documented. Not only were there very few written records, but the voices and perspectives of the women confined there were even less present, and what little could be found overwhelmingly emphasized Ireland's experience. This scrubbing clean from history of the Magdalene laundries motivated me to travel to Ireland in the hopes of speaking with former inmates.

Gathering accounts from this once-banished group proved complicated, for several reasons. For one thing, as sociologists Ridwan Nytagodien and Arthur Neal (2004, 467) have found in their research on trauma in holocaust survivors, "[t]alking about the 'unspeakable' engenders a sense of discomfort for either the speaker or the listener or both." The two-way silence this response provokes has left former Good Shepherd inmates isolated with their trauma, as it lives on in varying degrees of resolution in their memories and identities. Sociologist Kai Erikson (1991, 455) offers some insight into how trauma sets its victim apart; he describes trauma as a "blow to the tissues of the mind," one that comes from outside. "Something alien breaks in on you," says Erikson, "smashing through whatever barriers your mind has set up as a line of defense. It invades you, occupies you, takes you over, becomes a dominant feature of your interior landscape." In this way, traumatic experiences have lasting implications. They "move to the center of one's being, and in doing so give the victim the feeling that they have been set apart" (458). This sense of social separateness upsets relationships, as the survivor carries a feeling of being marked or damned and unable or unwilling to describe her or his trauma. For some Magdalene/reformatory survivors, as the stories in the following chapters confirm, their traumas created a sense of isolation. For others, the trauma drew them closer to those similarly affected, with whom there was mutual recognition, a shared symbolism, and a sense of community.

Both circumstances—disconnectedness from others and the sense of being drawn only to those who can understand or to those who have been there—made it difficult to find women who were willing to talk to me about their incarcerations. Their confinement had also conditioned them to believe that they were unfit to join respectable social ranks, a message regularly reinforced by the nuns. The power of this message remained with them throughout their lives. Many felt that they risked further judgment or stigmatization[27] by making their stories public and doing so risked validating what they had been repeatedly told—that they were bad people, delinquent enough to be removed from their homes and locked away. This message contributed to the silence of many former inmates.

The following stories tell us that enforced silence and the suppression of inmates' voices were central to Good Shepherd reform practices. Inmates were forbidden to speak to one another about their lives, nor could they write to anyone on the outside about their experiences within the institution. Barriers to survivors speaking about their confinement were thus deep-seated and numerous. Even decades after their incarceration, some women could or would not tell those closest to them about this part of their lives. For many former inmates, their suffering was, and continues to be, a solitary process but, as Erin Costello Wecker (2015, 266–68) argues, not necessarily a powerless one. For silence can also serve as a form of speaking back to the state's "oppressive discourse" about confinement and can serve to "shift control of the laundry narrative away from the oppressor." In this respect, it is vital to

27 "The term stigma ... will be used to refer to an attribute that is deeply discrediting" (Goffman 1961, 13) and causes people to be considered socially unacceptable and classified as undesirable.

consider former inmates' silence also "as a deliberate action" and not necessarily as a strategy to "deflect the past" (268). Those who told me their stories, however, felt that breaking their long-held silence was an important part of a larger self-restoration; for them, speaking back (by speaking aloud) to the systems that had demanded their silence contributed to freeing them from a long-held stigma.

The accounts that follow attest to the substandard (or non-existent) education that the school-aged inmates received during their incarceration. Those I interviewed deeply lamented the denial of their education, and in this they were not unique. Interviews from Irish laundry survivors, gathered between 2012 and 2016 through the *Magdalene Institutions: Recording an Oral and Archival History* project[28] and in the ongoing *Waterford Memories Project*,[29] for example, provide Magdalene survivor testimonies that make similar claims. Due to their poor education, many former inmates entered the outside world with basic literacy, at best. In addition to acting as a barrier to seeking formal support for the wrongs that they had suffered, this deficit left many feeling socially demeaned. Survivors' sense of degradation was complicated by an ongoing inability to publicly account for their lack of education, since doing so meant outing themselves as having been incarcerated. The combined effect seriously undermined the confidence of former inmates, driving many out of public sight.

Perhaps their earlier subjugation and their lack of formal education, taken together, became internalized by former inmates as a belief that as "disadvantaged" people they (as sociologists Francesca Polletta, Pang Ching, Bobby Chen, Beth Gharrity Gardner, and Alice Motes maintain) "are often less well trained in the requirements of telling an institutionally appropriate story, they are less likely to be seen as narratively competent, and their very experiences make them less able to tell the kind of story that

28 http://www.magdaleneoralhistory.com/index.htm. This project is led by Dr. Katherine O'Donnell.

29 https://www.waterfordmemories.com.

is required" (2011, 123). The issue of credibility haunts personal narratives generally, and those from trauma victims in particular. Trauma victims, Nytagodien and Neal (2004, 267) say, "face the twin imperative of truth-telling and maintaining secrecy." For they contend that truth-telling engages "a quest for justice and some degree of validation for beliefs about living in a just world. On the other hand, the emotional telling of stories by victims frequently results in credibility problems" (267).

In spite of the contested nature of trauma narratives, it is vital to the historical record and to collective healing that these memories be brought forward and given a wide audience. In this regard, Nytagodien and Neal argue that since individual and collective past traumas "refuse to remain buried ... they continue to have a living influence upon the contemporary present." It is critical to the course of healing on all levels that these stories be enacted and re-enacted in a process of enculturation. In so doing, the barriers of "denial and repression are removed ... [and] ... [c]reative energies are released. The challenge is to heal the wounds of the nation and, in doing so, helping to shape the future" (267).

For the above, and other, reasons, it was initially difficult to find women who would speak about their incarceration. During my first trip to Ireland in 2009, I spoke with several advocates for former Magdalene inmates but to only one former inmate. One of the advocates I interviewed in Ireland suggested that I participate in the JFM online survivors group as a way of meeting former inmates. I did so, introducing myself to the group as a former counselling therapist who had worked with sexually abused women and children, and as a cultural sociologist[30] who identified as a scholar-activist. I hoped that this context would convey to former Magdalenes that I was sensitive to issues of women's abuse and exploitation and that I was not there to manipulate them as research objects. Rather, I wanted to listen and learn from them. Ultimately, my gendered and professional perspective

30 As a professional sociologist, I would interview only with informed consent. Participants were made aware of that and I had received ethical clearance, consistent with tri-council policy, to conduct this research through the university where I am employed.

may well have permitted my entrance into a world from which others were restricted. Nevertheless, trust did not come immediately, nor was the more vulnerable content of these women's experiences readily revealed.

I spent over a year in this online group before one survivor, shortly followed by another, agreed to be interviewed.[31] They needed assurance that I was willing to critique the systems that had condemned them before I was considered trustworthy enough to bear witness to their stories. For good reason, these women initially had little confidence in my, or anyone else's, interest in them and were wary of manipulation by those in perceived positions of authority. I am reminded here of what Kai Erikson (1991, 467) has also observed, "People whose view of the world has been tempered by exposure to trauma can easily lose faith not only in the good *will* but in the good *sense* of those in charge of a dangerous universe." After having been silenced, abused, and negated, why should they freely place their trust in me? These exploitations, as their stories poignantly reveal, had culminated in a significant and sustained loss of trust; thus, confirming that "the hardest earned and most fragile accomplishment of childhood, basic trust, can be damaged beyond repair by trauma" (470). In combination with everything else that had been taken from them, why would they choose to break their powerful silences and risk losing more of themselves? And yet, ultimately, some did permit me access to their emotionally difficult

31 In time, a trusting relationship began to grow between me and one former Magdalene. In the course of our lengthy conversations, she conceded that I could hear and validate the harms that had been done to her, and she revealed more and more about her experiences. As many of these former inmates knew of one another through a transnational underground survivor network of sorts, she eventually also offered me the name of someone else to contact. In this way I also came to work very closely with others who agreed to share their stories with me. We communicated over a period of years: in face-to-face conversations, by telephone, in email exchanges, and through Skype. Ultimately though, for a multitude of reasons, not everyone who told me their stories wanted them documented; some simply could not bear to see them come to print. This is understandable, since these stories expose to scrutiny traumatic journeys involving ruthless and impersonal institutional practices within a still-powerful institution, the Roman Catholic Church.

experiences, and, once "inside," I came to share their indignation over their lost trust and the labelling of them as bad, shameful, and broken that accompanied it. Such characterizations, I learned, resulted in sustained psychic and social dislocation for each of them.

The interviews/conversations that unfolded with Rachael, Janice, Maureen, Autumn, and Chaparral between 2009 and 2016 comprise the chapters which follow. Their stories emerged out of recalled memories, some buried, some very much present and haunting. Returning to their time with the Good Shepherds required them to reconnect with the pain, anger, and vulnerabilities produced by their incarcerations. For some, this brought nightmares, flashbacks, and both physical and emotional disorientation. Yet, this group of women also considered their exploration of these memories to be an empowering process, partly because, as I was repeatedly told, my presence as witness served to both honour and confirm them. The process of interviewing and writing up their individual accounts involved years of drawing out and piecing together participants' memories and probing them for submerged details, associated feelings, and understandings.[32] I searched for common links and differences among their experiences and ultimately turned these findings into a more accessible narrative form.

I am comfortable characterizing our exchanges as what Mary Jo Maynes, Jennifer Pierce, and Barbara Laslett (2008, 98) call "intersubjective encounters." Viewing them as such acknowledges that they involved ongoing

---

32 My work in shaping the interviews into stories (or testimonials, as Rachael prefers to characterize her account) was a negotiated process in that those I interviewed were involved in decisions about what to include or exclude from the final draft. As I wrote each story, I checked back with each of my participants to ask questions, to verify details, and to ensure that they were comfortable with the content I was including. Some read versions of my chapters and commented on my interpretations, correcting my "reading" of their words as they saw fit. Others discussed content with me. Sometimes the deletion of content happened even before the writing stage, when say, following the divulging of vulnerable information, I was asked not to include that part or to include only certain parts of it. In some cases, I chose to omit content that concerned me in terms of potential liability issues.

attempts to understand one another's "subjective take on the world" (99). My commitment to responsible interaction within this context necessitated that I remain self-conscious about my influence and presence in the production of these stories and the privilege of my academic position. Moreover, in the course of listening and transcribing what I heard, my role was transformed. As Ruth Behar puts it, I moved "from listener to translator or mediator and then to story teller, from spoken to written word and from one cultural context to another" (Maynes et al., 108). This description broadly captures my work within the contexts of my participants' accounts, wherein my foremost duty in gathering these cross-cultural narratives was to uphold a version of each story that was shaped predominantly by the women themselves. I wanted, in other words, to allow them to tell their stories as spontaneously as possible and to leave a small footprint on their process. This, of course, simplifies a complex and reflexive interaction wherein, as Polletta et al. (2011, 113) point out in "The Sociology of Storytelling," the author can "never fully know her own role." I can and did remain conscious of my ethical responsibilities within this relationship, but as Gayatri Spivak (1996, 269–70) observes, the intersections of exchange always produce new and unanticipated outcomes: "We all know that when we engage profoundly with one person, the responses come from both sides: this is responsibility and accountability ... The object of ethical action is not an object of benevolence, for here responses flow from both sides."

Through the process of listening, translating, mediating, and telling, I have endeavoured to uphold what my participants expressed was their intention in relaying their stories to me; it was foremost political, they told me, to have me bring forward the injustices they had experienced and to have a hearing, a chance to detail for an audience how these injustices shaped their lives. The women who agreed to entrust their accounts to me did so anticipating that my position as a scholar could carry their voices into realms otherwise difficult to access, such as classrooms and other academic platforms. They, in other words, sought to benefit from my professional position, in an expectation that was deliberate and upfront. As former inmates they wanted my assistance in challenging the dominant story, the one shaped by powerful institutions, in the hope that their experiences might finally be considered credible (Polletta et al. 2011, 119–21). I brought to our exchanges additional interests. My questions, informed by my background as a therapist, attempted to draw out affective details, thoughts, and feelings related to these incarcerations. I wanted to know more about how these women perceived institutionalization to have affected their very identities—their sense of self, both as girls and throughout their lives as women. I wanted to know too about the nature of the human relationships within these places.

I furthermore sought to draw out of these accounts a sense of how these Good Shepherd institutions operated, in detail. To this end, sociohistorical research enabled me to contextualize the interview material and locate information that supported inmates' descriptions of their experiences. This research reflexively guided me by continuously re/informing the questions I asked of my participants. It likewise aided me in understanding stereotypes and falsehoods about the laundries, such as the common misconception that they housed only women who were pregnant or involved in prostitution. My collective research and storied findings together affirmed the authenticity and relevance of these lone accounts and rendered their descriptions—in the survivors' own terms—more understandable.

These stories, standing alone and as part of a collection, capture the understandings of those interned in these reformatories and offer intimate perspectives that help us to better appreciate the workings of such religious disciplinary environments. Moreover, they bring forth first-person insights into how and why girls and young women were confined and how their identities were shaped by this captivity. This is not to say that the following five accounts represent the experiences of all who were interned in Good Shepherd laundries and reformatories; no small group could possibly speak for the countless who were confined internationally. However, they are valuable in many respects, not the least of which is the insights they yield into the identity negotiations that accompanied forced confinement and its aftermath.

These stories defy the once-common stereotype of morally troubled girls and women in need of religious redemption and rehabilitation. Instead, they demonstrate that the "crimes" for which they were committed were often unsubstantiated or mislabelled and the punishments for their alleged transgressions, as "fallen women," were unduly harsh. As Senator McAleese (2013) contends, the stigma of the fallen woman is a "wholly inaccurate characterisation" that has done harm to former inmates and their families. Significantly, he adds, this characterization "is not borne out by the facts." The reality, said McAleese, "is much more complex" (ii). McAleese's findings also support what the women I interviewed told me about how they came to be institutionalized. Some were confined because they tried to protect themselves by running away from abusive family situations. Others were locked up to protect the social reputations of their fathers and/or stepfathers, who had sexually or physically abused them. Chaparral Bowman, mentioned above, was born into a laundry to a mother who was incarcerated for being raped. All the women whose stories are included here were handed over as children, with the support of priests or child welfare officials. Under this authority of the Sisters of the Good Shepherd, they endured years of great personal pain, deep loneliness, forced unpaid labour, and imprisonment.

While each former inmate's journey into the past was unique, their stories revealed significant common themes and understandings of their incarceration. One collective insight was that by being clustered together as a nameless, faceless group of bad, broken, or fallen ne'er-do-wells, the truth of their confinement was cruelly misrepresented. In other words, they and the pathways that led to their captivity, as McAleese observed, were more complex and nuanced than the labels that marked them. I hoped to counter such oversimplifications and distortions by describing former inmates' experiences, by drawing heavily on their words and details, and thereby shedding light on their humanity as individuals, *as persons* living and suffering under alienating conditions beyond their control. In so doing, we together hoped to shatter the nameless, faceless, and generic depiction of the laundry inmates and reformatory survivors.

While each of them had previously brought pieces of their stories forward to the public,[33] they hoped that my contextualization and consolidation of these longer in-depth interviews within a collection of accounts would further strengthen their individual claims and draw attention to their interconnectedness. Beyond the institutional similarities that these testimonials reveal, for example, we find comparable means of coping—or ways through what had been powerfully life-altering circumstances. For several, creative and biographical writing helped to reorient them and to make sense of their pain. Others had in common a need to work with those who, like themselves, had been rendered marginalized members of society. All of those I interviewed also share a preoccupation with gathering evidence of their incarcerated existence, and with rectifying perceptions of them, and those like them, as bad or

---

33 As the following three links indicate, Maureen Sullivan has advocated for compensation and recognition for Magdalene survivors by tirelessly sharing her story through media interviews. Here are three examples: http://www.bbc.com/news/world-europe-21345995, http://www.thejournal.ie/magdalene-survivors-nuns-radio- 825633-Mar2013/, and https://www.irishtimes.com/news/social-affairs/religion-and-beliefs/younger-magdalene-survivor-to-seek-compensation-for-loss-of-right-to-education-1.1580718. Chaparral Bowman published four works of autobiographical fiction under the name Georgina Williams: *Delcina's Tears*, 2005; *Beyond the Walls*, 2006; *Rehearsals in Madness*, 2007; and *Whispering Wildfire*, 2009, based on her Good Shepherd laundry experience in Saint John, New Brunswick. A sense of the scope of Rachael Romero's artwork concerning her Magdalene laundry experience can be viewed at http://rachaelromero.com/magdalene-laundry/4553654655. In addition, Rachael's short documentary, which makes poignant mention of her time in The Pines laundry, is entitled *In the Shadow of Eden* (Romero Docudrama Films on Full Frame Documentary Shorts, Vol. 4 dvd. http://www.docurama.com/productdetail.html? productid=NV-NVG-9778). In 2013, Janice Konstantinidis contributed parts of her story of incarceration in Mount Saint Canice, Australia, to a collective exhibit of Australian child institution survivors entitled "Inside: 'Life in Children's Homes and Institutions'" (*reCollections: A Journal of Museums and Collections*). Shortly thereafter (2013), she published "Life in 'The Mag'" in the *Journal of the Australian Catholic Historical Society*. Autumn has published two books, autobiographical in nature, under her legal name. In order to protect her identity, I do not list them here. Because of her concern with being stigmatized by her incarceration in a Good Shepherd reformatory, those published accounts of her life omit any mention of her time in the St. Mary's Training School.

amoral people. In this regard, each woman hoped that the power of their collectively wronged voices might shift the longstanding stereotypes of them as "bad" and untrustworthy by bringing attention to the far more significant social issue of their neglect and past abuse by the Church and the state and that this might finally free them and others from the historical stigma of disgrace.

The women who have chosen to speak here force open a crack in a once-closed system and call to us to look inside. The access they permit us to socially concealed spaces forcefully demonstrates how the "histories we live are constrained by larger cultural narratives"; their "tiny stories," in other words, capture a central feature of our macro social condition (Denzin 1991, 157). Their perspectives—from a banished culture—help us to interpret the hidden experiences of generations of Magdalenes and reformatory survivors. In this way their "reclaimed" selves are of great instructive value. They alter our sense of our shared social past by permitting us to observe the colonizer through the gaze of the colonized.[34] This inverted lens is invaluable, as Gayatri Spivak (2007, 237) contends, for helping us "to learn to learn from below." In this sense, their status, as unauthorized interpretations, makes the stories that follow extremely valuable. Indeed, one of the goals of this work is, as sociologist Peter Berger (1967, 11) once wrote, "to 'see through' the façade of society to find out what is really going on underneath it all." By exposing forced labour, educational deprivation, and identities permanently altered by stigma and emotional neglect, these former inmates' accounts actively resist and challenge the Good Shepherds' claims of a righteous mission in aid of the socially vulnerable.

As the interview process returned my participants to painful dimensions of their past and called them to revisit former perceptions of themselves, new meaning and understanding were generated. One result from this is that some of them have let go of parts of their stigmatized identities and reclaimed other parts that had been stolen from them. Repossessing

34 While it is distressful that, as Audre Lorde (1984, 114) says, it still falls upon the "oppressed to teach the oppressors their mistakes," this problematic arrangement provides formidable insights.

themselves in this way has provided postcolonial agency, that is to say, the colonized[35] discovered the potential for creative and expressive ways of overcoming or, at least, acknowledging past trauma (Jabri 2013, 133). In the act of recollecting and speaking of what had been denied them and suppressed, these "voices from below" (Kilty et al. 2014, 104) or "subaltern" (Gramsci 1971, 55) perspectives have been transformed. Their experiences—and once-forbidden voices—have been taken out of the margins and situated at the heart of their past.

The intimate vantage point that I have been granted, "inside" these Good Shepherd experiences, has shown me how the identities of this group of women, then girls, were deliberately crushed and reshaped by powerful external forces. But their accounts take us beyond that point by chronicling their ongoing attempts to redefine themselves following confinement. In so doing, they help us to make sense of how these women have managed to defuse the negative impact of institutionalization on their own lives. Their stories demonstrate that, despite a legacy of despair that so many unwillingly carried, some of them have managed to locate the resolve to resist and defy the attempts, as Rachael has said, to push them "to the bottom of the well" (Romero, interview, 2012). While intimately capturing dark journeys, these stories also offer hope in that they represent pathways for re-envisioning our cultural practices and creating space for the important alternative narratives that these experiences force us to confront.

---

35 In this sense I refer to Tracey Nicholls's work on violence against women as a form of bodily colonization. Here, the interpretation of colonization has been expanded from its strict previous association with imperial conquest (Fanon) to consider patriarchy, gendered cultural assimilation, and critiques of the bodily domination of women (Nicholls 2012, 6). Nicholls explores the colonization of women under patriarchal systems in which the structural violence that marks the everyday lives of women effects their very psychology as a breaking down of "the confidence and sense of self" (6). She views Fanon's theory of colonization as being "grounded in an analysis of power relations that is as applicable to gender as it is to conquest of foreign territories. He draws together political dominance, economic exploitation, and a program of psychological destabilization that convinces the conquered of their incapacity to resist" (7).

CHRONOLOGY

1641 • Formation of the Order of Our Lady of Charity, Caen, France

1835 • Formation of the Good Shepherd Order, France

1844 • Formation of Good Shepherd Order, Canada

1848 • Formation of Good Shepherd Order, Ireland

1860 • Opening of New Ross Magdalene Laundry, Wexford

1863 • Formation of Good Shepherd Order, Australia

1890 • Constitutions for the Religious of the Congregation of Our Lady of Charity of the Good Shepherd of Angers

1893 • Opening of Home of the Good Shepherd, Saint John, New Brunswick

1893	• Opening of Mount Saint Canice, Hobart, Tasmania
Late 19th c.	• Expansion of Magdalene Asylums in Ireland and elsewhere
1900	• Opening of St. Mary's Training School for Girls, Toronto, Ontario
1942	• Opening of The Pines, Adelaide, South Australia
1958	• Closing of Home of the Good Shepherd, Saint John, New Brunswick
1962	• Vatican II, reconsideration of the Catholic Church in the modern world
1967	• Closing of New Ross Magdalene Laundry, Wexford
1970	• Kennedy Commission on Irish industrial and reformatory schools
ca. 1970	• Closing of St. Mary's Training School for Girls, Toronto, Ontario
1974	• Closing of Mount Saint Canice, Hobart, Tasmania • Closing of The Pines, Adelaide, South Australia
1989	• Hughes Commission appointed (Hughes Inquiry into Mount Cashel, St. John's, Newfoundland)
1990s	• Growing number of charges of sexual abuse involving Catholic clergy in Ireland and Newfoundland

1991	• Hughes Inquiry Report released: Royal Commission of Inquiry into the Response of the Newfoundland Criminal Justice System to Complaints
1993	• Unearthing of Magdalene laundry burial site in Drumcondra, Dublin
1994	• Joni Mitchell song "The Magdalene Laundries" • Irish Catholic priest Brendan Smyth pleaded guilty to seventeen counts of child sexual assault • Resignation of Irish prime minister Albert Reynolds's government
1996	• *Sex in a Cold Climate*, televised documentary • Report of Royal Commission on Aboriginal Affairs, Canada • Last laundry closes in Dublin
1997	• Australia's 1997 *Bringing Them Home: The Stolen Generation Report*
1999	• Suicide of Rev. Sean Fortune • Documentary series "States of Fear" exposes child abuse in Church-run institutions • Apology by Prime Minister Bertie Ahern over child abuse in Church-run institutions
2000	• Commission to Inquire into Child Abuse, Ireland
2002	• Irish reparation board established to pay compensation to child-abuse victims in Church-run institutions • *The Magdalene Sisters*, film release

2003	• Article by Mary Raftery in *The Irish Times* on Magdalene laundries • Irish Education Department is charged with blocking probe • Formation of Justice for Magdalenes (JFM) to support survivors
2005	• Redress Board notes more than 14,000 victims seeking compensation
2008	• Australian prime minister Kevin Rudd apologizes for mistreatment of children forcibly removed from Indigenous families • Canadian prime minister Stephen Harper apologizes on behalf of Canadians for the Indian Residential Schools system
2009	• Ryan Commission Report • *The Forgotten Maggies*, documentary • Australian prime minister Kevin Rudd apologizes to forced imperial child migrants, institutionalized children, and wards of the state
2011	• National Museum and the National Library of Australia launch "Forgotten Australia" project, *Inside: Life in Children's Homes and Institutions*
2012	• Sinead O'Connor acknowledges that she was a former Magdalene inmate

2013	• McAleese Report, "Report of the Inter-Departmental Committee to Establish the Facts of State Involvement with the Magdalen Laundries" • Creation of *Magdalene Institutions: Recording an Oral and Archival History* project • Irish prime minister Kenny acknowledges Magdalene survivors as a distinct and wronged group
2015	• Report of Truth and Reconciliation Commission, Canada • *The Waterford Memories Project*
2017	• *The Final Report of the Royal Commission into Institutional Responses to Child Sexual Abuse*, Australia
2017	• "At the UN Committee against Torture last year, Ireland argued that 'no factual evidence to support allegations of systematic torture or ill-treatment of a criminal nature' occurred in Magdalene laundries" (Ó Fátharta 2017)
2018	• State-sponsored meeting of Magdalene survivors, Dublin, Ireland

CHAPTER ONE
Broken Up and Upside Down

In the early 1950s, Chaparral Bowman[1] ran away from the Saint John, New Brunswick, Good Shepherd Reformatory and Industrial Refuge Laundry. Her escape is a fitting entry point into her story because it marks a critical shift in her life, crystallized in her memory as an intensely frightening and emotional experience. Her emotions were amplified by an anxiety about the unknown world that she was escaping into and by the enormity of the rules that she was breaching in her escape. Chaparral climbed through an unbarred second-story window, crossed the reformatory's internal yard, and scaled a beam that supported the high fence enclosing the institution. After edging her way through a tangle of barbed wire at the top of the fence, she was shocked to find that there was no similar beam supporting the opposite side of the fence. However, Chaparral decided to jump down what she figured

---

1 In this chapter, unless otherwise indicated, all quotations attributed to Chaparral Bowman (nee Georgina Williams) are taken from a series of interviews between Chaparral and Rie Croll, which took place between 2009 and 2013. Georgina Williams is Chaparral's legal name, but she preferred Chaparral, and was called Chaparral by her friends. The story of her name change follows.

was the ten-foot height of the fence. She said she could not remember having seen the outside of the reformatory's fence prior to that moment.

Chaparral was born in 1934 to Delcina, then thirteen and pregnant from a rape. Her parents had apparently sent her to the reformatory upon the advice of a priest. This detail in Delcina's story was significant to Chaparral because it was evidence that her mother "wasn't put there by law." Her mother, she repeatedly told me, had committed no crime. And yet, after Delcina delivered Chaparral, she remained confined in the laundry for years, until she was no longer able to work. Chaparral too was detained there, for the first eighteen years of her life.

Like other Roman Catholic laundries, the Saint John Good Shepherd reformatory had been established as a mission "for the purpose of reforming women and girls who have lapsed from virtue" (Fenety 1895, 406). Yet, behind this mission was a thriving and lucrative laundry business, so successful that it posed a threat to similar Saint John businesses. In fact, as early as April 1896, competing business owners in the city were aggravated because, according to a report in the *Saint John Daily Sun*, the Good Shepherd's "steam laundry ... employed convict labor." In speaking about this on behalf of other "laundrymen" in the city, Mr. Ungar said that the labour was supplied by "convicts sent there by magistrates. A magistrate can send any Catholic girl there instead of to jail. The Sisters get three years' work out of her for nothing." The "girls sent to such places," added Ungar, "were rarely reformed" (*Saint John Daily Sun* 1896). Ungar maintained that the Good Shepherd business was thriving because its working conditions were exploitative:

> Any girl could be sent to the convent from any part of the province, either by her father or guardian if he found he could not control her. Then the sisters had the benefit of her labour. They did laundry work so cheap that their starting up had interfered, to a considerable extent, with the other laundries.

He claimed that the laundry had an unfair advantage by not paying taxes, even water taxes, and that he could take the girls at the Good Shepherd reformatory, provide them with better conditions, and still provide laundry services at cheaper rates. Chaparral's escape came more than fifty years after these criticisms were publicly lobbed at the reformatory.

Once free, Chaparral felt a sense of panic that would persist for years. She later understood this reaction to be rooted in "not knowing a thing and pretending to be normal." For she quickly realized that she was operating at a huge deficit regarding the "rules" of the society around her and assumed that everyone she encountered could see this. She felt that she wore the disgrace of the reformatory all over her. She had always been told how and when to sit, stand, and speak and had rarely made her own decisions. She had been provided with few skills for coping in a non-institutionalized environment and, as a result, the outside world was frequently a frightening and chaotic place. "At least in there," Chaparral said, "I knew what to expect, bad or not."

After her escape, Chaparral would sometimes creep back at night and "sit with a bottle of booze" in the dark outside the reformatory. Her Christmastime experience of doing this was a particularly strong memory; she recalled looking through the windows "at the lights and the nighttime rituals" of the nuns and inmates within. Those moments were frightening because, if she got caught, she might be re-incarcerated forever. And yet, the institutional routines were almost soothing to revisit because, given her childhood spent in captivity, they represented all that she had known. Despite the loneliness and dislocation that came with life on the outside, the allure of habitual routine did not entice her to return to captivity. However, for years, she experienced a profound sense of being overwhelmed by the chaos of society outside the institution.

As a young adult, Chaparral needed to develop ethics for situations she had never seen modelled. She was forced to steal food from a local market in her first weeks living on the streets in order to survive. She took vegetables mostly, convincing herself that, because they were "of the land," they did not really belong to anyone. She drew the line at taking meat because she felt that it would be stealing directly from a farmer. Rationalizations of this kind typify Chaparral's ethics as she tried to survive in a foreign social world, largely unprepared for its rules and habits.

Living on the streets of Saint John, Chaparral found refuge in a new friend who helped her find her first job and taught her some necessary life skills, such as how to cash a cheque. This young woman lived at what Chaparral described as a "whorehouse," where Chaparral also soon came to live. The matron and her workers' protective and "family-like" environment warmly embraced Chaparral, temporarily filling some of the void she felt. It was not long before she took up prostitution, which raised further ethical challenges. For example, while she was still eighteen, one of her regular customers was a police officer who was married with children. His illegal and extramarital sex with her produced a moral conflict that she begrudgingly lived with at the time, reminding her in some ways of earlier abuses by priests and nuns. Although as a child she had confused abuse with much-needed affection, as an adult she had come to regard each of these incidents as damaging and confusing violations by trusted authority figures. Abuse and neglect contributed to a storehouse of cynicism and hurt, which for decades she could only express as anger.

In the years directly following her escape from the reformatory, there was no way for Chaparral to understand or mitigate the harms of institutionalization. Nor did she have the time or the capacity to do so. What she needed foremost was to concentrate on her survival, which meant quickly absorbing the social rules she needed in order to pass as "normal." Even still, she experienced a chronic sense of incompetence. Chaparral described a time shortly after she had made her way to Toronto when the mere act of crossing busy University Boulevard was an overwhelming task. In her days in the laundry she had always been forced to walk in lines of inmates, and stepping out of those lines meant punishment. Following institutionalization, even the thought of stepping out of line, let alone "going in her own direction"—such as crossing a street alone—proved remarkably stressful.

Based on her Good Shepherd experience, Chaparral devised a way to approach unnerving urban intersections. She would wait for groups of pedestrians to gather and then cross the street with them, even if they were moving in a direction that initially took her out of her way. She did not feel "worth enough to have traffic stop for [her] alone," and so this approach helped her to maintain a semblance of normalcy and keep anxiety at bay. When she finally did cross by herself, "right across the whole boulevard without stopping," she experienced such a feeling of elation she thought passersby could read the triumph on her face.

Chaparral attributed her capacity to endure to what she called a surviving spirit, which she credits to her ancestry. "My ancestors," she told me, "were First Nations survivors, *big time.*" Chaparral knew little of her family, except that they were of Indigenous descent and had lived on a reserve on the outskirts of Fredericton before moving to Saint John.[2] Chaparral's grandmother told her that her grandfather did not want Delcina around during her pregnancy because her presence would serve as a reminder that white men had raped her. He feared, too, that her child would look white. In desperation, Chaparral's grandparents took their daughter to the local priest, who advised them to put her in the Good Shepherd reformatory. After Delcina gave birth, he reassured them, the nuns would find the baby a home and their daughter would be returned to them. Chaparral's mother never did return home. Delcina was exploited as a labourer until she was no longer useful to the nuns and a home was never found for her daughter. The nuns misinterpreted

---

2 In our earliest conversations, Chaparral told me that she was unsure about the specifics of her Indigenous ancestry beyond her family's migration from a reserve near Fredericton to Saint John, New Brunswick. This location could imply Wolastoqiyik (Maliseet) heritage but she variously referred to herself as Mi'kmaq and Métis. Joan Sangster's 2001 study of female delinquency in Canada from the 1920s to the 1960s provides an important consideration for reading Chaparral's story. As a female of Indigenous descent born into a Canadian Good Shepherd reformatory, Chaparral was, in a sense, doubly marked. This reflection aligns itself with Sangster's observation concerning the treatment of various categories of females who were said to have violated sexual norms. Prostitutes and Indigenous women, says Sangster, were seen as threats to the nation, whereas other sexually delinquent girls were viewed as redeemable (198).

Delcina's lack of English proficiency and her trauma from her beating and rape as intellectual disability. Chaparral said, "they got this idea that she was retarded; that the men beat her so bad they made her retarded." Chaparral's grandmother did not question this interpretation. "Back then," said Chaparral, "you believed what people in authority told you."

As a child, Chaparral worked alongside Delcina in the laundry and learned she was her mother only when Chaparral was a young teen. Before this discovery, Chaparral sometimes joined the other inmates who, steered by the nuns, cruelly derided and abused Delcina, who was punched and hit and ridiculed regularly. In the laundry, pregnant unmarried girls "were the scum of the earth," said Chaparral, and "an Aboriginal girl was even more so." While Chaparral's small role in Delcina's abuse ceased with the discovery that Delcina was her mother, it nonetheless created lifelong feelings of guilt and remorse for her. Chaparral also deeply regretted that she never grew to love her mother:

> Years later they said they knew that my mother had syphilis; they knew she was a diabetic, and they let it go on until her death. And that is a pain that I cannot express because I had no love for my mother, I mean, I still don't. I don't understand love between people. I have a lot of friends and I really like them but I've had some who have died and I don't feel what I see other people feeling or showing. So, I don't have that, whatever "that" is.

So, while Delcina and Chaparral had a relationship of sorts, it was distorted by institutionalization, Delcina's progressive disease, and the nuns' demonstrated contempt for Delcina. Without regard for her condition and lack of skills, Delcina was released from the Good Shepherd reformatory and put out on the streets, where she died in 1968.

When Chaparral was almost eight years old, her work assignment shifted from general cleaning to the laundry. It was there, she remembered, that she stole an article of clothing, Mrs. R's nightgown that had been sent in from the community to be laundered. "There was this pink nightgown," she said, "that had lace on the top and it smelled like what I thought a mother would smell like. And I stole it. I put it underneath my uniform, under my apron." The theft left Chaparral feeling sick with fear, since such an offence was immense by the nuns' standards and the consequences for her, should she be found out, would be likewise:

> And while I was in the bathroom I was physically sick because I knew I would be beat within an inch of my life for stealing something like that and then I went to the nun and I said, "Mother I am really sick" and she looked at my face and I guess it looked ... I looked so scared that she told me to go up to the infirmary and to go to bed. So, I went straight to bed and I took that nightdress out and I put it under my mattress. And I was a bed wetter and the mattresses were straw, so it wasn't long before that nightdress just smelled to high heaven. And I would take it out at night and I would hug that nightdress, and it became ... it wasn't Mrs. R's nightdress anymore, it became my mother's. It was my mother's nightgown.

This theft was an emotionally complicated act. Later, as an adult, its significance continued to resonate with Chaparral; she compassionately understood its meaning and what her child-self needed and lacked.

The Order of the Day

Each day in the Good Shepherd reformatory, the tolling of bells marked prayers and silences tied to the nuns' religious rituals. Inmates too operated under this regimentation, thereby ensuring around-the-clock order. This regimen shaped Chaparral's childhood and rendered her inflexible to change when, in the outside environment, she began to encounter unpredictability. The nuns regulated each day to the minute:

> Quarter to six the bells would ring. The nun would put the lights on and she would start with "In the name of the Father," and everybody would get out of bed, on the floor beside our bed, and we said about ten minutes of prayers. And then you lined up for the bathroom. And you had to line up in your rows, your bed rows. Beside your bed was a basin, and a bar of soap and your towel and you went over to the sinks and you poured water into your basin and brought it back to your stand and washed your face and whatever. And you went and emptied the basin and you emptied your basin in the same order as your bed rows.

Following this, inmates would make their beds and go downstairs to Mass. Chaparral explained that, once inside the chapel, the girls would check the altar for the number of candles: two candles signified a Low Mass and that meant that breakfast would be in half an hour; three meant High Mass and a one-hour wait until they ate. Following chapel, the girls filed in a line downstairs to breakfast.

The formula of daily life under the Good Shepherds rarely changed. Uniformity and conformity were rigidly imposed upon all aspects of everyday life. Inmates had no freedom to wander or even to step out of line. Meals were served at precisely the same time, most often with the same food, and inmates were always seated next to the same person. Choice in anything was rare, and there was little variety, even in terms of whom you could speak with. Chaparral remembered that when seated at the long dark brown refectory tables, "you couldn't talk to the people on either side or holler down the table, you just spoke to the one directly opposite you." An older inmate-monitor supervised conversation. More than anything else, they were not allowed to speak of things outside the reformatory's walls.

The many rules that uncompromisingly shaped each day did not provide Chaparral with a feeling of solidity or rootedness; in fact, she was left with a lifelong feeling of "not belonging anywhere" and of having little personal substance. She had no sense of ownership of either space or speech, and no sense of a control of her time, no prospect of anything personal or individual:

> You had no identity. You see if you were bad and you promised to be good, they'd change your name. There was no "you." There was everybody. I was baptized Georgina, I was baby Jane, I had Jean, I had Loretta, I was Gemma, I was Maria, I was Bernice, back to Jean, back to Loretta and when I finally left, I had been Jean for about five years ... So there is no you. There was no Jean, she was just part of that line-up. Everything the nuns say is "our." There was nothing personal.

Since a collective identity was all that Chaparral knew as a child, she had never questioned the fact that even her name was not hers to possess.

Following breakfast each morning Chaparral was expected to go straight to her cleaning assignment, which was dusting and cleaning until noon; she recalled that she was responsible for cleaning the large staircases. When she grew tall enough, Chaparral was assigned to a laundry machine called the mangle. She developed "great pride" in the strength that it took to do this job and in putting the sheets through the mangle properly. The machines did not wring the sheets out and when Chaparral handled them, they were dripping wet and very heavy. "And you hauled these sheets out by hand," she told me, and "you loaded all these wet sheets back in to another machine and they got wrung out there and came out still wet but not dripping." Hard and repetitive laundry labour like this created many short- and long-term injuries, especially in the younger inmates' bodies. As an adult, Chaparral needed to have surgery on her feet because of the substandard working conditions and long hours of laundry labour. It took four operations to attend to the damage that the years of wearing poor footwear on the wet laundry floor had caused to her growing feet:

> When the surgeon got in there he said my metatarsals were porridge and we would have been so much better off by letting the kids have no shoes on than to be in leather shoes and to be working in water where they'd get sloppy and wet. And when you went to bed at night and took your shoes off, the shoes would curl up and dry and, in the morning, you would have to force your growing feet into these shoes again. It would take until about 9:30, 10 o'clock for the shoes to get wet enough to loosen up again. The tightening up and loosening up is what destroyed the metatarsals in my feet.

Austere regimentation was expected of even the youngest inmates, and anyone whose body was unruly was humiliated and punished: "You were supposed to train your body to do your will, not you do your body's will."

In this and other ways, inmates' bodies conformed to the demands of the institution. Bedwetting, for example, which Chaparral did regularly until the day she left the reformatory, was treated with utmost severity, with inmates forced to wear their urine-soaked sheets on their back and bear the brunt of mocking from other inmates. Chaparral attributed her early bedwetting to fear. The nuns had told her repeatedly that the devil was always in wait. Chaparral came to believe that the devil was waiting underneath her bed and that, if she were to put her feet onto the floor to go to the bathroom in the middle of the night, he would grab her. So, instead of risking this, she would "lay there and fall asleep again and, of course, just pee the bed."

When reformatory rules were violated, or order was disrupted, the older, stronger girls frequently assisted the nuns in disciplining the inmates. The nuns would get these girls "to hold the small kids for 'the basin' or to put you in Saint Peter's room or anything like that," said Chaparral. "They would do it joyfully," she explained. "Because again, it's that thing [that feeling of], it isn't me this time." Chaparral described "the basin" as a form of punishment in which a girl's head was held under water until her resistance was subdued. This usually happened before a girl was confined to isolation in Saint Peter's room. There were supposedly five of these rooms, one for each class of girls.

The word "class" did not have the same meaning there as "classes" in a school system; rather, they were simply inmate groupings. As a younger child, Chaparral was in the Guardian Angel class. Her memories of Saint Peter's room from that time in her life were clear. It was a room, she said, about "6 feet maybe 4 feet wide and with all boards and no windows." What stood out most clearly about that solitary confinement room was that, when the big door of Saint Peter's room was shut, she was in blackness: "There were no windows and then this door would shut behind you and I remember trying to find the crack between the door and the wall and there wasn't any." Alongside the door was a little opening with a sliding door through which meals were passed. The bed was made of boards and at the end of the bed there was a pail that served as a toilet. Each morning the inmate was let out to empty and clean the pail and then put a disinfectant in it. As a bedwetter, Chaparral experienced Saint Peter's room frequently. She was also sent there for other behaviour infractions. Saint Peter's room was such a frightening experience that by the time Chaparral was fourteen she resisted it "like crazy," often putting up a physical fight when she was sent there.

Because of the repetitiveness of each day at the Good Shepherd reformatory, one day blended seamlessly into the next. Consequently, any events that departed from the monotony stood out in stark relief for Chaparral and became intensely memorable. During one of her isolation periods, she was prematurely removed from her cell and offered a deal of sorts:

> We had a visiting nun from Ireland. So, they got girls to sing these Irish songs and I was in Saint Peter's room and Mother Saint [name] said to me [that] if you can learn "The Minstrel Boy" in a half hour, you can come out. And this other woman

> came and got me, and we went up where the piano was, and she gave me the lyrics and the tune, and I was very good at hearing something once or twice and I could do it. And I remember singing that "Minstrel Boy" to that nun and feeling very privileged. But now that I know that those in Ireland were the same bunch of pigs we had there, and I think "oh, my god" and I sang for her because she was a visitor and we had to make a good impression and I was hidden in Saint Peter's room until they realized that I would be able to pick that up.

In hindsight, one of Chaparral's few special moments became a moment of repugnance. Her realization that the inmates were only as valuable as their ability to perform refuted her earlier hope that the nuns and priests had some love and compassion for her and other inmates. Despite the suffering inflicted upon Chaparral, part of her needed to and continued to believe that her caretakers cared about her. However, between her sexual abuse by nuns and priests (which is discussed in the pages ahead), and their later denial in court that Chaparral had even been in the Good Shepherd reformatory as an infant and young child, Chaparral's remaining faith in the nuns was broken. Instead, she came to see them as a ruthlessly calculating and self-preserving organization.

As the inner workings of other laundries, reformatories, and similar institutions such as residential schools became exposed in the media starting in the 1990s, Chaparral reassessed the cruelty of her own experience. With these public revelations, facing her experience of incarceration became almost unavoidable. What Chaparral once considered an atrocity that she alone bore, she came to see as a shared violence that persisted for many former inmates long after these institutions were closed.

Broken Up and Upside Down

Chaparral developed a deeply fixed perception of herself as damaged and distorted because of these childhood institutional abuses. The Good Shepherd nuns offered Chaparral no validation of her individuality, for attention to the individual contravened their reform methods. It was only in random moments, when attention was indiscriminately paid to Chaparral, that she gained a sense of herself as distinct from others. One such formative occasion occurred when Mrs. B, a children's aid worker, negotiated Chaparral's potential adoption in front of her. As the would-be parents surveyed the children lined up in their "feast day dresses," "all wearing [their] best 'take me' smiles," one woman took an interest in Chaparral. In a world where even smells were predictable, Chaparral recalled that she "smelled so good":

> I was probably five and she came and stopped by me and she said, "Mrs. B, what about this little one?" And she had her hand on my head and I remember I was praying "let me be adopted" ... I didn't even know what adopted meant ... they said these women were coming and they were going to look the kids over and some of you might get adopted.

In response to the woman's interest in Chaparral, Mrs. B, "with her pink lips and her rouged cheeks," checked her clipboard. Chaparral recalled being fixated on Mrs. B's hat, "a blue hat with a bird on it." As she spoke, "this bird bobbed its head and I was watching this bird and she looked at her clipboard and she said, 'no, no, not this one, the mother was diseased.'" Hearing those words, said Chaparral, the woman very suddenly "took her hand off my head ... I felt the static electricity—when she removed her hand—in my hair and I didn't know what that meant, and she just passed on to somebody else and two girls got taken that day." Chaparral was confused about what the exchange meant, and it disturbed and upset her because it registered with her as a blunt rejection, yet she did not know why she had been so abruptly rejected:

> Later, I went into the toilet. The water was always kept running in the bowl because many of the little ones forgot to

> flush. When I looked into the bowl I saw that my face was broken up and in pieces. At supper, I looked at the back of my spoon and I was upside down on the back and right side up but squished in the front. We didn't have any utensils to eat with other than spoons, and the bowl part of the spoon was enamel and the back was stainless steel, so I looked at the back and I was upside down and I thought in my child's mind that this is was Mrs. B meant, that I was broken up and I was upside down. And I carried that and I wouldn't look at anybody. That was what I thought everyone could see and why I was not adoptable.

Based on these self-assembled meanings, Chaparral equated being upside down and broken with "diseased." She concluded from this that she was not like the other girls. She was defective.

The memory of this rejection created a self-impression that Chaparral wrestled with even as an adult. Chaparral described this event as "one more pain [she] learned to push down and cover up along with the next and the next." She came to internalize the nuns' characterization of her as a bastard. This resulted in different treatment from the other inmates:

> They actually used the word "bastard" without telling us what it meant. But, we had to say ... the bastards all had to say ... fifteen minutes of extra prayers for the sins of their parents, and you were the sin. So, you got a feeling that you were not like everybody else, your skin was not like everybody else's. There were no mirrors. There was no way to tell that people couldn't see the evil in you. I believed that everybody who looked at me could see how evil I was and how ugly I was, and for years I walked around with my head down looking through my bangs. I absolutely refused to put my head up.

Chaparral knew that she was one of "those children," one of those who were considered to have been "born bad" and were made to atone for their mothers' out-of-wedlock pregnancies. "I think," she said, "but I'm not sure, that this was how the slave mentality was ingrained. By them making us feel that we were worthless and only worthwhile to the church as workers. That's how we could make restitution for what our parents did ... was by being, you know, good slaves." As a young child Chaparral figured out that, "as the lowest of the low," if she were to be considered worthy in the nuns' eyes, it would be through her work contributions.

With no one to modify or correct her perceptions, Chaparral's frightening self-evaluations grew in power and became fixed realities. She came to consider herself a broken bastard. "For one thing," she told me, "I'm different ... I'm still upside down and my face is broken up ... this is real. It's so hard to explain but it is still with me. It doesn't go away, ever." This stigmatization lingered throughout Chaparral's life along with her sense that she was somehow an embodiment of sin. This caused her to feel innately flawed and unlikable as a friend. Her skewed self-perception was partly shaped by the nuns' taboo around friendships between inmates. "If you were really friendly with a girl," Chaparral explained, "you had to tell the priest and then he'd tell the nuns and then if she was anywhere in your area like sleeping or eating or anything then you'd both be moved further apart because they called it the sin of 'particular' friendship." Chaparral felt that the nuns were concerned about lesbian relationships being formed, but the result was that "you never formed a friendship." Consequently, there were few supportive human bonds in the Home of the Good Shepherd and there was little camaraderie among the girls. This fuelled Chaparral's lingering "hang up" about trusting people. "I really like people," she told me, "but as soon as I think I like them then I sabotage the friendship. I don't answer mail, whatever, I just drop it. It would be too painful to face the sin of it, I think. You isolate yourself pretty much for being a sinner."

Deeply guarded secrets about her sexual abuse by nuns and clergy caused Chaparral to retreat still further from the other girls. Those abuses also aggravated her already complicated sense of being "broken up," with no bodily sovereignty. Her first memory of abuse is from around the age of three, when a bishop took a special interest in her.

> I clearly remember my first encounter with the Bishop; I was probably three. He gave me candy and cookies and told me what pretty eyes I had. I was the pet of the Bishop. He never hurt me. He just played around. He gave me pretty dresses that I could wear to go visit him. Other than that, I had to wear the uniform that everybody wore. So when I went to visit him, I got to wear these pretty dresses and I remember the little panties with lace on the butt and ankle socks with lace on them and patent leather shoes ... And he bought me these things, so I really liked him. And all he did was play around with me here and there and give me candies for showing him parts of myself and stuff. But he never hurt me. So, with him it was okay. I was the pet until a younger one came in. That was the day I lost my candy.

Chaparral identifies this rejection as the beginning of teaching herself not to care: "I taught myself I didn't care even when the Bishop transferred his pedophile attentions to a younger girl and I was thrown back onto the trash heap."

The repeated messages that she was born of sin coupled with ongoing physical and emotional exploitation caused Chaparral to bear personal responsibility for her abuse. This was confirmed once more when a nun sexually molested her and then directly blamed Chaparral for the abuse. While the abuse itself was emotionally damaging, the nun's accompanying message was even more destructive:

> I had this terrible hidden feeling that somehow, I had brought it on myself, and I made the nuns do it. I had this one nun tell me

> that the devil was in my eyes and caused her to sin. I carried that with me for a long time ... for years I walked around with my head down. I didn't have a mirror, so I didn't know what that meant. I didn't want to look at anybody because I didn't want to make anybody sin. As a little girl, you'd get punished if you walked around with your head down, you'd get punished for that because you were being sullen, and if you put your head up and looked them straight in the eye, you were being bold, so you got punished for that. There was no way to go.

When Chaparral was about seven, a priest singled her out for special attention. Again, Chaparral maintained that the priest, like the bishop before him, did not hurt her since his sexual contact with her involved petting and fondling, rather than intercourse. Chaparral interpreted this as his demonstration of love for her—at least, until she left the laundry and realized how exploitative the relationship had been.

The story of Chaparral's relationship with this priest began with the annual Children of Mary in May pageant. The pageant began with a procession that culminated in the priest's crowning a girl who had been "really good" that year, as the Blessed Virgin. Leading up to this highly anticipated event, the younger inmates' behaviour was monitored and charted with star-shaped stickers on a large piece of cardboard. All the girls' names were listed there and each day leading up to the pageant they were rewarded or punished with different coloured stickers assigned for degrees of "good" behaviour and no sticker if they were "bad." At the end of the month, the names of those who had earned only gold stars would be collected, and one girl would be crowned the Blessed Virgin.

For the procession, hoops serving as crowns were created out of wire covered in green crepe paper and embellished with green leaves and decorated differently, depending on how "good" the girls had been. The inmates who had received all gold stars wore hoops covered with big red roses made of crepe paper. This was the crown that Chaparral dearly wanted to wear but she knew that her bedwetting meant that she would not earn any stars. On pageant day, the priest found Chaparral crying at the back of the procession that was headed to crown the Blessed Virgin, and he asked a nun why Chaparral had only a bare wire on her head. Despite the nun's angry response, the priest decorated Chaparral's crown with roses and ribbons. This, she said, was the first time anyone had behaved like that toward her.

Chaparral said the next thing she knew she was the priest's pet: "I would sit on his knee during catechism. I was sure he loved me. Yah, I really did believe that." Although this priest did not have intercourse with Chaparral, he pursued sexualized contact with her from the time that she was a child until after she left the reformatory. As the relationship persisted, her internal discord increased. On the one hand, he gave her longed-for attention; on the other hand, he counselled the younger girls in the laundry to remain pure, like "his idol" the Virgin Mary. All the while, Chaparral said, "he's doing these things with the small girls so that they are sinful." This contradiction created hopeless conflict in those he assaulted, which they could not voice, and which left them feeling permanently stained. For Chaparral, as a child, this emphasized that her "face was upside down." Even as an adult, she could not shake the sense that she wore the signs of the abuse and "sin" externally. A fractured and contradictory self-image followed her when she left the reformatory and was reinforced through her continued relationship with the priest:

> Even after I left there, he'd take me out to Mispec beach and we'd lie on the sand and stuff like this you know. He never had intercourse with me ever but he pretended, which was worse, I think. He'd pretend that was what he was doing but he wasn't doing anything; when I became a prostitute and he found out about it, I remember him calling me a whore. That really hurt me.

The priest's angry rejection and stigmatization of Chaparral was deeply hurtful because she genuinely believed that he loved her. Because of this belief, it took her a long time to see the relationship as exploitative, and when she did, she felt his denunciation as yet another abandonment:

> I guess that I wasn't special to him. He was just satisfying some bizarre need and I happened to be the little girl that was handy. After I stopped crying, and got over it, I was kind of glad it was all over because then I didn't have any reason to pretend. That's what we used to do; he took me one time to a cottage owned by a friend of his and we spent the whole weekend. He was drinking wine and he was really drunk and he was telling me all these stories about his mother and the things she did and then a priest ... he was involved with a priest ... when he was just a boy. And this priest was telling him how women were evil and filthy and all this, and he told me how he used to go home and looked at his mother, and he loved his mother, and he couldn't believe she was filthy and evil, so he had this twisted sense of what women were. He was so drunk—he was crying and slobbering about. I didn't know it then, but he frightened the heck out of me.

For many decades after her escape from the Good Shepherd reformatory, Chaparral remained imprisoned in her sexual abuse: "I could not say the words ... I could talk about the basement and Saint Peter's room and beatings. Those things I could talk about but that was everyday life for me." However, the sexual abuse was a different matter. The nuns and priests had given Chaparral every indication that she was responsible for it, and so giving voice to those abuses opened her to blame.

What complicated things further for Chaparral was that she sometimes experienced sexual pleasure in response to these violations, even though she was a child:

> I don't know if you've ever talked to anyone who's been abused as a child but for me, by the time I was nine, my body was responding to these people. And, it was like a betrayal of your own body. We are sexual creatures and to those who didn't hurt me, I responded to it in a big way because there was no love, there was no outward sign of anybody caring about you beyond that abuse, so my body would respond to them at various times, and then I felt that I was the sinning one. And so, I never told anybody because I didn't want anybody to think that I had been a bad child. I couldn't tell anyone ... because I felt that I was the sinning one because my body responded to it.

Chaparral's need to view her wardens as caring and trustworthy protectors made taking responsibility for her own abuse preferable to admitting that they had used and molested her.

As an abandoned child, a "bastard," a victim of sexual abuse, and a prisoner, Chaparral carried multiple stigmas that made her a social outsider. But, it was how the nuns taught her to see herself that most fragmented and disconnected her:

> And, you are the sinner! That carries on into your adult life. It doesn't go away. You have to make a conscious effort not to dwell on it because if you do, it's there. It is there! There's a feeling always of being lost. Disconnected would be a better word I think. Disconnected from what everybody else is. And, even though I truly believe it had nothing to do with us as kids, we were not sinful and all that, but it's there. It's there, as though you don't really belong anywhere because people are good and you are evil. And you have to hide that because if they find out about it then no one will like you or want you or whatever. It's a really bad thing that they do, to do that to children.

Chaparral's sense of sin and bodily disconnection was exacerbated by her one and only visit to her family, when she was seven or eight. This visit, she later understood, was related to a decision to phase out the admission of children to the reformatory. At that point, they began farming out the youngest children to orphanages or attempting to return them to their families. Chaparral was sent to family members in the hopes that they would take her back. She vividly described that "terrifying" day when she was released into her grandmother's care. After exiting on foot through the back of the reformatory, they passed a place called Lady Hazen's castle, which Chaparral had only ever seen from the yard of the reformatory. She recalled that her grandmother walked her up the hill overland, not by the street, to get to her house.

Once at her grandmother's, Chaparral entered an even more foreign world. She was left outside with other children, some of whom were half naked because of the summer heat:

> I remember they were doing strawberries and my grandmother gave my cousin Marilia and I each a bowl of the froth that they take off berries when they are making jam and left us sitting out in the back yard ... It's kind of all unreal because I had to go to the bathroom and all they had was an outhouse. I was terrified because I had never been in one ... and the foul smell ... and so I came out of there and I had peed on the floor in there because I couldn't sit over that hole. I didn't know I wouldn't fall in. Anyway, my grandmother was trying to be kind, I think, and she got me to go lay down on the bed and I had never been in a bed by myself in a little tiny room, you know, what a single bedroom is like. I'd never been in one and I was absolutely petrified. And then I woke up and I had to go to the bathroom, but nobody had told me I could leave the room, so again I just peed where I was. And I remember my grandmother coming in and saying, "jeez who's going to want you, all you do is cry or pee?"

Her grandmother then cleaned up Chaparral and sent her with an older girl to get ice cream at a nearby store, about seven houses down the road. Chaparral had never had an ice cream cone. She remembered intensely the smell of the store. "It was so pungent," she recalled, "and outside the store there were all these little straw baskets of strawberries. They were all on this shelf outside the store and everything smelled so good." The girl asked her if she could find her own way back to her grandmother's, cautioning her to stay on the side of the road that they were on, because there were moochers in the woods:

> So, I am walking up the road and I'm licking this ice cream and really enjoying it and a man came out from between these houses and called me Jean and said, "come here, I want to show you something." So, I went across to the woods and he raped me. I was used to being abused ... he wasn't hurting me any more than Father [name] had done or the bishop, so I wasn't afraid of him, and I'm licking this ice cream while he's doing his thing, because I had learned I had the ability to separate myself from myself, and the ice cream was more important than what he was doing.

The man who sexually assaulted Chaparral warned her to stay there for a long time or he would tell her grandmother, and she would be sent back to the Good Shepherd. She did not know what he meant by a long time, so she stayed there until she heard people calling her name.

When Chaparral got back to her grandmother's, supper was being served. She tried to eat, but threw up. She remembers someone saying it was the heat that had made her sick and her grandmother putting her to bed again, this time in the living room on an old black leather couch:

> And I heard some talking ... and they were trying to decide what to do with me ... and someone said, "nobody is going to

> want her, all she is doing is pissing and throwing up and crying. What's the matter with her? Is she crazy?" And I remember hearing that.

The next thing Chaparral recalls was waking up to hear her grandmother on the porch talking to a man, who, it turned out, was the man from the woods—and a relative. The next day, a woman fetched Chaparral and brought her back to the Good Shepherd.

Upon returning to the reformatory, all of Chaparral's "pretty" clothes, including a gold locket of her mother's that her grandmother had given her, were taken by the nuns, and never returned. As a nun was getting Chaparral back into her uniform, she said, "such a shame that you couldn't be good, for one day, Jean, you might have had a home of your own. You must not talk about your day out." It would be many years before Chaparral spoke of that rape or the abuses that she had endured from the nuns. The following day she was moved directly to the prisoner's class, or the laundry.

Considering her prior sexual abuse, there was nothing to alert Chaparral to the fact that the assault she endured that day was not the norm or, more importantly, that it was not her fault. Completely alone in a world of enforced silence, Chaparral had no one to help her interpret these abuses. Cycles of abuse and abandonment thus contributed to her "broken" self-perception. It was excruciating for her to put words to those abuses:

> Putting it out there you know? Even inside my head, I had a hard time putting it into words ... IN MY OWN HEAD! Even admitting it. It was as though somehow, they could still harm me if I told about it; that the person ... could still somehow reach out, although they are dead, and harm me—harm me mentally more than physically.

Ultimately, it was the intangible mental, spiritual, and emotional abuses that most deeply injured Chapparal's sense of self.

No Personality

Renaming herself was a symbolically important part of Chaparral's identity reconstruction. Her lack of a definite sense of self, she told me, went back to her birth and to her first name, Georgina, given to her by the Sisters of the Good Shepherd. Georgina was but the first of many names the nuns assigned to her. It was significant to Chaparral that it was not a name chosen by her mother: "Some nun gave it to me when she poured some water on my head to keep me from hell. So it means nothing. It's not like I was named for a favourite aunt or a grandmother. It's a nothing name." When she finally changed her name from the ones that the nuns had assigned her to Chaparral, this name had significance for her.

In addition to having multiple names, Chaparral was also numbered. I asked her what purpose assigning numbers to inmates served; she had no idea but, despite the Church's testimony to the contrary, all inmates had numbers.[3] Chronic renaming and renumbering took a toll on Chaparral, the worst effect of which was having "no firm identity." After careful reflection, she chose the name Chaparral for herself, after the chaparral plant, which she described as "an unassuming plant" and "not particularly beautiful":

> It is now considered to be the oldest unchanged plant on earth since one bush in China was discovered to have a twenty-five-acre root system. This plant supplies food, shelter, and cover for a number of forms of life that are completely dependent on it for survival. It is medicinal in many ways, it can withstand years of drought, years of killer weather including storms and freezing temperatures. It can withstand it and it just keeps on. Then, within a day of sunshine it will rebound and send out shoots of new growth, and flowers. It is aromatic

3 In 1999, Chaparral took the Sisters of the Good Shepherd to court, suing for the damages that she suffered while in their keeping, but she lost the case. While under oath, the nuns denied much of her experience in the reformatory, including the changing of her name.

> in the extreme. It has been maligned as a "stink bush," creosote bush, and a pest; all these terms I feel were applied to me at one time but, like this amazingly hardy plant, show me the kindness of the sun and I thrived.

Choosing a name that had significance for her, and that expressed her intended identity, helped Chaparral to find her bearings. The chaparral plant, she told me, defied domestication, a characteristic she intensely identified with. She would not be institutionalized again.

Many years after her escape from the Good Shepherd, and following a suicide attempt, Chaparral began seeing a psychiatrist, who diagnosed her as having "no personality," which she learned by peeking at her file when he stepped out of the room. At seeing this diagnosis, she was hurt and outraged and challenged him with it when he returned to the room:

> And I said, "I have definitely got a personality. Don't say I haven't got a personality." And I was angry and he said, "no, it's not that you don't have a personality. What it means is that by the time the child is two, they have a very definite idea of who they are, where they belong and who belongs to them and what belongs to them. And that's why two-year-olds are called terrible twos because they are asserting their right to their toys, to their mother, to whatever ..." And he said, "with you there wasn't any of that identification, so whoever Georgina is now that is not the Georgina that was meant to be. Your personality was crushed at birth."

Through their further discussions, Chaparral also learned that the psychiatrist's diagnosis of "no personality" could be attributed to the many years in which her attempts at self-expression and displays of independence were suppressed. Her institutional self was one that had been constructed by others, for the needs of others. Choosing her own name was a response to this;

she characterized this act of self-definition as a necessary step toward creating an identity denied her by the nuns' ideology.

Another step in the process of declaring a definite identity involved Chaparral's location of a formal, documented record of her existence. Chaparral had discovered that the nuns who raised her had never registered her birth. She realized this when she applied for a birth certificate, and her application was denied. The response from the government officials who handled her application was that, essentially, she did not exist. This fact did not seem to distress anyone except Chaparral, who felt it was a denial of both her and her mother's existence. Learning that she had never officially existed was a catalyst for getting beyond how she had come to characterize herself: "a non-person" or "the product of sin." She felt an urgency to get past these negative self-concepts. "You have to figure it out as an adult, you have to," she emphasized. "There are no two ways about it, you have to get over it, or you're lost again."

Chaparral's defence against losing herself again was to unlearn what she had been taught by the Sisters of the Good Shepherd. Replacing some of the injurious messages from her childhood helped to free her a little from some of her immobilizing inner dialogues. While ultimately empowering, her progression through this unlearning and relearning process was uneven. Since the negative beliefs she carried were associated with deeply instilled insecurities, it was all too easy to return to them. For instance, Chaparral said, "I had an awful sense of not even belonging here, you know? Like I was an accident that got here somehow. I've come to see that it [her existence] is not haphazard and I am worth it." She recognized that she no longer needed to live in fear of Christianity or any of its manifestations. Separating herself completely from that faith was a necessary part of divorcing herself from that fear but doing so made many people uncomfortable. "The so-called Christian people," she said, "don't understand how I could do this without a god, theirs or whatever—it's usually theirs—their interpretation of what God is, and I tell them I have a personal reciprocal relationship with my creator. I don't need a Bible, I don't need a priest, I don't need anything."

After years of suffering intimate partner violence and grappling with addictions, Chaparral gradually began to untangle herself from those destructive forces. With the help of a trusted doctor, Chaparral probed the previously unspeakable abuses she had suffered and the debilitating inner dialogues that had defined her. Gaining insight into her childhood sexual abuse brought Chaparral to some life-altering realizations. Importantly, it negated the perception that she was the product of sin. When she rid herself of that notion, she began to see herself in more compassionate terms, and "not made up of the trash they told us," an important turning point in her healing.

Time and again, Chaparral tried to summarize for me the lasting effects of the nuns on her, yet so much of it seemed beyond words. The cruelties of their institutionalization practices were still felt physically, emotionally, mentally, and spiritually, and they immobilized her in unexpected ways. For example, when she heard thunder, she could sometimes be reduced to a terrified five-year-old. "Because I was put underneath a tree at five," she said, "in a wet nightgown, because I wet the bed in a thunderstorm and was told that if I moved from that spot God was going to strike me dead." In later life, when Chaparral heard thunder, even though her rational mind would try to soothe her, she was right back to feeling like that frightened five-year-old.

Chaparral could only fully recognize what institutionalization had done to her once she was free of it. Yet, when she was on the outside, she became deeply resentful of what she had been denied, an education in particular. "That's where the anger kicks in," she told me; "they didn't give me grade one." One point that Chaparral repeatedly returned to in our conversations was that the Sisters of the Good Shepherd was not a teaching order. Their lack of credentials in this area was critical because it supported her claims about the very low level of education she received in the reformatory. Chaparral's resentment was twofold: not only did the nuns not make her education a priority, they also were unqualified to teach. Despite this educational deficit, Chaparral described one saving grace that came in the form of a relationship she formed with an elderly bedridden nun who taught her the basics of reading. This relationship, which Chaparral described as something of great value in a place that offered her little else, lasted until the nun's death. In her adulthood, Chaparral built on these skills through ongoing self-schooling that continued for the remainder of her life. Even at her most self-destructive low points while living on the streets, Chaparral carried a book under her arm, sometimes as a prop to demonstrate to herself and others that she was intelligent and worthy. But even after years of dedicated self-schooling, Chaparral considered her lack of credentials a major deficit; she did not have "the piece of paper"—the high school diploma—that demonstrated social belonging.

Chaparral knew that formal schooling would have made her more like others. Her sense of not fitting, of being a chronic outsider, was tied to this deficit. Diplomas, a mark of social standing, indicated a past with friendships, clubs, societies, a sense of normalcy, and a community to belong to. "It means you've been part of a family somewhere, that somebody knows who you are," Chaparral explained. "Nobody knows my name anywhere. I didn't know my name." Moreover, she was denied the common learning milestones offered by a public education, the shared terms and references, and the forms of play and socialization that come with schooling. These were a part of Chaparral's larger social deficit, something that she was ashamed of and tried to hide, for fear that people would think she was, in her words, stupid.

While her lack of formal schooling was something that she was never able to fully bridge, Chaparral filled in some of the holes it created in her life with the resources available to her. Having been denied all possessions as a child, for example, Chaparral described herself later in life as a hoarder, citing her marble collection, which numbered in the thousands. As we talked about the significance of those marbles, Chaparral had a revelation. "They're mine," she announced suddenly. "I don't have to share them with anybody. That's it. I just got it. Wild. They're mine. That just hit me like a ton of bricks." An early denial of personal possessions had created a deprivation that Chaparral needed to correct. She also collected teddy bears, or, as she put it, she rescued them. This began with an abandoned stuffed toy bear that she and her partner, Kacy,[4] found in the dump. Chaparral strongly identified with the bear's abandonment and "just had to take it home." In this and other ways, she began, piece by piece, to fill in experiences that had been denied her and had left her feeling incomplete.

One effective approach to righting herself was by writing about herself. The point when Chaparral knew that she must write her story came in 2006, following a judge's ruling that invalidated her Good Shepherd laundry existence.[5] Of the various hurts and violations Chaparral had endured, it was this blatant and official negation of her experience with the Good Shepherds that fuelled her desire to begin writing about her life. Having finally garnered the courage to legally challenge the Good Shepherd Order about the abuses she suffered while in their care, this formal rejection of her claim was a devastating blow to her credibility and to her faith in the state's ability to protect her. The judge and testifying nuns effectively denied that she had even been in the laundry as an infant and child:

> So right in this courtroom, he said this stuff never happened. They even denied the name changing, even Mother A [on the stand] called me Jean, which wasn't my name, and she referred to my mother as Henrietta. And when they said that, I thought, you don't want to know so I'm going to force the truth on you. So, I started writing it. I'd go to bed sometimes for two days and just wake up crying my eyes out, take a Gravol, go back to sleep. It was horrendous writing that first book because that's the child, right? The second one and all

4 The last twenty-five years of Chaparral's life, until her death in 2014, were spent in a loving and supportive relationship with her husband, friend, and artistic collaborator, Kacy Bowman.

5 In an email to me, Chaparral referenced her legal case as Georgina Williams v. The Religious of the Good Shepherd and the Bishop of Saint John New Brunswick, 2006. Justice John Turnbull presiding.

> the rest are all books where I stood up and closed my fist and said you're not doing it anymore to me. That first one was so difficult because it was like tearing my heart out, remembering how I felt as a child. I would write it and be crying as I wrote it, because it was so real.

In the face of this final blow from the combined powers of Church and state, writing was Chaparral's way of authenticating her and her mother's existence.

In the aftermath of this formal denial, Chaparral needed people to admit that her mother had lived and to know as well *how* Delcina had lived. Above all, she wanted to write a testimonial to her mother's life, to make it known that her mother's name was Delcina, and to honour her own complicated relationship with her mother. "She wasn't crazy," Chaparral told me. "She was just a very hurt human being that I couldn't have feelings for. I mean I pitied my mother and I would never have hurt her, but I didn't have that mother/daughter thing ... it's a missing piece."

Recording her life had other motives that were not entirely clear to Chaparral when she began writing. Her desire to validate her life also meant getting distance from it. Getting "clear of it" required Chaparral to step backwards into some of her most painful and confusing memories. Through revisiting her past, she was able to look critically at how the Sisters of the Good Shepherd had shaped her and, beyond their constraints, see who else she was, or could be. Chaparral's new, slowly emerging "I" revealed her as far more than an "evil" child or the self-destructive person who had been treading water for years. Putting that time of her life into writing gave her a new perspective and helped her to validate her existence. Doing this, she found, allowed her to honour her life, as she had lived it. "I was just writing it in scribblers," she said, "and then I realized, why don't I publish it?"

Exposing details of her own life in writing, fragments that she had tried to conceal for decades, was liberating for Chaparral. Making these parts of her life transparent helped her to stop evading the judgment of others. The things that had been done to her, and her subsequent ways of coping, she realized, were who she was. Writing about her life gave Chaparral a more compassionate perspective on her own situation. It helped remove some of the self-blame and judgment that she carried and gave her an understanding of how her harsh upbringing contributed to her own frailties and vulnerabilities.

Of the many obvious damages caused by the Good Shepherd nuns, the harm to Chaparral's sense of spirituality was one that she only gradually recognized. As an institutionalized child, she did not develop spiritually; instead, she came to despise the belief system that so diminished her. Once Chaparral was rid of the Sisters of the Good Shepherd, she did not wish to go near anything that was remotely connected to religion. Over time, as she began to take stock of the nuns' negative actions in the name of God, she could not bear any further association with Christianity. Even her prayers, as a response to fear, stopped. "I absolutely despise it," she admitted, "because I've watched how it works around me. It hasn't changed." Chaparral explained to me that what others glean from Christianity does not resemble her relationship to it:

> Whatever Jesus means to everybody else is not what it means to me. What it means to me is the Bishop messing with me when I was three years old, or Father [name] lying on top of me. That's what Jesus means to me.

The worst of her abuse stemmed from the manipulation of her mind and body in the name of God: "You do a terrible thing when you use people in the name of God … a terrible, terrible thing and then they get away with it. They do. People say they'll pay for it when they die and stuff. No, they don't, they just walk away, scot-free."

As an adult, Chaparral deliberately avoided organized religion but eventually found some measure of inner peace through her own form of spirituality. This progression began with her growing respect for nature.

Chaparral came to understand herself as a dimension of nature and was able to extend the respect she held for the natural world to herself: "I am conscious of it and it may sound silly but from a meal I always make sure that some of it is placed on the earth. It reminds me to respect what I am. I am the universe." This sense of a greater and grounding connectedness remained with Chaparral even as she continued to uncover areas of unresolved pain and outrage related to sufferings inflicted by those upon whom she had depended. An anecdote she shared from her time in the Home of the Good Shepherd epitomizes that hurt:

> There was one woman, who was named J, who came there at eleven years old and when she was over ninety, when that place closed, they put her out on the street. She had never been outside that wall. But after all those years of working in the laundry, from the age of eleven, they put her out when they closed those doors, like we put the garbage out. We don't need it anymore. They just put these women out.

This sense of being disposable and of no value to others was something that Chaparral struggled with her whole life. But the credo she came to embody, "I am the universe," balanced this perception in her later life. She also incorporated it into her work with at-risk Indigenous youth. In speaking in high schools about suicide, the cornerstone of her message was what it took her decades to learn: "they are the universe; alive, conscious and thinking about themselves and that they do matter." Chaparral's eventual awareness that she too mattered in this way helped her to get past trying to kill herself:

> And then I tell them what I believe, that when I was born, the minute I was conceived, that good or bad, the universe was changed. The whole molecular system of the universe changed because I was born, and that I do matter and they matter. They

> are the same materials as the rock, as the water. They are everything. They are the stars. And they are worth everything they need to work through in order to stay here. They are worth it.

Keeping this message close helped Chaparral move beyond the ongoing sense of estrangement she once felt, and the sense of "non-being" that the Church and the state had instilled in her by denying her experience. This conviction sustained in her a connectedness and harmony with life by providing a sense of belonging where there had once been none. As with her message to vulnerable youth, she tried to remain ever conscious of her connection to a greater, sustaining life force. This awareness, together with her self-discovery writing process, helped her to separate what she was once told she was made of from who she really was. In 2012 Chaparral was awarded the Queen's Diamond Jubilee Medal[6] in recognition of her courageous work as a writer in making her story of institutionalization with the Good Shepherds public.

6 Chaparral's acceptance of this medal in her then-hometown of Dryden, Ontario, along with a brief write-up about her life were covered in the *Dryden Observer*: http://thedrydenobserver.ca/2012/09/a-moment-to-savour/.

CHAPTER TWO
Baptized in Disinfectant

The STIGMATA
of
religiously tattooed
Magdalene
Slaves
scourgings of
"fallen women,"
scars from
inmate labour
laundry work
hard physical
against the will work,
disfiguring injury
to hands and minds
now and always

Branded and
besmirched by
vituperative
nails through the palms

language
religious scourgings
marks of experience
onto legs
bellies

Branded by injurious insult
religious tattooing of the mind
forced
physical labour
such as laundry work
against the will,
side by side nail marks
Christ inflicted pain
Magdalene self-injury
cigarette burns to
know what Jesus felt.
PENITENCE
the identifiable stigma
of slaves
hard labour institutions,
stigmata people
ancient
branded
on my body
the same wounds
symbols of pain
and slavery
marks of ancient inmate identification
by order of the church,
state order.
(Rachael Romero)

The Home of the Good Shepherd in North Plympton, Adelaide, South Australia—"The Pines," as it was known locally—operated from 1941 to 1974[1] by the Catholic Church's Order of the Good Shepherd Sisters under the control of the Children's Welfare and Public Relief Board. According to the Order:

> Girls committed to this home are accommodated in good wholesome surroundings, and keen interest is taken in their welfare by the matron and staff. During the weekdays the girls are fully occupied with various phases of laundry work, and their leisure hours are carefully provided for by means of concerts and other features. (State Children's Council 1944, 88)

In September of 1967, having just turned fourteen, Rachael Romero was sent to The Pines for one year of hard, unpaid labour. The offence that produced this conviction was running away from her sexually, mentally, and physically abusive father and, then, with nowhere to go, ultimately surrendering to child welfare. Rachael later discovered that her mother, who was named runner-up for a Housewife of the Year award during her incarceration, chose to have Rachael committed to The Pines rather than bear the indignity of making her father's abuse public. Apparently for her mother, it was a choice between protecting Rachael's father—and, by extension, the

1 According to a Government of Australia website, in 1941 the archbishop of Adelaide asked the Sisters of the Good Shepherd to establish a home for teenage girls with "behavioural problems." As a result, a convent named The Pines was established the next year. "This home was originally owned by the John Martin family. Set on nineteen acres of grounds, it was remodelled to accommodate up to eighty children. By December of 1942 The Convent of the Good Shepherd was proclaimed as a private reformatory school for girls. This proclamation enabled the Home to receive children who were wards of the State." https://www.findandconnect.gov.au/guide/sa/SE00029.

family's reputation—or defending Rachael. The decision seemed clear-cut to her mother: "She told me that she had to choose between her husband and me and she had to choose her husband" (Romero, interview, June 2013).[2] Ultimately though, her parents' manoeuvre to protect their reputation resulted in an intentional discrediting of Rachael's own reputation. She explained that, when she was sent to The Pines, her father checked himself into a psychiatric ward. This way, he could circumvent responsibility for his abuse of Rachael and maintain control of the situation. Rachael saw this tactic as typical of her father's strong survival instinct:

> [H]e was afraid that I was going to out him about the sexual abuse because I had run away and the police were involved and welfare was involved.... He had taken me to the police before to say, "take her, she is a delinquent, take her," and I think he was trying also to besmirch my record; so that I would be a liar and a cheat ... so I was not credible if I said anything against him. So, then he could cover it by having a nervous breakdown. But he did it [committed himself] because there was talk of committing him and because he did it himself he could leave when he wanted to. He wasn't stupid. He was a survivor too. And my mother wasn't ready to leave him, and I was refusing to come home while he was there. So, she thought well what am I going to do? I am going to do the easiest thing for me.

In running away from home, Rachael said, "I ran away for my life." But, this act of self-protection led to her incarceration as a juvenile delinquent in the Magdalene laundry. This shift in her role from "the family black sheep to their sacrificial lamb" temporarily masked the family's problems by turning the focus to the supposedly deviant Rachael. In addition to

2 In this chapter, unless otherwise indicated, all quotations attributed to Rachael Romero are taken from a series of interviews between Rachael and Rie Croll, which took place between 2009 and 2016.

bearing the disloyalty of her mother, close family members, and, more broadly, state authority, Rachael now wore the stigma of delinquency, and, as she later understood, of "the fallen woman." Then, as now, personal integrity was paramount to Rachael, and she suffered deeply from this invalidation. She recognized that once she had been designated a juvenile delinquent, she lost all authority to assert the truth of her reality. And since neither friends nor extended family members were told where Rachael was, there was no one who could come to her defence. In one conversation, she described her integrity as all that she had and spoke of being rendered powerless as it had been stripped from her.

At The Pines, Rachael and others were told by the nuns in no uncertain terms that they were "the scum of the earth" and "not to be trusted." The message instilled in them from the moment they entered The Pines was that they were "wrongdoers" and "bad" people. Rachael saw the stripping away of inmates' integrity as part of a broader plan to deny them all that had been theirs, beginning with their names. The surrendering of their names was one part of the process of making inmates nobodies. "I don't think they thought we were that human," said Rachael. "They would call us 'girls' or our names, which were the names they gave us." While sitting in a "disinfectant" bath on her first day at The Pines, a compulsory practice for all new inmates, Rachael was told by a nun to "choose" a new name. In telling me about this, Rachael laughed ironically at the harsh symbolism of an experience that she portrayed as being "baptized in disinfectant." In that moment, naked and vulnerable, she picked the name Rachael, based on a dark-haired character she had once seen on the television show *Peyton Place*. It was "a TV show I had briefly glimpsed," she told me, laughing again at the absurdity of the source and the randomness of her choice. One of the nuns overseeing her bath asked her whether she wanted the Old Testament spelling of "Rachael" or the New Testament "Rachel." She chose the old, "more mysterious" spelling, and has kept that name to this day.

Although the name has negative connotations for her, Rachael felt so distorted by her experience of imprisonment in the laundry that she had difficulty identifying with her former self, and especially with the name her parents had given her. "I just didn't feel like I was that person anymore," she told me. "I thought it was kind of obscene to call me [former name] after what I'd been through ... after being called Rachael how could I possibly go back to that other name?" That she could choose her new name rather than having it assigned to her made keeping it possible. Rachael maintained that if she had been allocated a name by the nuns, as others had, she would have renamed herself following her incarceration.

Following her antiseptic bath, Rachael was stripped of her clothes and subjected to a forced shaving of her armpit hair. The nuns themselves performed this act because, as Rachael said, "they wouldn't have given me the razor or I would have killed myself." With hindsight, Rachael considered the removal of her hair as an even more invasive act than the enforced bathing and renaming. This bodily violation, the results of which she characterized five years later in a poem as the "plucked chicken skin beneath my arms" was a symbolically important defilement. In that poem, one of many she wrote attempting to come to terms with her Pines experience, she returned to the symbol of hair, associating it with nature, and its removal as an artificial rupture from her own nature. The shaving signified an eradication of her spirit and her life force or, as she expressed it, "Life abbreviated. Life as I knew it ended there."

After the removal of the remnants of her identity, Rachael was reissued clothing which she described as "very old ... that somebody else had worn forever ... long enough and shabby enough with aprons and everything, making you one of everybody. You didn't have your own clothes." Rachael's footwear consisted of second-hand nun's shoes with heels, so large and dilapidated that she held them together at the back with safety pins. This demeaning outfit, like one from a Charles Dickens novel, removed any sense of her own individuality: "You lose your name, you lose your appearance, you know you have to tie your hair a certain way, you have to wear things down to your mid-calf, you have to wear long sleeves even when it is 100 degrees under a wrought iron roof in a factory situation." This stripping-away procedure, as Rachael and others described it, was part of a process of becoming both everyone and no one.

Before entering The Pines, Rachael thought the abuses she had endured at home were the worst that she could suffer, but she soon understood that the laundry was crueller. Among other privations, she told me, she had "never known such loneliness" as she felt while in The Pines. I asked her how it was that physical and sexual abuse by her father could pale in comparison to incarceration. The difference was in the physical environment. There was no respite from that setting of total confinement, in which her every movement was regimented and watched, whereas in the rural setting of her family home she could often escape her father:

> I didn't spend my whole day with him or anything. I was out on my own with animals and everything. I was wild and free a lot of the time. So, I blocked out all that stuff ... I stuffed it, I blocked it, I erased it, I went out of my body. But you couldn't do that in The Pines. You were constantly under surveillance, constantly in danger of getting beaten up by one of the other girls or ... it was so dangerous and so horrible and not a thing to alleviate the stress, nothing!

In the years marked by her father's abuse, Rachael found ways to sustain herself, such as escaping into a deep relationship with nature and a rich and creative inner life. These connections gave her agency and a reason to live. But, institutionalization impaired her self-reliance and the spontaneous connection with herself and others she once had. In the laundry, working with potentially dangerous equipment, she was forced to be always present, always alert. This life-preserving hyper-vigilance extended to the rest of the prison environment, to the dining hall, the dorm, and even the bathrooms.

Yet, in The Pines, Rachael was separated from the strategies that had once ensured her some distance from abuse—the physical competencies she had honed as a child that enabled her to survive the physical threats posed by her home environment and to feel strong in her body:

> I felt completely powerless. I felt completely disempowered and thwarted by everything around me, so that I didn't trust that I had that aliveness to overcome it in that intense imprisonment. Because before that I always thought, well, I can run away, I can climb a tree, I can hide here, I can go there but, when you're in a prison, you can't. You have to keep doing what they say.

The physical resiliency and resourcefulness that had been her saviour at home were at odds with the nuns' mission to break down inmates' wills. Once incarcerated, Rachel and others were forced to submit their bodies and minds to a system, remote from their own needs, which contradicted their individualized survival strategies. Severing them from their coping capacities likewise created a disconnection that, as Rachael later experienced, would prove harmful once they were no longer institutionalized.

Although Rachael would, out of necessity, develop techniques to survive the harsh conditions of her imprisonment, she at first found herself defenceless in a terrifying environment. Most significantly, The Pines "took my own trust in myself ... because ... I couldn't rely on myself for safety." Rachael could not speak or she would be brutalized, and she could not escape. In sum, "I couldn't do anything ... It was totally unsafe ... It just completely dropped me off my feet." While the factory-like setting of The Pines was inhumane, it was the accompanying "mixture of shame and defilement ... that was the most abusive thing of all." A dehumanizing condemnation of inmates was delivered at every opportunity, expressed blatantly and uttered repeatedly. The nuns told the inmates that they "were absolutely impure," which is why they were in there.

The nuns' characterization of inmates' impurity was not subtle or inferred; they were told, said Rachael: "There is a God and He hates you."

For most of the inmates, this continual emphasis of their unworthiness coloured how they perceived themselves. A painful and damaging judgment was delivered to them at every meal by the head nun. While they ate, she would browbeat them with the details of their defects:

> Every day this woman … this bulldog head Nun Mother A.… would lecture us … her favourite expression was "so what?" She would say so you are mongrels and you fight and you do all these things and you are sloppy and you are ugly and you don't dress neatly and you don't do this and you don't do that … "So what?" So, Mr. tall, dark and handsome comes along and he won't be interested in you and nobody will want to be your friend and you won't get a job … over and over and over and over … "so what?"

"She knew we all stank," Rachael added. "She kept at it every day. I mean it was indoctrination."

Convincing the Magdalenes that they were all equally worthless, Rachael believes, was one of the nuns' objectives. It was apparently important that this exiled population realize they were "vile, disgusting, and unacceptable to society." This message was particularly effective because this "really negative, negative, negative, negative" denunciation came at "a very formative time in most of our lives, our early teens and mid-teens." The clear allegation by the nuns was that, "Well, you were fallen that's what you were. You're a scourge. Defiled and defiling by your presence."

This organized breaking down of inmates' self-esteem was part of the nuns' undertaking to expunge the inmates' previous selves and remake them in another image: souls worthy of saving. To withstand this attempt to break her, and many other daily threats, Rachael kept her head down and conformed to the system. Fortunately, she could maintain this strategy because her sentence was relatively short. I asked her though if she thought the parts of herself that she kept hidden, out of the nuns' reach, would have been in danger of being snuffed out if she had been in there for two years or three. "Yah," she responded, "I think I probably would have killed myself. I did try to kill myself. So, I was depressed. Obviously, I was depressed." Compounding her sense of despair was the fear that she might never be entirely free of re-institutionalization. Rachael remembered the nuns telling the inmates upon their release, "you'll be back, you'll be back. You're just hopeless, hard, and you can't help yourself." The repetition of this message ensured that it became internalized; even long after leaving The Pines, it was difficult for inmates to free themselves of the fear of re-incarceration.

Inside The Pines

> *As I was still new I had not learned that in this place there are a set of unwritten laws: Keep clean, keep alert, keep your eyes open, keep your ears open, keep your mouth shut.*
>
> (Romero, pers. journal, 1967)

Although The Pines was located in a relatively urban section of Plympton, Australia, it was set back from the road on a sizable property, removing it somewhat from the surrounding community. Rachael recalled that it sat in the middle of ten acres of land with a row of commanding pine trees leading up the driveway to the front entrance. Immediately surrounding the building structures was "barbed wire and then clearing." Apparently, there could be no doubt that this was a prison. Given the fencing and barbed wire, I asked Rachael about the prevalence of inmates' attempted escapes. There were attempts, she said, but the institution was set up for surveillance. "There was clearing all the way around. It was like a penitentiary ... the barbed wire on top of the very high fences." When someone tried to escape, Rachael recalled, "they would get the dogs. You had to climb this high fence over the barbed wire and I remember a girl called Freddie got caught on the barbed wire and she was hanging there with the dogs underneath her." On another occasion a girl that she knew attempted to run away:

> She was somewhere in Mother A's room or something and somebody turned their back for a moment and she ran out what was the opening for the convent and she got out and she was caught by the police and brought back. When they [inmates] were brought back they say they added a couple of years to their time. So, it was a heavy thing.

Apart from the dreaded lengthening of the inmates' sentences, there were other punishments for breaking institutional rules. Like most Good Shepherd reformatories, there was a "punishment room," designated for solitary confinement. Rachael laughed as she told me that, at The Pines, the nuns called the isolation room the "Cosmetology" room. "What a name," she added; "there was no cosmetology going on, let me tell you. It was just a plain room with nothing in it. And we just got locked in there as an isolation thing. It was a daytime thing. There wasn't anything to sleep on." This room was one of three that inmates glimpsed upon entering The Pines. The first was Mother A's office; the next, where incoming inmates received their antiseptic bath; and third, the "Cosmetology" room. That room, Rachel told me, because it was designed for inmate isolation, "was heavily locked with no windows."

There were between seventy and eighty inmates in The Pines when Rachael was there, ranging from quite old women to pre-teens. The Magdalenes were divided into three groups under different supervisors and, as Rachael put it, a "senior snitch." Each group slept in an open room that contained three rows of beds. This arrangement, designed for optimum surveillance, took precedence over the inmates' need for privacy. Privacy, in fact, was forbidden and so inmates' sleeping, eating, bathing, working, and praying were monitored. The Pines' physical structure was ideally suited to the regulation of these routines—a fact that Rachael found disturbing. This was no coincidence; The Pines' physical structure was remarkably like other Good Shepherd asylums, complete with a quadrangle design and an internal, walled exercise yard, which provided the inmates' only contact with the outside world. There were no trees or flowers in this space, and Rachael mourned this forced separation from the natural world.

Rachael described institutional conditions in which every minute of every day contravened her will, her choice, and her freedom. There was "total scrutiny and control every minute of the day. We would never be alone up in the bedrooms or anything, ever. We were always being watched. You had to be on your toes at all times because they would scream at you." She described this routine as a cookie-cutter-like formula, calculated from bottom to top with girls and women working as slaves, with the proceeds of their labour going directly to the bishop, and further up the Roman Catholic hierarchy.

The type, degree of routine, and surveillance at The Pines was, according to Rachael, akin to policing. "I mean there was no observation," she told me, "there was no reflection—it was you do this or you're in trouble." This lack of "reflection" was a troubling point for her. The nuns who oversaw the inmates' every movement did not perform this service in a wise, guiding, or thoughtful capacity; they were perceived as unconscious and unfeeling enforcers. The nuns' lack of reflection was one of many characteristics that distinguished the laundries as institutions of incarceration from the "homes" that the Good Shepherds claimed to provide. In contrast to the more nurturing atmosphere and idiosyncratic rhythm of a "home," Rachael's daily life at The Pines was deeply lonely and repressively regimented:

> We got up, I can't remember the precise time, but it was very early like six or something. And we were in silence in the large dormitory. And we had to straighten our beds, wash our faces, la la la la … line up, go down to the chapel and then there was a service and then we filed around to the dining room and had breakfast in silence. And then we had I think

> some small amount of time like ten or fifteen minutes to do chores like our laundry or have a bath. There were 70 girls and there were four showers ... so there were fights about things like that. Then we went into the laundry. And we worked in the laundry and then there was lunch and then we went into the laundry again. There were a few of us who were under age who went for a couple of hours to do the correspondence course and then back to the laundry.

When I asked Rachael about how precisely schooling fit into her daily routine, she explained that it was an extremely basic form of education, begrudgingly delivered, primarily through correspondence courses. The nuns wanted her to work in the laundry full-time, until she insisted that, under the law, she was entitled to an education until she was fifteen. School-aged inmates were apparently sent to a classroom for upwards of two and a half hours a day. "It wasn't very long," Rachael told me; "it didn't stretch us at all. We didn't really learn anything. It was there because it was the law. They were just covering their butts." Because the nuns discouraged education, Rachael was not taught per se: "they would say read this and write this and we would do it and it would get sent off and a month later, or something like that, we would get A, B, C or D ... you know what I mean?" Despite the nuns' resistance, Rachael willed herself to learn. Her education could not be externally provided, given that their teacher was a nun who had joined the Good Shepherds at age fourteen or fifteen and had not received a formal education:

> But we sat there because of the whole system of the place ... we did what we were supposed to do ... you know? The place had bars on the windows and so forth. And, uh, we were locked in. And so, each of us was at a different level, and so she couldn't help us, so we just struggled along on our own.

Fortunately for Rachael, at the time she was at The Pines, there was an anomaly in the system in the form of a woman named Mrs. L. This woman, a Catholic layperson, "wasn't part of the institution" but became "very important" to the inmates, especially to Rachael. She arrived about seven months into Rachael's sentence, when the regular teacher had to be hospitalized. Mrs. L, who was invited to take her place in the classroom for a few weeks, was the first person Rachael had met there who was humane—"extraordinary":

> I mean she talked to us. She listened to us. She was like this fairy godmother kind of person. I can remember girls telling her their story of having been gang-raped and things like that and expecting her to say "oh you filthy despicable person no one will ever want you," which is what the nuns would say, and she said, "you keep going and you're a good person" and stuff like that and we were just looking at each other with our eyes popping out.

Rachael was so influenced by her brief brush with this woman's compassion that she looked her up when she got out and visited her several times before Mrs. L's death. After Rachael's release, Mrs. L cared enough to bring Rachael to where her daughter worked, a place for intellectually challenged people. In so doing, Rachael explained, "she kind of was responsible for getting me into the kind of work that I do. She also spoke to me after I got out about how the nuns were in such a mess and fighting and everything." Mrs. L alluded to bullying and power struggles between the nuns and described their living/work environment as generally unhealthy. This perspective, "from an adult point of view," helped to break the authoritarian hold that the nuns had on Rachael and clarified something that had been a mystery to her and other inmates. "We saw them as a solid block and of course they weren't." Mrs. L, who had an independent insider perspective, saw the system more critically than the nuns could. She saw the chinks in the armour of what seemed to Rachael to be an impenetrable and powerful machine. These insights, from a Catholic who "wasn't biting the bullet," as Rachael put it, helped, retrospectively, to partially disarm the nuns' power. This was beneficial because, even after Rachael's release, the institution continued to hold her in its grip.

Although their time together was short-lived, her post-Pines conversations with Mrs. L altered Rachael's outlook. Rachael described her as "a pretty liberal person" who had "pushed the box a lot of times and she had done it in many ways." Following the cookie-cutter formula of The Pines, with its categorical views of good and evil, it was important to Rachael that Mrs. L seemed to value people on their terms and was genuinely concerned with the perspectives of marginalized people. At a time when Rachael was beaten down and numb with depression, Mrs. L was one of the few with whom she could connect. Just following her release from The Pines, Rachael described herself as "frozen ... fifteen and frozen ... I was impenetrable." But, Mrs. L connected with her and honoured her in a way that Rachael felt was immediate and real. "We could get down right away," Rachael told me, grateful that this woman could see her worth and tried to reach her in her condition of pain and disconnection. This much-needed contact, at such a fragile point in Rachael's life, taught her something that her later experiences in working with (and reading about) marginalized people validated:

> One of the reasons that I work in the areas I usually work, with people who are disregarded, put aside, marginalized, and children too, is that in study after study they say that people who do survive and thrive have somebody, an adult, who believes in them. If only for the shortest time. You can see why when Mrs. L came along she was like a ray of light in the darkest of night.

Under conditions where Rachael and the others were considered as people not to be believed and less worthy than other humans, Mrs. L was a significant presence and a hope. "She was very important for all of us," Rachael explained; "she couldn't protect us but she at least acknowledged us as human." After a short period, the regular teacher returned. Very quickly, those breaks for school, an hour in the morning, and perhaps an hour and a half in the afternoon, became little more than time spent away from the laundry. Then, it was back into the laundry until 5 or 6 p.m., just in time for dinner:

> There might have been again a couple of minutes to go to the bathroom or something and tidy your locker or something but again you weren't allowed to talk. And then we went in to eat, in silence, and sometimes we would have chapel again. It depended on the day and I can't remember really. There was a lot of church and I can't always remember how they fit it all in. Oh, I forgot. After breakfast, we had to do a cleaning job. So, I used to wax the floors and clean the sick room. And then after lunch I did the pig slops. So, we had these extra chores besides the laundry. We did all the work. Different people would have been cleaning the dormitories. That sort of thing would have been taken care of by the girls.

The menial work of the institution, as Rachael points out, was done completely by "the girls," while the nuns' primary task was surveillance. Inmates endured these routines, uninterrupted, for the duration of their sentence. And, for some, it was a life sentence.

For those Magdalenes who had families with the means and/or the resolve to visit the inmates, half-day passes were permitted after an initial six months of incarceration. Upon entry to The Pines, inmates were made aware of the minimum length of their sentences. Rachael, for instance, was told that she could not get out in under a year. "If I ran away," she told me, "it would be more. That's what I knew … they read that to you when you came in … forget about it for a year … and after 6 months if somebody comes to get you, you know your parents or someone, they'll let you out for an afternoon. And then after two [more] months you get another afternoon."

After not having seen a familiar face for six months, Rachael's sense of isolation and loneliness was intense as she anticipated the first visit from her mother. This outing meant so much to her that she was literally counting down the days. But, when the time came for the visit, Rachael told me, "you know you're waiting and waiting and waiting for the day out, and my mother cancelled because she had a garden party. She was not able to deal with my pain I think. She finally did come and get me on another week and what does she do? She took me to the movies and then brought me back."

Rachael felt that her mother, like most people at the time, was in denial about what went on within The Pines. "It was possible for family members and others to deny conditions at The Pines," Rachael said, "because of a social climate of 'don't ask, don't tell,' as we say today, in which the Church was above questioning." Rachael tried to tell people about the atrocities that she had experienced in the laundry, but they could or would not hear it. "When I tried to say anything about it, they were always like, 'ohhh the good Sisters.' I was the juvenile delinquent. Kids had no cred anyway." The inmates, branded as delinquents, were not believable. So, the community knew nothing of what went on in the institution beyond the front parlour, where families were sometimes permitted to visit. "Nobody admitted it happened," said Rachael; "nothing ever happened outside of the room that they came once every few months to see me in, this shining wooden-floored room, so that they had no idea what was going on outside of it."

It was social welfare representatives such as police and social workers that brought many of the inmates, including Rachael, to the laundry, yet no representative checked on them once they were placed there. No one, it seems, ventured beyond The Pines' front rooms and offices. "Oh no," said Rachael sarcastically, "no, nobody came in. The good Sisters knew what they were doing. No one checked." Yet, in searching for records of her incarceration, Rachael discovered that the institution was government supported, and it had been their responsibility to know about and to record what was happening there:

> When I did my research on them at that time I saw that they answered to the government. They got money from the government. And yet they never kept records and they wouldn't allow us to have our records. I tried to get my records and they said all we are going to give you is the date you went in and the date you went out.

Government reliance on the Good Shepherds empowered them and left families vulnerable to their authority. Under these terms, parents and loved ones had little power to inquire about where their sisters and daughters ate and slept and worked.

Rachael's experience shows that it was not only parents who were prepared to take the nuns' window dressing at face value. She described, for example, an annual event where the inmates performed a play for visiting representatives from the Church and Social Services. This was the only time in Rachael's memory of her time there that Social Services stepped inside the reformatory. On this occasion, the nuns displayed oranges in bowls for the visitors, a touch of nutrition and homeliness that the inmates never experienced. The "girls" performed the play *HMS Pinafore* for the assembled visitors. One nun, who had had training as a hairdresser, curled, teased, and tied up Rachael's platinum blond hair in rags for the performance. Following the play, the same nun approached Rachael excitedly because a priest had taken a special interest in Rachael's hair and had asked this nun to cut off some of it so that he could keep it as a memento. This demand for a donation of her hair revolted Rachael, a revulsion enhanced by the nun's eagerness to objectify Rachael by honouring the priest's wish. Although Rachael eventually evaded this request, the incident disturbed her and stressed her lack of safety from predation. It became even more powerfully clear in this moment that she was The Pines' property.

In effect, the Magdalenes were expected to operate as nameless and voiceless entities whose worth was based solely on their contribution to the operation of the institution. They were, as Rachael perceived, objects with no control. Under this system of incarceration, their identities were not their own to control. For example, their lack of freedom to communicate evoked an array of strong feelings and responses in those I interviewed. In addition to robbing them of self-expression and self-definition, the silencing of their voices denied them an important social tool and source of connection in an alien environment. In the moment, Rachael did not reflect much on the compulsory silence at The Pines; it became her new "normal" and therefore an unquestioned state. "I was in shock and busy trying to keep my mouth shut and my eyes and ears open so I wouldn't have talked much anyway." As a means of survival, Rachael "yoked [her]self to the rhythm" of the institution. Moreover, because she had grown up with a great deal of silence, "alone on a farm with no one to talk to," it was not a completely foreign experience for her to work silently in the packing room at the laundry. "Everyone else was working too," Rachael said, "and we were afraid of being yelled at if we tried to talk." In that relatively dangerous work setting, "there was no room to fool around, linger or hide."

The Sub/Culture of The Pines

There were times when inmates were permitted to speak and times when they did so in secret. Rachael recalled Sunday afternoons as a period when inmates were allowed more speaking time—"an hour or so." The girls would also sneak a word or two with one another when the nun left the classroom "to go to the bathroom or something. But it was mostly a kind of foul-mouthed, bawdy bravado gag or two. No conversation. We were scared. That's where I learned Aboriginal swearwords." These words were later understood by Rachael to have greater meaning than they did at the time. Together, with other shared expressions of anger and self-harm, these words became the inmates' language of signification and survival—small but significant escapes from control—part of an insider's culture, one created in an environment where little else belonged to them, including language:

> There was sort of a patois that the girls used in The Pines and there were a lot of people who had Aborigines in their family or were from the outback ... and some of it was quite explicitly foul language ... but you know it was how we referred to one another and others. There were pejorative words for sure but that was just because of the self-hatred that was endemic. We enjoyed saying things that the nuns didn't understand. And also ... we were such a closed society there wasn't any input. So that the culture itself had to be learned and that was part of the language.

This prisoner subculture was formed in opposition to the authorities that treated them as beings unworthy of their own identities. In an environment where they were all equally unworthy, they built small connections between themselves—brief moments of expression and human connection in a world where that was forbidden.

Another strategy that the inmates devised for circumventing the nuns' surveillance and building scraps of community was through the authorized exchange of holy cards. These small collectible cards, which typically displayed a religious image on one side and a prayer on the other, were appropriated by the inmates for their own communications. "Always watched," said Rachael, "we could buy the cards for pennies from the nuns and sometimes we were given them as gifts. We could not pass notes or letters unless the nuns read them first, but the holy card was ok. It carried our 'voice' however coded, however muffled." The cards represented a "currency—emotional currency—in a place where expressions of contempt are the norm; where you can't trust anyone because of coercion and it is unwise to share secrets." Rachael described the holy cards as "a sanctioned ... purified, way of showing loyalty and caring between people." Since these and only these exchanges were completely authorized by the nuns, they were above suspicion and eluded censorship. The holy cards thus allowed the Magdalenes "to say what otherwise may not be said, to give each other courage."

At The Pines, as in other Good Shepherd reformatories, communication with and about the outside world was forbidden. The nuns vetted any ingoing or outgoing letters. So, upon an inmate's release, contact with another ex-inmate was essentially terminated because they had no way to track each other's whereabouts. This communication censorship also blocked any validation of one another's stories of incarceration and of thereby lending credence to one another's accounts. Ultimately, Rachael came to perceive the holy cards that she kept as a meaningful corroboration of her and the other inmates' incarceration and an indication of their shared humanity.

In addition to controlling inmates' voices and communications, the nuns regulated the inmates' bodies well beyond their initial disinfecting procedures. Enforced physical modesty, which entailed ensuring that the inmates' bodies were always covered, was one manifestation of this regulation. The strict rules about dressing and undressing were enforced similarly across Good Shepherd institutions:

> We were told when we undressed in the dormitory, because of course it was all open, that we were to undress discreetly under our … you know we would put our nightgown over our heads and then took our clothes off under it and things like that. I also was used to sleeping with no sheets in the very hot weather and I learned very fast that I had to cover myself with a sheet. And I still to this day have that in my head, you know.

Outdated and heavily concealing uniform dresses further enforced modesty while simultaneously emphasizing the expectations of Magdalenes' penal and religious servitude.

The nuns' insistence on modesty went beyond the regulations on inmate nudity and clothing. Rachael noted that they also "never went into the bathrooms because of course they would be seeing us naked, and that would be sinful for them." In their effort to evade this perceived sin, the bathrooms became one area of inmate life that was uncontrolled. As a result, unsafe and unsanitary conditions prevailed there. One filthy bathroom was particularly dangerous:

> It was old and the walls were slimy ... concrete walls ... and there were broken shampoo bottles in the shower stalls and so forth ... And it wasn't cleaned and there was a hierarchy of people who had been there for years, so it was the seniors [among the inmates] who were in charge ... One particularly depraved girl actually used to sexually molest girls in the toilet ... She was about twenty-three and she had been there for about twelve years or so. And she was very strong and athletic and masculine and really emotionally very immature, like a fourteen-year-old boy or something. She coerced one of my friends to meet her in the bathroom at night and stuff like that. And she was a frightening figure. You wouldn't mess with her because she had a lot of power.

To cope with such threatening conditions, Rachael hurriedly found strategies for staying away from the most overt forms of physical harm. Of the senior inmate described above, she said, "I kept away from her. In the beginning, I was threatened by a bunch of girls because I opened my mouth and I was pinned up against the wall with a teasing comb at my throat and so forth, and I realized that I had to completely not trust anybody and completely stay to myself." However, The Pines was particularly dangerous because the nuns gave senior inmates power over newer inmates:

> If you had been there for a long enough time, if you sucked up to the nuns long enough, there were a couple of people who were given more power and they would have been in charge and if they told you to do something and you didn't do it, they could be really cruel and get away with it. Never go to the nuns about it because the nuns had put them in power. And if you said anything, there were times when they were in charge and they could really hurt you and the nuns wouldn't be around and nobody was going to come on your side because they were afraid of these people.

Given the condoned inmate power hierarchy, the rules around silence, and the nuns' fear of same-sex attractions, "there was no community." Inmates "were always pitted against each other" to see "who could be most self-effacing, who could grovel the lowest, who could appear to debase themselves." Such competition to win a glance of moral approval from a nun was damaging and intensely demoralizing. Rachael perceived it as a competition for scraps of caring, where no genuine caring existed. "Can you imagine," Rachael asked me, "being in that environment and knowing that, if you were alive or dead, they would probably prefer you dead, you know what I mean? There was no sense of the sanctity of our lives."

Rachael could not tell whether the nuns colluded or were unaware of the abuses occurring between inmates, but, she said, "I think they wouldn't have cared. They just thought that we were all so capable of horrid things that we brought it on ourselves." In that aggressive environment, rather than lashing out at the nuns who were oppressing them, the inmates attacked one another:

> It's always the way you know? They go for somebody weaker than them and so they persecuted each other. There were a few scuffles with the nuns but … if somebody tried to hit a nun there was going to be somebody who was besotted with

> that nun who would kill them for it. You know what I mean? So that kind of crazy situation. Don't touch my mother; you get away from my mother.

Rachael felt that the phenomenon of the abused child who protects his or her abusing parent described precisely some of the dynamics between nuns and inmates. Playing on this reaction, the nuns could maintain order by pitting the most aggressive against the most vulnerable. In this way, the nuns remained relatively safe from physical harm, protected by the inmates and one another. "Lines of defense" was Rachael's term to describe the human barrier established to ensure the nuns' immunity from inmate aggression. However, there was little in place to protect the more defenceless inmates.

In addition to the dangers of inmate culture, the physical perils of the laundry setting were formidable. At The Pines, girls and women carried out the entirety of this business from washing, ironing, and operating the mangle (or wringer) to packing and preparing for shipping. Rachael depicted the mangle operation as "very dangerous, extremely hot, and loud." The mangle "had two feeders and two catchers at a time." Inmates from other laundries similarly described the mangle—with its two massive rollers—as a constant threat to hands and fingers, especially for younger girls who were less experienced in laundry work. For a time, Rachael received the hot sheets coming through the window, which she then had to stack. This was "very heavy work," done repeatedly for hours on end. She described loading "these great big baskets and then hauling the baskets to the outer gate. The guys would put them on the trucks to take them where they were going. And my hands got calloused; they were really hot and starchy." Behind those working the mangle were "the folders preparing wet sheets for feeding and on the other side folding to go to the packing room. There would be others folding small items like hankies."

This Magdalene laundry serviced not only its own church but its labour was apparently contracted out as well. "We also did church vestments from all over town," she told me. The Pines' laundry served the "Hotel South," the oldest and "the most expensive hotel then in Adelaide," whose patrons were "old school money, government visitors, etc." Various other restaurants, hotels, and institutions "also relied upon the Good Shepherd laundry." The clientele for the laundry was meaningful to Rachael, as it was for the other laundry inmates I interviewed, because it verified that the Church was running a commercial business on the backs of unpaid and sometimes underage forced labour. Rachael, who perpetually gathered evidence throughout her experience, even kept laundry receipts from such clients, as they reaffirmed the reality of her experience.

Considering the absence of compensation for work, the dangerous work conditions, and the problem of underage labour, Rachael remains outraged that there was no government supervision of the laundry. This lack of state accountability confirmed that Rachael was on her own at the age of fourteen—fed to the wolves, so to speak—with no one to aid her:

> What I think it did was it squarely placed me in the category of you're on your own sister, that's it. I was on my own before [The Pines] but then okay so no welfare system, no mother, no country, no friends, no family, no godmother, no grandparents, no sister, nobody is going to come to my aid. And the incarceration was a conspiracy of silence.... because they all agreed to look the other way, and to say what you don't know doesn't hurt you.

This rapid severing of all levels of support was nearly lethal for Rachael. Once institutionalized, she realized that not only had her family officially ceased to care for her, but, as the unmonitored hazards of her new living conditions demonstrated, it quickly became plain that so too had the Government of Australia.

Beyond her own sense of peril, Rachael was also deeply affected by the mistreatment of some of the more vulnerable inmates around her. Some of them, she said, belonged to Australia's "stolen generation." These Indigenous and so-called mix-raced children were taken from their homes and either institutionalized or brought up as white people by other "white people." They had been brought to The Pines from other reformatories and orphanages, so that by the time they got to The Pines, they had been institutionalized multiple times. This atrocity, for which the government has since apologized, and which Rachael calls government-sanctioned genocide, has resonated with her: "Um, they thought they were being kind." They operated under the assumption that the Aborigine people "don't know how to live," said Rachael, and so "we're going to show them how to live, and if they forget who they are that's fine." She described the prevailing attitude as "a form of imperialism entering into education"—that "whole empire bullshit."

In addition to the Indigenous inmates of the "stolen generation," Rachael compassionately described others at The Pines against whom the forces had been unusually stacked. These girls and women were discarded there with no hope of having someone on the outside waiting for their return. Given that no state official was checking on them either, this meant absolute abandonment. Of this group were women "in their thirties, forties, and fifties" with intellectual disabilities who had been "dumped there":

> There was one woman who had Down syndrome who used to fold hankies in the laundry. And she was very sweet but quite old for someone with Down syndrome. She must have been in her forties. And she couldn't speak very much. She used to talk to her mother who had died on her shoulder. She would mumble to her shoulder. And she used to give the excuse that she had a headache all the time ... to get out of the laundry because it was so loud. And then she would wait with her little handbag on Sundays for someone to pick her up and they never did.

The image of this gentle figure waiting for years in vain for someone to take her from the institution conveys the absolute sense of desertion and emptiness that most of the inmates shared. For those who were eventually able to leave The Pines, re-entry into their social worlds created a new set of problems. As Rachael said, "These ways of institutionalizing the treatment of people so often go awry. Big errors like this have so many results. I struggle with it in my work with street people." Like the marginalized people that Rachael has worked with for years, former inmates carried a heavy sense of abandonment and stigmatization. Many harboured a nagging fear of re-incarceration. For Rachael, it felt like her "time there never stopped ... those who have been INSIDE can never fully be outside—because the inside, and the fear of being inside again, however unlikely, stays with us forever, like a brand that only we know is there. This is a great loneliness" (Romero, pers. comm., February 13, 2011).

Stigma/ta: The Moral Residue

In the eyes of the Sisters of the Good Shepherd, Rachael and the other inmates were morally stained and in need of salvation, if indeed salvation was possible. This condemnation was especially hard to remove once implanted: "It was a stigma for a long time." The difficulty of shedding this powerfully discrediting judgment stemmed partly from The Pines environment, which reinforced the judgment through daily routine. Inmates were made to believe that they were inherently defiled by their nature; they were all "fallen girls." "We were Eve," Rachael added. "We were the image of the laundry, the cleaning that never finishes. I can still smell the dirty laundry. The smell of the dirty laundry, yah. And also the starch on the fingers. Hot starch and the sheets on the brazen, brazen fingers." This hard laundry labour combined with the repeated messages about the inmates' impurity cemented their negative perceptions of themselves. The smell and the physical sensations still linger with Rachael, as does the moral stigma. For better or for worse, that experience played a role in defining who she is.

Rachael was under no illusion that the nuns, as they claimed, were actually turning the Magdalenes' lives around. It was about punishment and nothing else; Rachael could not see it any other way. Her life in the laundry was marked by a series of depletions:

> Because here they were taking away our education and making us slave in the laundry ... We lose our hearing, we get our hands mangled because they didn't care about safety, you know, bust our backs. We're not hearing music; we're not reading any literature. Were they possibly thinking that they were improving our lives? They weren't. They were basically not, and they didn't make any attempts. We were just the sludge of the earth.

When Rachael was released from her period of institutionalization and attempted to reintegrate into her school community and a broader social life, she felt different inside—an altering that has "been sustained" ever since: "I always felt besmirched. I felt maladjusted to the rest of society and I felt like I was a misfit because of that." Equally concerning was the related sense that her body and mind had become detached from one another. They no longer worked in unison. That sensation began when Rachael entered The Pines and remained with her until she reached mid-life. Because this discord was so complex to understand, let alone to bridge, Rachael "didn't really incarnate till [her] forties." She ascribed this initial split to her effort to survive in an unsafe environment where the many physical dangers demanded that her body be alert and present, but where, at the same time, it was dangerous to exist emotionally.

This sense of disconnection and the stigma that had tarnished Rachael remained largely unaddressed until 2003, when she brought her past into the public eye in an autobiographical documentary. This creative undertaking enabled Rachael to give form to the abuses she had suffered, first in her home and then at The Pines. Creating the documentary was an emotionally gruelling and complex process that forced her to revisit tormenting memories and express long-held secrets. However, making these parts of her life public also helped to break her longstanding sense of being an outsider by connecting her to others who identified with her experiences and shared her outrage. This process, while healing, did not rid her entirely of the spectre of her incarceration, or allow her to put it behind her. But, it did give her insight into, as she put it, "how it frames my life."

Rachael had kept her incarceration private, not out of shame but to avoid judgment and the re-visitation of a painful past. Unlike most other inmates that I have spoken to, she refused to bear a sense of shame about her incarceration. She adamantly maintained that shame was not hers to accept: "I felt branded, I felt tarnished, I felt dirtied, but I didn't feel ashamed." I asked her what the difference was; to her the distinction was obvious, simply, "because I didn't do it." She explained that she would only have been ashamed if she had committed an offence worthy of incarceration:

> If I'd hurt somebody or if I'd let myself down I would have been ashamed, but I didn't think I had ... I felt besmirched and I still do. But shame is a very different feeling to me. Shame is when I do something wrong that I know I shouldn't have and my conscience bothers me until I remedy it. That's different. If I had done some terrible thing in order to be put in The Pines I might have felt shame, if I'd murdered somebody or even stolen a car. I just felt this sense of extreme injustice and that that injustice was endemic. And that's how I set myself on the political trajectory that I was going to change the way that was for people. Because how could children be so un-empowered and left to the wolves like that?

Rachael likened the discrediting that she and other Magdalenes were burdened with to the religious phenomenon of stigmata—a branding worn externally for all to see: "You know, like I felt tattooed. There was something that may not be apparent to everybody on the outside but they damaged us … our sense of our own value and our potential." For decades, Rachael felt that everyone could see this damage, that she not only carried her Pines experience internally but "had signs all over [her] of defilement."

Some inmates reified the pain and alienation of their degradation by cutting and tattooing themselves. In Rachael's view, there was a parallel between such behaviours and stigmata: "They [the nuns] were saying that we were defiled and so forth and then we were hurting ourselves externally, as they were hurting us internally. Do you know what I mean?" Self-harm was fairly widespread among inmates. With no one to confide in, in a world of enforced silence, it was an autonomous response to being defiled:

> There was a lot of cutting going on amongst the girls and tattooing. I got muscled by some … to give them my Indian ink. And then they would prick themselves and made tattoos with knives and all sorts of things on their legs and all over. It is not uncommon to see red scratches up a girl's arm or initials carved on her legs. One girl in particular made quite a habit of inflicting pain on herself to quell the pain elsewhere.... (Romero, pers. journal, 1967)

As a member of the inmate culture, Rachael perceived cutting and tattooing as "a sort of individuation thing," a personal expression in a place where all self-expression had been denied. She did it too. "It was like having a hole in your life," she explained, "an absence of experience or emptiness." Making the emotional pain more tangible through physical pain and self-produced images brought temporary relief:

> I remember my sister and my mother coming to visit me for the first time and I was telling them how horrible it was and begging them to get me out of there. And my sister said, "oh you deserve it, you slut." And I ran out and I went to the

> bathroom and there was all this broken glass and I just scored my arms up and down. And I didn't know that other people did it and then I saw that all these other people had scars. We had to wear long sleeve shirts, so the nuns didn't see it.

The self-cutting and marking by Magdalenes was also an attempt to regain some control in a place where it had been completely taken from them. Rachael described the effect of The Pines on her development as an emotional "cauterizing"—an effect which sealed off her emotions and made it difficult for her to re-enter society. The sense of disconnection she felt on leaving The Pines was a cut-off point. "They broke my will," she said, "they really did."

Rachael returned to the outside world much altered. With no information about how society had changed in her absence and with no one to support her in undoing the negative self-perceptions that formed there, she had a sense of not being "on the same map anymore." She spoke of this as "losing the code somehow." Part of the "code" that had been lost was her once spontaneous ability to read and adapt to her social world. Losing this resulted in a social distancing, yet another "gap to be negotiated" following her release:

> I just realized that I had lost ground ... and I didn't know if I had the energy to regain it or just keep going in my own way. And the clothing and everything was all wrong. I mean not knowing the Kennedy assassination and all that. It's like "where were you?" You know what I mean? "How come you didn't know," you know? ... It was very difficult. I was flummoxed ... Yeah, no radio, no TV, no newspapers. It was kind of embarrassing as a teenager to have not heard songs for a year and things.

The sense of difference that came from not having passed the same cultural milestones as her peers was worsened by her sense that the deeper changes imprisonment had created in her were visible to them and others. "I thought everyone could see that I was scarred and twisted and changed by this experience. It didn't occur to me that other people saw me as other than that ... I looked like a cheerleader if there were such a thing in Australia. And yet I felt completely tattooed."

The sense that she wore institutionalization externally for all to see caused Rachael to socially withdraw. This was but "one result of being cut off at such a tender age." In the early months following her release, confiding in others about what happened to her in The Pines was not an option, given that her trust, particularly in authority figures, had been deeply marred. Vulnerability with anyone was likewise difficult, given the dangers and humiliations of prison. Rachael tried to attend to these effects by isolating herself, but social retreat emphasized her sense of being a misfit. So she kept moving—in jobs and physical locations, and in relationships—but this did not ease the interpersonal issues caused by incarceration, nor did it quell the unexpected flashbacks triggered by such sights as a nun or a priest on a bus, or the smells of ironing or dirty laundry. In these and many other ways, incarceration was *in* her and *on* her and *with* her. Rachael is still sifting through the personal results of her incarceration and realizes that it continues to affect her in complex and unanticipated ways. "To me," she said, "the biggest horror is to be incarcerated."

Rachael's Lifeline: Barbed Wire and Roses

After years in perpetual motion, of moving from country to country, and job to job, Rachael finally planted herself in New York City. But while continual movement had buffered her from focusing too directly on submerged memories, staying in one place allowed them to flood in and overwhelm her. Consequently, when Rachael finally stopped moving, she broke down. Her overriding sense then, and for many years, was anger, which she tried to channel by attaching herself to a collective outrage:

> I went through so many layers of it. Basically, I transferred my rage to trying to stop the Vietnam War, to marching and all those things. The first thing I did when I came to this country was take a bus to Washington and march against Nixon and I transferred my rage to the perpetrators of all wrongs. So, it was very simplistic; I wanted power for the oppressed. It's denial too; it's denial that I felt besmirched. That you then get fired up by the idea of many people enraged and you get empowered by that.

In the bleak immediate aftermath of The Pines, Rachael completed her public-school education. Winning a federal scholarship allowed her to skip her final year of high school. The educational track she chose was art school, with a focus on printmaking, a medium through which she felt she could best communicate her own and others' suffering and thereby make the most effective social change. In political posters, for example, she depicted the homeless and the dispossessed—people who, like her, had been abused or disenfranchised within the social system. Rachael likewise served as a voice for the stigmatized through her art outreach with populations in street-level clinics, drop-in centres, and workshops. Rachael felt that this work enabled people to regain their voices through their own artistic assemblages.

Aligning herself with the marginalized helped Rachael to communicate her own wounds. Together, she and those she worked with represented a collective injury. By harnessing herself to a wronged collective, Rachael's isolation and sense of powerlessness were eased. Having suffered the stripping away of her integrity, she could relate to those on the social fringe. Rachael felt like the artist Henri de Toulouse-Lautrec in gravitating "towards the outsiders of society," because the only people who would understand her were those who had "been there." This, she added, "I continue to do."

As Rachael's work with disempowered people grew to take centre stage in her life, she recognized that it, in some ways, framed how she saw herself. Her strong identification with discredited identities caused her to see herself primarily through that lens. For instance, even when opportunities for educational or career advancement were presented to her, she found them difficult to pursue, out of concern that she would somehow be revealed as unworthy:

> I remember when I was going back to school this woman was trying to tell me to go to Harvard. And I couldn't see myself there; I couldn't see myself getting in there. She was saying "yes but you can" because she had ... It was that I am not legitimate, and they'll know. That's part of the tattoo and the stigma. Because it is as if you have been branded, and the "Mother A's" of Harvard would know.

This sense that she might be outed as an imposter considerably influenced how Rachael shaped her work and social environments. Certain seemingly straightforward expectations of her, such as the ability to function under particular types of authority, or hierarchical systems, were difficult for Rachael to realize. She connected these and other responses to incarceration and related post-traumatic stress symptoms. The abuses she had endured within the Good Shepherd system left her feeling like an outsider within social structures in which others seemingly flourished. Hence, while she might have pursued career advancement and the associated security, such as health benefits, that it could have provided her, moving up the hierarchy was an uncomfortable prospect.

Nevertheless, Rachael's art thrived and deeply informed her career in outreach work. Gradually though, she recognized that her work as a representative for subjugated populations was not enough, alone, to heal her wounds. What was required was to bring a certain focus "back" to her "own ego." Rachael realized that the kind of work she did compelled her because "these people's voices needed to be heard because [her] voice needed to be heard," and "nobody was hearing it." Rachael described herself and the dispossessed people that she felt most comfortable working with as "a public malignant, apparently not believed or believable." When she spoke to those outside that circle about the conditions that she had endured in The Pines, no one believed her. "They thought I was exaggerating," she told me, "but it meant that I was questionable to them too." Their lack of trust in her credibility hurt and alienated Rachael and further fuelled her identification with those similarly marginalized.

Working artistically with the content of her most harmful life experiences both grounded and validated Rachael's reality. Part of this process included her methodical visual and written recording of her time in The Pines. As an artist, comfortable in visual and poetic forms of expression, she portrayed, and continues to depict, through multiple forms, the effect of The Pines upon its inmates. For example, in an etching she made while in art school several years after her incarceration, Rachael recreated the "fear, agony of incarceration, and derangement" suffered under those conditions. This piece's seething and distorted human figures capture the pain and violence inflicted upon inmates' psyches. It symbolically documents "a kind of bedlam experience … set in The Pines." In there, "there were all these people in deranged agony." The anguish that Rachael captured in this early image was rooted in her sense of hopelessness and loss, including the loss of her once-free nature.

Rachael's creative documentation of The Pines, together with her practical chronicling of names, times, artifacts, and event details, created substantial proof of her existence within an unbelievable reality:

> Sort of like the way people use photography now … they went on vacation and that was the proof. I was in a [broader] world of denial but this happened to me and it felt like this was a record. Everyone around me said don't exaggerate. Nobody had a clue. Nobody had a clue. They didn't want to know. They thought I was confabulating.

Because no one had believed her about what went on at The Pines, this was one way of defending her credibility and disseminating the truth of what she had endured there. Then, and still, one way to prove to others that it had happened and to allow herself to fully feel it was to make it visible to all:

> I resurrected them. I drew them. I had this thing when I got out that I had to do. I drew maps ... like totally ... this is where the barbed wire is, this is where this is, this is where that is ... I drew it and I wrote down everybody's names and I just documented it. And I drew the people that were in there and I drew this woman with her handbag, and I drew the retarded woman who did the cooking who used to love *Bonanza* ... she used to sing *Bonanza* [theme song].

She described her compulsion to actualize these people, places, and events as "a kind of evidence" building that she was compelled to collect:

> I kept these things. I still have this little box from The Pines, a very strange thing. In that box was a tiny little wooden box from the Catskills where I now live. God knows how I got that. It has the holy card that the kids gave me when I left, and you know like I don't want to see you back here ever again kind of I am sorry you are leaving for me but I'm glad for you ... that kind of thing.

This scrupulous documentation of evidence served multiple purposes for Rachael. But in the aftermath of The Pines, it validated a reality that had been denied by many and, in so doing, served to clear her sullied name.

The social discrediting of Rachael began in court,[3] when her father

3 Bell v. Bell (No. 4014) (1972) (page 161) Supreme Court of South Australia, Adelaide. Judge Walters presiding.

attempted to deflect the focus from his abuse of her by depicting her as a delinquent. The judge accepted this assessment. "I was a defiled person and it was like having a prison record so that everything I said was questionable," she told me. "That kind of vilification is very traumatic for a teenager," and it was rendered more painful still, she said, because it was "public ... like the witches or something." Much of Rachael's life since then has been a response to this denigration, including her life-long project of manifesting what others distorted and/or denied about her incarceration experience.

Rachael's self-assurance in her artistic outputs was never shaken or diminished, despite external assaults to her integrity. Her capacity to give terrible and haunting events both words and forms that she could then integrate and disseminate helped her to disarm the stigma that she was burdened with. In this way, her creativity essentially sustained her during captivity and afterwards. The only way she could explain herself was with her art. "I wrote poetry," she said, "and stuff like that and documented everything with drawings, all the people and all the situations, and I did it as a reification because I was in and out of my body in those years ... it was if I was at an angle to the rest of the world and I wasn't really in it." For Rachael, art became her one constant: her survival strategy, her liberation. "It's what I have. It's how I have confidence in myself. In that I know I can metabolize it and I can reify it. And that I have such confidence in myself to be able to do that."

In addition to freeing her, over time, the art forms that Rachael shaped to these experiences rendered them more understandable to her. Content that she could not process during the shock of her imprisonment became more accessible retrospectively through continuous engagement with it. But even during her incarceration, Rachael had put her surroundings into a tangible form while, to outward appearances at least, she was complying with the orders of the institution. "I put on the outfit of The Pines," she told me, "and I went along and they all thought I was a perfect inmate. But I wasn't, you know, from their point of view." While her external persona may have been one of obedience, religiosity, and compliance, the nuns knew little of what was stewing beneath this demeanour.

In hindsight, Rachael saw her practice of chronicling life inside The Pines and her appearance of compliance to be strategies that made her captivity more bearable. In a world with few choices, these self-developed tactics for self-preservation gave her agency:

> I realized early that being a loud mouth and saying what I thought was going to get me beaten up, or more prone to, so I tried to act like I was really compliant, so I could get away with what I could get away with, in terms of time and so forth. I got to paint roses for the nuns and I got to be *alone* to do that. They locked me in the schoolroom to paint these bloody roses. They used them as greeting cards or something. But that was a coup because it got me out of the laundry you see. They [the roses] were quite symbolic ... it was therapeutic in that I was doing lots of thorns ... [laughter] ... back to the stigmata thing.

While painting roses for greeting cards was, by her standards, not a particularly creative activity, it allowed her to be less vigilant for brief periods and it provided her with occasional relief from unbroken surveillance, wherein she could let her defences down.

The Pines created in Rachael an emotional disconnection that became outwardly apparent before she realized it herself. She described the moment when she was ridiculed into an awareness of her numb detachment. While this moment was not atypical of the harassment inmates received, it became significant to Rachael decades later.

> There was this one woman that ... she was a layperson that came in briefly to do some sort of bullshit that they were trying to inculcate us with, and I used to present a blank face. I

> really wasn't there. I would just turn off. She used to look at me and she used to say "deadpan, deadpan, deadpan!" in a mocking tone, and sneer at me.... but I wasn't there. And you couldn't get me. But it was very difficult for me to come back into my body; it took me until my mid-forties, I think.

As an adult reflecting on the mockery of her fourteen-year-old demeanour, Rachael reconsidered her blank face and what it protected. She realized that she had not been deliberately presenting a blank face; rather, it was her way of operating. "I was back there, in there somewhere," she said, "but I wasn't going to show it." She could not risk exposing defenceless parts of herself in that unsafe situation. In the years closely following her release, she found it difficult to convey a former, more vulnerable self, for she had been unsafe for too long.

Rachael described her fourteen-year-old "deadpan" face as "the mute thing, the empty face. Go along to get along." This attitude was suited to the values of the institution, for she was surrounded by nuns who "were going through rituals, without any self-reflection," and the inmates were expected to do the same. While the mockery of Rachael may have been a strategy to cut her down and render her more compliant, it did not entirely succeed. She remained well protected until her forties, when she realized that her defences had developed into a liability, and a more complex range of emotional expression became emotionally necessary. However, in letting her Pines demeanour go, she needed to acknowledge and pay respect to its purpose. Submerging her subjective, vulnerable, and creative dimensions behind a blank wall had been her only defence against the nuns' mandate to break her will and make her compliant. Even with this strategy in place, she said, they still got to her—The Pines "changed my equilibrium forever."

Rachael's reconnection with the deeply shielded dimensions of her identity and to the natural world that had sustained her came much later, largely through intensive work with her writing and art. With the making of her first documentary, Rachael began a process of deliberately reconnecting with her self-described "heritage of pain." Through this and successive artistic work, she embraced and adapted the Australian Aborigine notion of the songline in the creation of her own lifeline.[4] The songline, Rachael explained, derived from the Aborigine's bond to ancestry and place, is a song that is handed down through ancestors. It is "an outline of what is yours ... given to you by your ancestors. And it's only for you ... you have to own them." Rachael recognized in this potent ritual a reminder of place and belonging that she had lost because of the forced severance from her body and the land on which she grew up. As a child she felt that she had a close relationship with the rocks and trees surrounding her family farm and was aware that earlier Indigenous inhabitants had been violently driven out of that place. She described being fascinated by the hand stencils of the first inhabitants in caves and she played in trees they had hollowed out as shelters.

The songline, with its emphasis on honouring her unique social and material heritage, was an emancipatory concept in the wake of Rachael's incarceration. Folding this ancient tradition into her experience enabled Rachael to possess her incarceration differently and served, at least partially, to re-root her. Rather than living annulled by rage or stigma, or trying to renounce it, she drew this legacy closer, viewing it as a hard-earned sense of herself forged from the place of her branding. By reclaiming her past in this way, both the good and the terrible memories, Rachael essentially chose not to live dispossessed. True to the songline tradition, she created an outline of what was hers and, in doing so, lessened the sense of groundlessness that abuse and incarceration had bestowed on her.

Along with her personal adaptation of the songline, Rachael brought to her recovery process artist Joseph Beuys's notion of "owning material."

---

4 Songlines are oral maps that supported the Indigenous people of Australia as they traversed the land. By singing certain ritual songs in a particular order, they could navigate the landscape, without getting lost. The details of the landscape were embedded in their songlines. See Bruce Chatwin, *The Songlines* (London: Picador, 1987).

This concept, which evolved from Beuys's symbolic integration of his survival tools following an alleged near-death experience, deeply impressed her. "That got me," she said, because her incarceration had similarly produced an emotional death-in-life condition. The idea was to reconsider the images and events of her past that resounded in her with the idea of making them central to her symbolism, and, in doing so, ultimately reclaiming them:

> So, my material would be what is with me, not necessarily what transformed me. Like the roses that I am drawing, the tattoos and barbed wire and all the little truisms and the Aboriginal language and that sort of thing that was amongst the girls. I've recorded all of that and I consider it part of my life.

In her art and writing, she reclaimed and reconstituted some of the most painful words, occurrences, and objects from The Pines that had contributed to the making of her. She reclaimed that which was most "resonant" for her. All the material that she had once dislocated herself from was given a symbolic repositioning in her identity. "I've recorded all of that," she said, "and I consider it part of my life."

The importance of Rachael's developing a new relationship with those parts of her experience that she had been forcibly alienated from in The Pines cannot be overstated. This process helped her to reinstate authority following a life-altering loss of it. But, reclaiming what had been dispossessed necessitated that Rachael return to a psychic place that was riddled with pain and trauma, the point where her life course was destructively altered:

> What happened to me at The Pines ... I died, and I came out another person ... forever changed ... you go through a gateway and you never return. I was cut off from my family, a complete severance, and from then on, I had a different trajectory. But it was not given to me by the Church; it was forced out of me by the Church.

In our conversations, Rachael was careful to clarify that the nuns could not be credited with anything of worth that she reclaimed for her recovery process. All that she retrieved from her imprisonment and symbolically adapted to create something of sustenance was her own doing. The nuns, Rachael repeatedly made clear, had contributed nothing productive to her life.

Upon her release from The Pines, Rachael slowly recognized that she had become a stranger to herself. The nuns' efforts to re/form her had included a seizure of her voice, her hair, her body, her labour, and her dignity. Outside that system, Rachael found herself alone, trying to re-assimilate and reinvent herself, unsupported even in finding language with which to express the inexpressible. Yet, instead of doing what the nuns said she should do—"shut it off, forget about it"—she relocated a means of expression through art and writing, which provided her with a way of communicating these formerly private horrors and making them public in repeated acts of signification. In these ways, Rachael has worked intensively to understand and rid herself of The Pines' defining power over her. But still, she told me, "[i]t's as if I never completely cleared myself, not completely, of that sense that I was an object to be oppressed by the rest of society ... And so that plagued me and still continues to. I still have difficulty operating." The Pines marked her "so indelibly" that it changed the trajectory of her life, with negative and positive consequences:

> They broke my sense of connection with the world, you know? And you know that wonderful confidence that a kid has in their own body and everything. I remember being acrobatic and everything, knowing that I could run up a hill. You know, swim across a river, that kind of feeling. I came out; who cares if I can swim across a river, I was just broken.

Rachael's determination to draw something productive from her experience in The Pines remains active as she continues to work as an artist in New York and devote herself to the plight of socially marginalized people.

In both areas, she remains devoted to challenging the kind of institutional oppression under which she, and others, have suffered. Rachael also persists in fighting for public exposure of the laundries and accountability from the Church and the government for the damage they caused generations of Magdalene inmates. She wants recognition for those, dead and living, whose "life trajectories" were also altered by incarceration in the laundries. Rachael believes that an official acknowledgement is important, as a sign that former inmates have been listened to and understood. But, at the same time, she wonders what compensation for damages to the Magdalenes could look like: "How do you compensate for the sense that you have been relegated to the bottom of the well? And that they have poisoned the water above you?"

CHAPTER THREE
Behind the Clock

Janice Konstantinidis was sent to the Sisters of the Good Shepherd in Hobart, Australia, when she was twelve. She had been told that she would be attending a nearby Catholic boarding school, Mount Carmel, and recalled feeling excited as she and her grandmother prepared her for her new school. Janice's grandmother was not well enough at the time to take her into the city to shop, so they purchased her school supplies from local stores. Brown, her grandmother told her, was the colour of Mount Carmel's uniform. They found three pairs of brown socks and some brown underwear at a local Catholic school supplies shop, and a few other things they thought she would need at boarding school: "I had shampoo and a toothbrush, toothpaste and some other items of toiletry in a red toilet bag. I felt quite important," Janice told me.[1] Janice's great-grandmother, who lived close by and

1 In this chapter, unless otherwise indicated, all quotations attributed to Janice Konstantinidis are taken from a series of interviews between Janice and Rie Croll, which took place between 2009 and 2015. Janice has since told me that my bearing witness to her Good Shepherd experiences served to validate and, in so doing, free her from some of the shame she carried about her incarceration. This affirmation in turn motivated her to join others in making public parts of her story which she had borne, unexpressed,

with whom she had a special connection, was openly distraught about Janice's leaving for school. Janice tried to reassure her by telling her that she would be home for a visit the following weekend. "I could not see why she was so tearful," said Janice; "she said to me as I was leaving her house, 'This is so wrong.' I recall wondering why she would say this." What Janice did not know then, but her great-grandmother apparently did, was that her father intended to have Janice committed to a reformatory that doubled as an institutional laundry. This place, Mount Saint Canice, was known locally as the Mag. There, Janice was institutionalized, performing forced laundry work from 1962 to 1965.

Once inside the reformatory, shock and disbelief at first prevented Janice from realizing that she was not a student, as she had been led to believe, but a prisoner. The damaging effects of the nearly four years of incarceration that followed took a toll on Janice that she is still working to overcome. Foremost was "the belief that [she] was bad." The stigma of having been locked away from society as a "bad" person when she felt she had done nothing to deserve that label or punishment caused her "humiliation at every level."

Janice, born in Tasmania in 1950, was raised primarily by her paternal grandparents. Her parents, she said, especially her father, often mistreated her. Janice linked their neglect and the chaos of her early life to long-lasting anxiety and coping difficulties later in her life. These problems were exacerbated by incarceration. For the first year of her life, Janice lived with her parents in her paternal grandparents' home. There she was relatively well cared for. "I would have been fed well, and [kept] clean," she added. "I was a healthy baby by all accounts." While living under her grandparents' roof during that first year of her life, Janice's father drank heavily. His excessive

---

for decades (see 46n33). Shortly thereafter she contributed a slightly elongated version of that autobiographical piece to the *Journal of the Australian Catholic Historical Society*. While most of what is now published in the two publications listed on p. 46n33 Janice also told directly to me, I cite these publications where she used the same words or phrases that she used in conversation with me.

drinking continued for as long as Janice knew him. When he was drunk, he was often verbally and physically aggressive toward Janice's mother, and later, toward Janice too. Janice was told that her father had extramarital affairs while her mother was pregnant, and "in general made a public disgrace of himself with his drunken bouts [on] the weekends ... He would fight with [Janice's] mother. He would vomit in their bedroom."

Janice's father's behaviour became so upsetting to his parents and their younger daughter that they asked him to leave the family home. "So, my father rented a two-bedroom house," she said. "I recall it quite well. We moved there some time towards the end of 1951." But without her grandparents' care, Janice was often neglected. She recalled feeling cold and having a sore bottom from wetting her pants and frequently wetting the bed. Janice also remembered her grandmother's annoyance with the way she was dressed; every now and then, she would declare that Janice was filthy and take her back to live with her for a few weeks. In travelling to her grandmother's place, Janice recalled, she "would not want to touch me—I know this. She was afraid I would make her good coat smell of urine."

Of her life with her parents, Janice remembers primarily chaos and neglect, and very few happy memories. Her mother would frequently be gone, and with the addition of a new baby to the family, the situation grew more stressful. When the baby cried, Janice often became the victim of her father's rage. When she was still under four, Janice would occasionally wander into the heavy early morning traffic on the main street near their house. She recalls lying on her back, on the road, with her legs in the air as the oncoming vehicles approached. Just as they came dangerously near, she said, "I would get up and run to the side of the road. At times, I would hear the drivers' car horns. I loved to feel the anxiety that this made inside me, the adrenaline." Janice later understood this behaviour to be a response to the stress within her home. As a toddler, and for many decades to follow, Janice pursued adrenaline-producing experiences. They represented for her a normal, and even desirable, state.

In the summer of 1954, Janice's father woke her up in the dark and told her, "Mummy's gone." She cannot recall what she felt or thought in that moment. Janice's only solid memory of that day is that a neighbour, Mrs. H, brushed her hair: "I remember it hurting and that my mother did not hurt me when she combed my hair." Janice recalled her mother as kind and gentle, who, in contrast to her father, never seemed to be angry with her. Just after her mother's departure, Janice was sent back to her grandparents. Her father made the two-hour bus trip with her and she can still picture her grandparents waiting at their gate as the bus let them off. "My grandmother took me from my father," Janice said. "I remember my father leaving early the next morning on the bus back to Hobart. This was the last time I would live with him." From that point on, until her father had her committed to the laundry, Janice lived with her grandparents. Their growing resentment toward her, her increasing anxiety, and mounting angry outbursts from her grandfather were, what she suspects, the catalysts for their having her sent away.

It was at the midterm break in her school year, just before she turned thirteen, that Janice departed for what she thought was her new school in Hobart. She remembers leaving that day with her grandparents to meet up with her father. He always did the driving whenever they went to the city, since her grandfather felt confused by the new one-way streets. This, from what she could tell, was the only reason for her father's involvement that day. While Janice's grandmother would no doubt have eventually been aware that she was committing her granddaughter to a reformatory, Janice justified this "betrayal" by saying that her "pious grandmother" no doubt believed that the presence of nuns would enable her to flourish anywhere: "I know my father was asked to find a boarding school for me and he chose Mount Saint Canice, and in fact lied to my grandparents about where I was going. I know he knew where he was sending me and this makes me sad."

Janice has disjointed memories of the events that unfolded in the next few days, but what she does remember, she remembers strongly. She recalls driving with her father and grandparents to a very large grey and red brick building. At the front of the building, a clock tower stood high above the main entrance. Janice remembers too that, while her grandfather said goodbye to her, her father remained silent. The men stayed in the car while Janice and her grandmother walked to the door to ring the bell. They were invited in by a woman who, Janice would later discover, worked with the sick and elderly nuns in the convent. Janice and her grandmother sat waiting on upright chairs in a long corridor of shiny blue linoleum, surrounded by religious statues:

> We were approached by a ruddy-faced nun in a cream and black habit who introduced herself ... and she invited my grandmother into her office. Not long later, she came out with my grandmother and said to me that I should say goodbye to my grandmother. My grandmother and I said goodbye, and I went with Mother [nun's name] into her office.

The first thing that the nun said to Janice was that her father had sent her to the reformatory because she was uncontrollable and that this was intolerable behaviour. The nun then asked her if she had had sexual intercourse with a man. Janice was speechless in the face of this question, and the nun's insinuations about her behaviour, and it took her a moment to understand and respond to it. Once she absorbed what the nun was implying, Janice told her that she had not had intercourse. She was nevertheless told that a doctor examined the new girls to determine if they had any sexually transmitted diseases. From that point on, Janice was so overwhelmed by the conversation that it fell pretty much "on deaf ears."

As they left the nun's office together, Janice heard something being said about taking her suitcase to be searched. The nun then led Janice through two locked doors, which she opened with a key from the big bunch that hung from her waist. Although it had not yet dawned on Janice that she was not in a boarding school, it quickly became evident that Mount Saint Canice was prison-like. To this day, Janice resents hearing the Church deny that it was a place of incarceration. "It had bars on the windows," she said firmly, and she is still sometimes haunted by "the image of nuns with heavy keys on their belts." There was never any doubt that she was "a prisoner."

As the two walked from the convent into a long hallway filled with lines of girls, Janice felt emotionally overcome. Seeing her distress, the nun ordered one of the girls to take Janice to tea, which was about to begin. There, to her surprise, Janice recognized a girl who had lived in her hometown. This girl had frequently been in trouble and had been sent away to a home for bad girls. "I said to her—in my naivety—thinking I was in a boarding school, 'What are you doing here?' To which she replied, 'What are you doing here?'"

On that first night in Mount Saint Canice, Janice was assigned a bed in a large dormitory with about forty other girls. All the inmates in the reformatory, regardless of their age, Janice later noticed, were referred to as girls. In her view, this was a way of levelling and humiliating them. As they were short a bed when Janice arrived, she initially slept in the dormitory used by some of the older women and auxiliary nuns. Her bed was in the centre of the room, in the middle of a line of beds. Janice felt unnerved by her simultaneous enclosure and exposure.

That first night, like every night, the main lights went out at 9 p.m. Because Janice had been reticent to shower in front of the others, she found herself in darkness just as she was about to take her turn. She recalls spilling her new shampoo all over the tiles, and she remained quite shaken even after someone helped her clean it up. Later, lying in her bed with wet hair, Janice felt so frightened that her face went numb with anxiety. She recalled laying there crying from loneliness and watching the moon through the dormitory's barred windows. In that moment, she told me, the significance of the bars had still not fully registered with her.

Her first full day with the Good Shepherds began in the darkness of early morning, with the toll of a bell followed by the rattle of keys in the door. In addition to the pitch-darkness, Janice recalls that it was cold. The lights were then abruptly switched on, hurting her eyes, and a nun came through the dormitory loudly calling out, "In the name of the Father, and of the Son and of the Holy Spirit." Janice learned on the spot that this was the signal for them to drop to their knees at their bedsides and recite the

Lord's Prayer in unison. The girl whose cot was next to Janice's gave her quick instructions in a hushed voice on dressing and bathing. The girls then lined up and were led through several doors. Each door they approached was unlocked for them to pass through and then locked again behind them.

The group's numbers grew as additional inmates from other dormitories joined them and all together they filed toward the convent church. There, the girls and the nuns from the reformatory were segregated from the rest of the congregation into two distinct sections. When Mass was over, the girls reassembled in the order by which they had originally assembled and filed to the refectory for breakfast. As with chapel, silence was maintained during meals. Janice remembered feeling exposed and vulnerable during her first meal at Mount Saint Canice, seated at one of many long tables amid what she estimates were about 200 inmates. She sensed that everyone was looking at her, the new girl. This continued when, after breakfast, Janice was brought to a vast ironing room that contained approximately twenty ironing stations. She described the sheer size of that room, where many girls were working in silence, as overwhelming.

Janice was assigned a position at one of many long tables alongside a nun who instructed her to begin ironing, handkerchiefs at first; she would be given more complicated ironing later. Although confused by this turn of events, Janice did as she was told, in silence, until a bell rang and she was collected for school. Because no one had yet told her otherwise, Janice still thought she was in Mount Carmel. But doubt crept in when, being fitted for a uniform, she noticed that the colours were not those that she and her grandmother had anticipated; these were navy and white. Once in her uniform, Janice was taken to a room where the other school-aged inmates were being taught to cook. It was there, seated next to her new classmates, that Janice realized she was in a reformatory. Out the classroom window, in the distance, her eyes had settled on what she thought was a swimming pool, and she asked the girl seated next to her if swimming was to be a part of their school day. The girl, who was clearly taken aback by Janice's question, told her to look again. When Janice realized that what she was seeing was the metal structure and barbed wire of the Mag's reformatory complex, she was devastated. Mount Carmel had been a lie.

Janice only recently learned that Mount Carmel was a day school; it had never been a boarding school as she had been led to believe. Uncovering this subsequent betrayal by her father was upsetting and it caused her to question the times, after she left Mount Saint Canice, when former classmates asked her how she was enjoying her boarding school. She wondered if they had known all along that she had been in the Mag. With that thought came a renewed sting of humiliation. She reflected on that time and the vulnerability she felt as the full hurt of the betrayal washed over her. She described herself as feeling overwhelmed by a sense of betrayal and humiliation. As the reality of her situation set in that day in the classroom, Janice must have looked as distraught as she felt, because the nun in charge of cooking brought her into another room to sit down. There the nun informed Janice that her family had placed her with them and that she had to stay there for some time. As it turned out, Janice would not see her family for even a short visit until Christmas, eight months later. But in that moment, she said, "I can't describe what was in my mind ... it is too sad for me to contemplate."

School ended each day with a bell at 3 p.m., at which time the girls filed out in line to the refectory for a brief afternoon tea. From there they returned to their respective places in the laundry and worked until 5 p.m. When the school-aged girls got out of the laundry each day, they were allowed back into the dormitory to quickly wash themselves before dinner—cleanliness was regularly emphasized. As with the other meals, there was no talking during dinner, except when they were told they could. Janice remembered that the diet in Mount Saint Canice contributed to weight gain in the inmates, primarily because of its high starch content. Bread and potatoes were staples but, unlike some other Good Shepherd institutions, the farm produce provided a supplement of carrots, onions, and other vegetables to the inmates' meals. The institution, said Janice, was remarkably self-sufficient. Fruit, however, was not part of the inmates' diet.

At meals, Janice was seated beside an auxiliary nun who wore a grey habit with grey stockings, and black lace-up shoes. Her uniform was different from those of the other nuns because she was not a full-fledged nun. As Janice understood it, auxiliary nuns had usually been in the home for many years and were considered reformed Magdalenes. They had been sent to the Mother convent in Melbourne to train as nuns, and while they would never be eligible for formal orders, they considered themselves nuns. Janice recalled that some of these women oversaw groups of girls and did a good deal of the institution's work.

Sitting at Janice's table as well was a young woman whom Janice described as "challenged." At nearly twenty years of age, she could not speak and would not be separated from the teddy bear that she carried. The care of this young woman was the auxiliary nun's responsibility, but some of her daily upkeep soon became the responsibility of Janice and another inmate. They were assigned to take her up to the dormitory in the evenings to be bathed before the other girls came up. Janice was initially frightened of her because she would often attempt to scratch and bite when Janice had to take her teddy bear from her at bath time.

The dining area, or refectory, segregated the inmates based on age, ability, and the work they performed in the reformatory. Janice noted that the older women ate together in one area. She later learned that many of them worked together too. Some of those not working in the laundry laboured, along with the intellectually challenged inmates, to grow food for the Good Shepherd reformatory farm. These women were sturdy of build and "smelled of cow manure" (Konstantinidis 2013, 103). Janice thought it was sad that some of them could not remember a life outside the confines of the reformatory, partly because her memories of roaming free in nature were what sustained her during her incarceration. These women would sometimes sit along one corridor together with those who could no longer work. As this was an area of the institution where the sun shone in, they gravitated to that spot. Janice knew of one woman in her late thirties who told her that she had not been outside the institution for over twenty years.

As far as Janice knew, "this woman had come to the home in her youth and had not left."

Janice also remembered a family who lived at Mount Saint Canice, three girls and their mother. She was not sure of their story and often wondered about how they had ended up there together. Janice referred to this family and most of the other girls who were sent to the home for various so-called crimes as "the fallen, the wretched, and the shamed" (Konstantinidis 2013, 101). The girls' "crimes," the reasons that they were incarcerated in the first place, "were things like giving cheek to their parents, smoking, maybe drinking or having unmarried sex." From what she could tell, few were legitimately "bad," as they were called by the nuns. Their rebellious behaviours within the institution, as Janice later understood, had a lot to do with their being institutionalized. When she was incarcerated, she also saw herself "as bad, and without worth or entitlement"; everyone, she noted, responded to this levelling in different ways.

While Janice's memories of certain events and the daily structure of Mount Saint Canice are quite clear, she finds it troubling that she is unable to connect with most of her emotions from this time. She has tried hard to feel what she must have been feeling back then. With effort, she can attach a word such as "confused" or "frightened" to an event, but she cannot connect to the feeling behind those words. Decades after her incarceration, in counselling for post-traumatic stress disorder, Janice worked intensively to reconnect her emotional responses to her laundry experiences. While she has had limited success in realigning these dimensions, it has been helpful for her to understand that the shock of incarceration, and the cruelties she was exposed to there, caused her to suppress her emotional responses.

Despite not having access to her emotional memories, Janice vividly recalls the physical pain associated with having a burned neck the first week she was there. Her burn was the result of being deloused and disinfected, mandatory practices for all girls upon entry. While aghast at this bodily inspection, Janice was forced to endure it. She was given a bottle of some awful-smelling substance and told to shower with it on her second day there. Although this intake procedure was normally performed directly on arrival, Janice had arrived late in the day, so it was postponed. The next day, though, another inmate washed Janice's hair in kerosene, creating the burns on her neck. But since there was no treatment for the burn, she had to endure the intense discomfort until it subsided.

In addition to the painful and humiliating delousing procedure, Janice recounted other violations from that first week, including the thefts of her underwear and the watch her grandmother had given her. Her watch was never returned, and the nuns replaced her stolen underwear with pink, institutionally issued undergarments that she described as odd and outdated. This foreign underwear, while not in itself significant, represented a loss of the last of her familiar touchstones. Wearing these slightly humiliating and ill-fitting clothes, together with her burning neck and the violation of thefts, left Janice feeling increasingly alienated. In the intense loneliness of her first days and weeks in the reformatory, she recalls keenly hoping that she would be able to go home. She yearned to tell her grandmother, among other things, about her burned neck, her stolen watch, and the long hours of laundry work. But, she knew that trying to write to her grandmother about her circumstances was futile, since all ingoing and outgoing mail was searched for forbidden content, including descriptions of life inside the Mag.

Marks and Order

Janice entered Mount Saint Canice with random impulses to perform self-soothing rituals such as repetitive counting. This behaviour, which in her adulthood was diagnosed as obsessive-compulsive disorder, was thought to have been further fuelled by the institutional setting, particularly by ritualized and heavily structured religious and prison routines. For one thing, she explained, the environment served to both incubate and camouflage her ritualized behaviours. In there, "[her] obsession needs were rampant," and the routine tolling of the bells agreed with her need to perform rituals. "Being in [a] convent is a good place to have such needs," Janice told me, "as no one looks twice if you genuflect many times a day. Or at least I didn't think they did." Janice described a life governed by the bells: "we lived by them." The bells rang late at night and first thing every morning. When the bells tolled, "all nuns stopped whatever they were doing ... even if it was to dot an 'i.'"

As months turned into years in Mount Saint Canice, Janice developed a dependency on the bells for structure and became used to doing things in synch with others. Permission to function as an individual in that environment was rare, so operating independently of others grew increasingly uncomfortable. With hindsight, Janice feels that the bells halted her capacity for independent action, as each step that the inmates were expected to take throughout the day was regulated by this sound. Today Janice claims that she is not "a self-starter" in any other place except her home, and even there, it has taken her a long time to try new things. She believes this is the direct result of being allowed to act only when she was told.

Janice conformed to institutional rules, but she constantly longed to be free. In her confinement she reflected on the freedoms she once had and felt empathy for those fellow inmates who had only sparse memories of freedom. Unless they went out into the walled reformatory courtyard "and saw the light of day," Janice gathered that it was possible for them to live their whole lives in the reformatory without ever going outside. Looking back on those years, Janice views herself as being held "in a place of sensory and other deprivations." Despite the detrimental effects of the numerous absences inmates experienced, such as the withholding of touch and affection, fresh air, and intellectual stimulation, one of the most significant injuries she suffered was the loss of her individuality. "Even if this was not one deliberately contrived by the nuns," she said, "it was certainly sanctioned by them for they continued to do it." She described the inmates as "powerless" in terms of "what they ate, what they wore, when they bathed, what they read—there were very few books—or watched on TV." More importantly, Janice said, "I was not allowed an opinion."

As a rule, inmates were not allowed to speak unless otherwise instructed.

The enforced silence is "a good metaphor" for the low value ascribed to the inmates; "it works well for me," she continued, "and strikes a chord." The suppression of inmates' bodies, voices, and emotions was partly maintained by a system of reward and punishment. Each fortnight the girls were assigned a total of three marks based on their conduct in the areas of work and/or school, general care of themselves and cleanliness, and overall behaviour and adherence to rules. If an inmate had been "good" in all three areas, she would receive four shillings biweekly. A loss of marks meant a loss of shillings. While four shillings every two weeks was a meagre sum, it was still a powerful motivation to conform to the rules. Not earning those shillings meant public humiliation, as every two weeks the wrongs of those who had not earned their money were read aloud, including such details as their lack of hygiene. The "marks" system was applied to all disobediences, large and small, including violations of the rule of silence, and was extended to all girls irrespective of age.

Having those few shillings meant that inmates could purchase a "luxury item" such as deodorant or shampoo from the tuck shop. The convent supplied only the most basic clothes, shoes, and personal hygiene products. There was an institutionally issued shampoo, for example, but Janice said that it did not smell very nice. The only other thing that the nuns provided were sanitary pads, one packet per menstrual cycle, which they referred to as "bunnies." Janice found it humiliating that inmates had to request sanitary pads and saw this as evidence of the nuns' larger dissociation from the bad and shameful bodies of the inmates.

The money associated with the mark system was, in Janice's view, extremely important within the inmate culture. It contributed to their underground economy and allowed some to gain control over others by undermining one another to the nuns. This worked in the nuns' favour, since it led to the inmates' policing of one another. Since none of the inmates knew what other inmates had reported about them, the biweekly reporting system was a "nerve-racking" process. No one knew if they would receive their three marks until their "every 'wrongful' act [was] described in public."

This, said Janice, "was very humiliating for me at least"; it was a "highly demeaning" system of regulation. In response, "the girls were always talking about themselves as slaves," working for nothing and being treated in a debasing manner. Although Janice was then too numb to agree or disagree with this viewpoint, she now fully agrees with it. The girls who could work "worked long and hard hours primarily in the laundry, and the sum of four shillings every two weeks was an insult to them."

After being in the reformatory for an indefinite period and conforming strictly to the reformatory rules, inmates might be permitted a biweekly family visitor. Keeping this hope in sight, Janice did precisely what was expected of her. However, she did not receive a single visit from her grandparents or her father while she was incarcerated. Once, though, some distant relatives took Janice out for an afternoon. She remembered that they were kind to her and she could tell they felt bad about her being locked up. "Obviously," she said, "people somewhere in the family knew it was wrong." Beyond that one act of compassion, Janice felt completely abandoned.

Before turning thirteen, Janice was given the additional duty of monitoring several severely epileptic girls. These girls slept in a large room on mattresses which were placed on the floor to protect them if they seized. Janice was locked in the room alone with them for three nights a week; another inmate monitored them for the remaining four nights. The girls had frequent seizures, so an undisturbed night was unusual. For every seizure that occurred, Janice was instructed to leave the room (she was given a key) and pull on a bell to alert a nun, who would then come with an injection for the girl. The years spent caring for these girls took a toll on Janice. Ever since she had experienced a grand mal seizure before entering Mount Saint Canice, she lived with an often-unmanageable anxiety that it would happen to her again. Even witnessing a seizure could cause her body to go numb. Janice remembered that when she would wake to one of the girls seizing, it would take all the focus that she could muster to unlock the door so that she could ring the bell. "I still have dreams," she said, "where I am trying to open these doors. I was terrified."

Janice wondered why the nuns put her in charge of girls with seizures when she had told them repeatedly about her own fear of seizing. Looking back on it, she found it "shocking" that they knowingly placed her in that situation. "I can't describe the anxiety," she said. "It was pretty dreadful of them to do it. It was most inappropriate really, and cruel. How dare they." One small advantage of Janice's caretaking responsibilities, though, was that she was relocated to a smaller dormitory of nine beds in which she got a bed by a window. This was a relief from her exposed position in the other dorm. And while her window had bars on it, the view from her bed allowed her to mentally escape each night, which, in turn, helped her to survive the harsh and chronically monitored day environment.

On Saturday mornings, inmates could sleep in until 7 a.m. They went to a later Mass and spent the morning cleaning their dormitories in preparation for inspection. Inmates' beds had to be made neatly and their sleeping area kept clean and tidy. Inspection was held on Saturday afternoon before the marks were assigned. Janice remembered that one tactic used by the auxiliary nun for getting inmates to sweep properly was to randomly throw tea leaves under their beds. After sweeping, the girls would then wash and polish the floors on their knees. In like manner, they cleaned the bathrooms. This cleaning went on until lunchtime.

Janice worked in the laundry Monday to Friday from 8 a.m. to 5 p.m., with school breaks in between. When she turned fourteen, she worked Saturday mornings as well. Mount Saint Canice was reputed to have the biggest commercial laundry in southern Tasmania, taking orders from hospitals and other businesses. They did some private laundry, too, recalls Janice, which was mainly sent to them from priests and the archbishop's residence. The laundry facilities consisted of the ironing room, where Janice worked when she was not in school, the machine room, and the folding, packing, and drying rooms. The machine room, as in other Good Shepherd laundries, contained very large mangles and rows of large washing machines. The heat from these machines was so intense, Janice told me, that a wet sheet would only need to be fed through once.

It was Janice's job to iron dozens, if not hundreds, of pairs of underwear, shirts, and hankies each day. During this rote work, she emotionally "switched off," for her own survival. Sometimes, in her mind's eye, she "walks the corridors of Mount Saint Canice," trying to re-connect with what she was thinking and feeling while incarcerated. Although her feelings from then are difficult to re-engage, some are returning: "I see myself ironing in the laundry"; "I feel trapped and angry. I don't want to iron all day. I hate the school that they have there. I know all they have to teach me because I have done it before."

The injustice of incarceration was extremely difficult for Janice to reconcile within herself. "We were prisoners," she said; "we were locked in our dormitories at night, and we could not go outside." Their only contact with fresh air was a brief daily break in the internal courtyard. There, she could see the sun but no grass. It still pains her that some women had been there all their lives and this was their only contact with the outdoors. Keeping the inmates always out of the public view shielded them from outside influences but, Janice believed, keeping them out of sight also rendered them out of the public's mind. She feels strongly that the state should have been held accountable for them, but, according to her, state presence was negligible in Mount Saint Canice. They were aware that cruelties were taking place inside the reformatory but did nothing to intercede. "I know that to be the case," she said, "because the girls who tried to run away were hunted down like dogs and brought back by the police and the social workers, and their heads would be shaved then and there." This harsh practice was widely known and accepted.

Janice recalled that the nuns not only shaved the runaways' heads but cut their nails. It was her understanding that the purpose of those practices was to take from the inmates what they "treasured about themselves," thereby levelling all ego and vanity. In addition to those humiliations, the nuns also confiscated runaways' clothing and forced them to wear "the punishment dress," a dress assembled from sacking or burlap material, with the edges trimmed with coloured binding. Those who had worn the dress told Janice that it felt starchy. The length of time the punishment dress was worn varied. Janice knew of a few girls who had to wear it for twelve months "because they had fought a nun as they were being brought back or had not followed orders in the weeks following their recapture." Wearing it on "parlour visits" and to Mass was, in Janice's estimation, the most humiliating part, because the public could see you.

For the duration of their punishment, runaways would also scrub the long and drafty "red corridor" each day on their hands and knees. If inmates were caught talking to or helping a girl "in punishment," as it was called, they would immediately lose all their marks. This, Janice explained, was out of the nuns' fear of escape plans being devised among inmates or of friendships being formed between them. Regardless, "we used to be quite sensitive towards the girls when they came back." The inmates did what they could do to make the runaways "feel a bit better," mostly through small gestures. Some of the girls, for example, offered "support by action, food given as we passed and looks of sympathy, but not a lot of talk as we were not permitted to talk." Inmates knew the further isolating effects of shunning and so, even if the girl "in punishment" was not particularly liked, they felt compelled to be kind to her. In one incident, Janice felt genuine sympathy for an inmate who had regularly bullied her. Following this inmate's runaway escape, and the shearing of her hair and the cutting of her nails, she seemed "cowed and broken." Janice was sensitive to the humiliations this girl had suffered, and hugged her. "You can't kick a dog when it's down," she said, although "this is what the nuns did to us."

Another runaway attempt that remains strong in Janice's memory ended with the shearing of one side of the inmate's head. Janice and the other inmates recognized that a half-shaven head was intended to be more humiliating than a completely shorn one and that this girl, "who would not be broken," was being used as a cautionary tale. However, in a bold move to restore some self-dignity, the girl countered this violation by styling the unshaven side "in a French roll." Janice clearly remembers how the inmates responded to this act of defiance by clapping in admiration of her spirit.

Janice described the nun's response to this forbidden show of solidarity as potent. "And to see the nun," she said, "who saw what she [the inmate] had done, and our open admiration for her when she walked in, take to her hair again with scissors and cut the rest off, was horrible. I see this as twisted and vindictive."

Another way that solidarity was expressed among inmates was through a code of silence. Nowhere was this more evident than around inmate's escape plans. Such a plan usually developed over weeks, unless it happened spontaneously, in response to an upset of some sort. Janice recalled that the days and weeks prior to an escape created an odd sort of exhilaration among the inmates. Most of them could identify with the longing to escape and knew the dangers that an attempt posed. There was thus increased camaraderie, as those who knew about it kept quiet and waited for it to unfold. On one such occasion, an escape being plotted by three inmates ended with one of the girls jumping out of an upper-story bathroom window and breaking her back. Janice was in her dormitory that Sunday night, helping to bathe her charge. In anticipation of their escape Janice kept an eye on the window, hoping to see them jump. Their plan, known widely among the inmates, had been to make their escape through a third-floor bathroom window, one of the few windows in Mount Saint Canice without bars. From there, they had planned to navigate their way from one ledge to another, before jumping to the roof of the first floor. But, the first girl to jump lost her footing and fell as she tried to land on the first ledge. Janice heard her hit and saw that she lay motionless on the first-floor roof. Janice later learned that the girl had broken her back in the fall and would never walk again; she never returned to the reformatory. Janice has still not fully absolved herself of the guilt she carries for not telling what she knew about the escape plan, yet remaining silent had saved her life from being "made quite hell" in the laundry. The credo among the inmates in the laundry was that "you don't 'lag,' you don't lag on people." If a girl snitched on a fellow inmate, she would be "pinched and beaten up" and sent to "Coventry ... a form of purgatory in which nobody would speak to you."

In addition to running away, girls who wanted to escape from the laundry would attempt to hurt themselves so that they would require hospitalization. For some, even extreme injury was preferable to life in Mount Saint Canice. After the girl who had her head half-shaved had been recaptured, she was working with Janice in the ironing room one day when a nun momentarily left the room. The girl, who was working on a shirt-press, lay her hands on the machine as though she was flattening a shirt. The memory of what happened next still plagues Janice:

> I then noticed with horror that she let the press down on her hands. I ran to her, thinking that it must have been a terrible accident, and I stepped on the release foot pedal. But this was a mistake as her hands were stuck to the top lid of the press. She screamed, I screamed, and an older girl raced to help us. The burned girl was taken to the hospital and did not return until sometime later.

Despite how deeply disturbed Janice was by this incident, she was expected to immediately carry on with her work as if nothing had happened. This detachment was expected of the inmates, as the order of the institution was valued above all else. When the girl was returned to Mount Saint Canice, she told Janice that she had put her hand in the press on purpose so that she could get out.

Even though such dramatic injuries occurred during inmates' attempts to escape—injuries that gave Janice nightmares for years—there were still no interventions from the police or Social Services. The superintendent of police and representatives from the welfare system attended the institution's large annual concert put on by the inmates, but, according to Janice, apart from this ceremonial show of interest in Mount Saint Canice, there was no external presence in the institution. She maintained that the welfare and policing systems knew "the low that the girls were in, but nobody stepped in."

The Slag from the Mag

From the moment that she arrived at Mount Saint Canice, Janice was discouraged by its school curriculum; the nuns covered only the most basic arithmetic and spelling and emphasized sewing and cooking. This offered her no challenge and "taught [her] nothing." Prior to her incarceration, school had been a place of refuge and a source of accomplishment; she had done well in her subjects and enjoyed being there. The realization that school had become no more than a diversion from endless hours of laundry work was one more blow. Several weeks into Janice's incarceration, the nun in charge of inmate education noticed that Janice was more advanced than most of the other girls, and made her their tutor. From then on, tutoring became all that she did in school. Janice felt dejected about this because she knew she was not learning and that she was slipping behind her classmates at home.

In 1965, two girls who were younger than Janice arrived at Mount Saint Canice. Shortly thereafter, for reasons unknown to Janice, a psychologist administered IQ tests to her and these girls. Following this evaluation, Janice was asked if she would like to attend school outside Mount Saint Canice. Janice had apparently done well on her test, and there had been a recommendation that she and one of the other girls attend an external, local school. Because Janice was interested in going to "a proper school," her father was contacted about paying for her uniform and books. After some time, Janice was told that her father had refused to pay anything toward her schooling and that external schooling was therefore not an option for her. By that point, Janice recalls, "I was down so low I did not really care." Perhaps that is why she remembers little of that time, beyond continuing what was to her the terrifying work of monitoring the epileptic inmates at night and spending Christmas in Mount Saint Canice. The depression she experienced then and long afterwards left her with an inability to find happiness in anything outside of her imagination.

Early in the New Year, Janice was beckoned to the Reverend Mother's office, where she was told that she would attend the external school after all.

They had decided to pay for Janice's uniform and other school needs. Apparently, the psychologist who had tested Janice had been concerned about her "nerves." In addition, she was thought to be exceptionally intelligent and would benefit from both "a good education and interaction with children in a proper school." Janice and the other girl who was chosen for the external school were to sleep in a room near the convent infirmary and have their own study room. Janice would be supplied with keys to the side door of the convent so that she could come and go from school. She was told that this had never been done in its history, and she was expected to be a credit to the convent.

Even in her depressed state, Janice recalls feeling slightly buoyed by this turn of events. She was taken by an auxiliary nun into the city to purchase her school uniform and supplies—an unheard-of outing for inmates. From there, they went for an interview with "Mr. Brown," the high school principal. It was important to Janice that he "welcomed [her] to the school," as it was a dignity that had not been shown to her in a long while. Once officially enrolled, Janice found that she had been placed in the lower end of the academic stream in a grade 10 class. This demotion, she maintains, resulted from the low level of instruction that she received at Mount Saint Canice. Despite feeling discouraged by it, and the fact that the nuns confined Janice to a strict route to and from school, with no lingering allowed and no extracurricular activities, the thought of no longer being a constant prisoner was uplifting.

Some inmates were hostile to Janice's new privilege, which created conflict for her in the Mag. However, she found a way to soothe their resentment by making her new situation beneficial to all of them. She agreed to sneak in cigarettes to some of the inmates and, as word spread, she was posting letters and making phone calls on their behalf. In retrospect, Janice viewed these illicit communications, to mothers, sisters, or other family members, as "quite sad"—as desperate attempts at human connection in a world where all intimacy was denied. Cutting the inmates off from these relationships "seemed so wrong," said Janice.

Janice's messenger role created conflict for her. Because she felt some gratitude to the nuns for giving her a chance at schooling, doing forbidden favours for the inmates felt like a betrayal of their trust in her. Simultaneously, she was loyal to the inmates and wanted to both remain in their good books and share some of her privilege with them. Janice could also identify with their desperation and isolation and wanted to help alleviate it. But, as Janice's first semester in her new school progressed, she grew increasingly self-conscious about her status as an inmate from the Mag, and she wanted to distance herself from that identity. Because of these conflicting roles, she said, "I found myself anxious most of my waking hours."

Janice's anxiety was complicated by her growing sense of inadequacy. Soon into the semester, even the freedom of attending school could not offset this. Only with hindsight could she express what she was experiencing, that institutionalization had taken her identity:

> I did not do things well independently; I seemed to need to know that I had the structure of "the home" close to me. I was very nervous and kept to myself where possible. I tried to keep this hidden and I think I was successful at this, as people have said later that they would never have guessed I was under such a strain. It is amazing what a "clown" can cover.

Access to a library and new English books were two of the greatest pleasures of attending an external school. Countering this satisfaction, though, was Janice's recognition that she was in trouble academically. Because of her time in Mount Saint Canice, several subjects were now beyond her grasp. Complicating this deficit was the fact that she had become a target for bullies.

As Janice was walking to the bus after school one afternoon, a boy blocked her way and said, "How about a shag, you hag from the Mag?" His friends joined him in this taunt. Janice ran onto the bus feeling sick, but she could not escape them. They repeated this degrading insult every time they saw her. In the schoolyard, at recess, or lunchtime, they would catcall and jeer. Janice began eating lunch by herself on the rocks near the sea. It was out of school bounds but it was more important that she get away from her bullies. Although making the acquaintance of several girls at the school eased Janice's isolation, the students generally kept their distance from her, and she also distanced herself from them. "I did not fit in," she told me, "and I was so very upset about the names the boys called me."

The boys' bullying escalated. Another taunt came in the form of the chant "spit, spag and spew reminds me of you" and they threw stones at her each day as she made her way to and from the bus stop. This caused her intense anxiety and destroyed any motivation for learning, "which was hard enough as it was, given that [she] had not been in a regular school for some time":

> I was known as "Haggy Slaggy from the Maggie." Most places I went I was called Haggy, and I knew what the rest was. The gravel and small rocks hurt my legs, and sometimes made small cuts, which bled. This was to go on for months. I can't describe how I felt. When I try to see into my mind at this time, it is actually blank. I used to think I didn't care and that I was a hard person because I can do this at times. But I think I have a mechanism whereby I can compartmentalize this pain somehow.

Janice was unable to thrive under these cruel conditions. The chronic harassment made going to school nightmarish, and she developed anxiety attacks on her way to school each day. Soon, Janice was unable to focus on even the part of the work that she should have done well, and she began failing her courses. When the school holidays came, Janice was relieved to return to the Monday-through-Saturday, 8:30 a.m. until 5 p.m. laundry routine of the "working girls." She did not want to go back to school. She blamed herself and felt ashamed for not being able to catch up with the curriculum. She had not told the nuns about slipping behind. She saw herself, as her father did, as "[n]ot worth a pinch of shit."

Janice's fifteenth birthday came and went with only one card to acknowledge it. This came from her grandmother and included a happy birthday message from her great-grandmother. When the semester resumed, Janice began practicing for the school play, *Pygmalion*, in which she was given the role of Eliza Doolittle. The nuns unexpectedly allowed her to attend play practice in the evenings, but she had to be escorted by two older girls who had been in Mount Saint Canice for years. These girls were referred to as "trustees," and Janice described them as "raucous." While she practiced, they stood outside the school smoking as much as they could in their brief freedom from the Mag. Janice was acutely aware of their company and their difference from the more refined children at school. Soon, word of their presence reached Janice's primary bully, whose gang had grown substantially by then:

> Everywhere I would go there was a whispered "Haggy" and the odd snide remark about me being the "local bike." I am so glad I didn't know what this meant at the time. I think it would have broken me. The girls who came to get me were named "The Bitches of Magbeth," and they became the flavour of the teasing for some time. The students knew the home as the Magdalene home and this is where the names were generated. I understand that some students were told not to go near me by their parents. This was not kept from me by the gang. They told me that the rocks they threw were to take the "Crust of Gonorrhoea off me." I did not know what this meant, but the rocks hurt me. They also used to hold their noses as I passed any time.

Even now, the "spit, spag and spew" taunt occasionally runs through Janice's head. It has been extremely difficult to get past the pain caused by this bullying; she has concluded that "you do not get over something like this all that well."

When Janice's principal heard of the bullying, he asked her about it, and she told him she would like to leave the school. He convinced her to stay by assuring her that he would handle the bullies, which he successfully did. Nevertheless, between the bullying and the academic setback, Janice was unable to salvage her school year. The nuns expressed their deep disappointment in her failure to honour the privilege they had granted her and they would not support her in returning to school. It was time, they told her, for her to get a job, and they helped to set her up in a boarding house in town. Nothing had prepared Janice for this sudden transition to the outside world—a place that had become "extremely confusing and frightening" to her. Because of years of institutionalization, she was ill-equipped to navigate her life on the outside, alone and without structure. Nevertheless, once freed, she knew with certainty that, while the outside was daunting, she could never survive being sent back to Mount Saint Canice—back "behind the clock."

"Behind the clock," a threat Janice's father used to keep her in line once she was released from Mount Saint Canice, referred to the large clock that sat atop the brick entranceway to the reformatory. The crux of his warning was that he could have her readmitted if she got into any trouble, particularly sexual trouble. Janice's father had been a taxi driver in Hobart for many years, and he and his fellow cabbies had delivered many girls to the reformatory. Janice recalled their referring to certain fares as "such and such a girl" and saying "[they were] going to take them behind the clock." He knew what the expression meant, said Janice. "Certainly, there was a broad perception that the girls who were in the Magdalene home were sexually active, easy to get along with, and were bad."

Janice carried the fear of being sent "behind the clock" into her adult years. "I didn't want to go back there," she told me. "I knew girls in there that were so old. I had seen them brought back in at twenty. And that's terrible. The residual fear of being sent back in was there even after I was twenty-one.

I don't think it ever fully leaves." Janice's dread of re-institutionalization proliferated on discovering that she was pregnant at sixteen, months after leaving Mount Saint Canice. Late in her pregnancy, Janice's fear became a reality when her father and his girlfriend brought her to an interview at a maternity home called "Elim House." She was terrified of the place, because she knew of its reputation from girls who had been there when she was an inmate in the Mag. Janice recounted the story of a young woman who returned to Mount Saint Canice and hanged herself following her stay at this maternity home. Janice was so disturbed by the accounts of the young pregnant women who were sent there that, during her interview, although she was in the late stages of her pregnancy, she scaled the fence surrounding Elim House and escaped.

Despite Janice's escape, the delivery of her child brought another unwelcome and life-altering state intervention. Alone and unaware of her rights, Janice was eventually coerced into giving up her newborn infant by persistent social workers who visited her in the hospital and at home. What Janice now views as a forceful and manipulative removal of her child is a regret and a deep loss that continues to distress her. Because of this treatment, Janice described herself as "a victim twice over" of a society that had no regard for her welfare. Even today people suggest that it is a good thing that her baby was taken from her: "Don't you think it was for the best for everyone? You couldn't have raised her. And I think well why couldn't I raise her?"

Janice told me that getting pregnant had been part of an inevitable progression that began with her incarceration and its associated stigma. Apart from the low expectations that her family and surrounding community had of her, because she had already been incarcerated as a bad girl, she had received no sex education from anyone, let alone her grandparents or the nuns. In addition, her public schooling had been so disrupted that if family planning or sex education was normally provided in the curriculum, she missed it. The one thing that she did learn from the nuns was that she "shouldn't be unclothed in front of a man." "Which," she said, "I wasn't really."

Complicating her lack of understanding about sex was her perception that being married would protect her from being sent back to the laundry. The social message she received was that marriage, even early marriage, was a defence against re-incarceration. In keeping with this view, she explained, one notable thing that Mount Saint Canice did for her was that it caused her to marry her first husband. "When I got married," Janice told me, "the first thoughts I had were 'well this won't last but at least it will keep me out of the home ... now my father won't be able to put me in the home.'" For a long time, Janice avoided telling her spouses and her children about her incarceration, and she was not alone in keeping this silent. She told me of a friend from Mount Saint Canice who, out of fear of judgment, has yet to tell her husband or her children about her time at the laundry.

While Janice now speaks about her time in the laundry, she is sympathetic to those who chose not to disclose this part of their history because she knows what people thought of former inmates, even, as she learned, children on school playgrounds. "Everyone at that time in Hobart ... if a girl was from the home ... then they thought she must have been very bad. I was conscious of that." This evaluation of inmates reinforced Janice's sense of inadequacy and, in turn, it eventually caused her to misbehave:

> I acted out ... and I was not even conscious of it ... you see bad is bad, isn't it? And if society sees a girl who gets pregnant as bad and I did get pregnant within a few months of leaving the home ... that just vindicated their notions that I was just hopeless. It was the most terrible thing that a young girl could do.

With hindsight, Janice does not view herself as "bad" or her behaviour as terrible. Rather, she perceives her post-Mount Saint Canice choices as an understandable outcome of her environment. In explaining this, she relayed a dream she had had in which she was a marionette. She said that she identified with the symbolism of the puppet, saying that for a long time she was almost completely controlled by others—they were operating her strings. Institutionalization was like this, she said; it left her unable "to function in [her] own right."

The Internalization of Mount Saint Canice

> *I am in the dormitory now, lights are out, and it is a Saturday night. I can see from my bed down to the main street of lower Sandy Bay; there is life, cars, people. I want to be part of it, it seems wonderful to me. Looking back at the darkened room and rows of sleeping girls, I feel depressed.*
>
> (Konstantinidis, interview, 2012)

"To be locked away and be expected to live like one of a flock of sheep," said Janice, "is very much how Mount Saint Canice felt." This denial of her individuality deprived her of the ability to set personal boundaries. As an inmate, she had no say in what was done to her and, for decades afterwards, this led her into one damaging relationship after another:

> Most of the people I associated with in later life and with whom I was raised were dysfunctional. And this led to layers upon layers of dysfunction for me until I was enmeshed in what I see as madness. I did not attract, and nor was I able to connect with functional people. I was weak and I was the ultimate victim that would choose people who I thought would rescue me. These choices led me further and further into dysfunction, intellectual paralysis, self-loathing, and a total lack of regard for myself, a total lack of any confidence that I could live alone—and this is the most poignant damage as I see it; I had become institutionalized and a creature who simply survived. I was buried. So, I think I can honestly say that

> being in Mount Saint Canice thwarted my ability to grow and become self-sufficient.

As Janice develops in these areas, she more fully understands how being considered an insignificant person, manipulated for and by the institution, left her vulnerable to being controlled "like a puppet" later in her life.

Janice's puppet dream stands as an important metaphor for her loss of agency and self-worth. Being forced to operate as one of a flock, without opportunity or permission to act independently, has permanently altered her ability to make choices. "What the home didn't do for me," she said, "was give me a sense of having the ability to choose what you want to be. We weren't identified as a person with a future ... And that makes me very sad. Nobody asked me, nobody taught me." In Mount Saint Canice, and for decades after, Janice felt ill-equipped to make sound choices in relationships and life options. "I tended to accept the thinking of other people without questioning," she said; "I did not know that it was important to think about what I did before I did it."

It has been difficult to separate the harm that happened to Janice in Mount Saint Canice from that which she experienced prior to entering there. Only after decades is she beginning to untangle the various abuses and understand their distinct effects on her. In doing so, she has realized that what was done to her in Mount Saint Canice was at least equally as harmful as the abuses she endured within her family. "While I was not verbally abused or beaten in the convent to the extent that I had been at home, there was a reinforcement of the sense of myself as not a person, but perhaps just something that lived." Although Janice struggles to express the effect that this dehumanizing experience had on her developing self, one consequence is being left with "no idea of [her] own sense of being."

Entering Mount Saint Canice, said Janice, was akin to "Alice falling down the rabbit hole." Her incarceration perpetuated a bottomless sense of fear and loss of control. But, unlike Alice, she said, "I feel as though I have never landed." With incarceration, Janice lost her potential to regain stability and has never since felt completely on solid ground. "The home was horrendous," she maintained. "I imagine an amorphous hole with gray walls, windy tunnels and ... I felt lost and fearful there." This place was scarier than anywhere she had lived. "To have been put there," she told me, "was almost murderous."

Janice maintains that the few freedoms the girls might once have possessed were stripped from them when they entered Mount Saint Canice. Certainly, the freedom of movement and communion with nature that Janice once experienced living on her grandparents' farm was stripped from her. "I can remember," she said, "times when I longed to be free and I visited this image of running through the fields. I wanted to run, just run through the fields. I think a lot of it died because I got very depressed. I know a lot of me got very numb by the institutionalization." Janice sometimes revisits the intense feeling of immobilization associated with the reformatory. When her memories of Mount Saint Canice return, she often emerges from these distressing recollections feeling disoriented. Looking at photos of Mount Saint Canice has a similar effect. "They are [a] horror," she told me. "I could never understand that I was locked inside and not allowed to run about as I had previously. I wanted to run about in the bush as I had all my life. I felt shackled."

Janice maintained that absolutely nothing was done by the nuns to nurture those who suffered emotionally: "there were so many girls there with so many different problems and I don't think there was anything actually ever said to anyone about anything that worried them privately." Inmates were not allowed to touch the nuns, and the nuns did not touch the inmates in displays of affection or consolation. Nurturing and counselling of any sort were denied. As a result, Janice withdrew emotionally and coped using whatever means were at her disposal. She internalized her feelings of loneliness, fear, and anxiety to the point that they became unspeakable. Even memories of these feelings are still almost completely inaccessible to her.

Janice only started to talk about her feelings when she began therapy in her fifties. Prior to this, she had little insight into her emotions. She described herself as being "pretty closed down." Even today, she tries to re-engage her feelings from her years in Mount Saint Canice:

> People used to really have to prompt me to say, "but you must have felt that surely," or "didn't you know that ..." and I'm thinking well, I can't remember feeling that. I can't remember feeling. I was numbed for many years. But you could say it was disassociation or, yah, I could really compartmentalize my brain. In that way, I was like a turtle putting its head inside under its shell.

Janice is still quick to compartmentalize experiences if she wants or needs to, but she reminds herself not to because she is committed to staying mentally and emotionally present.

The environment of Mount Saint Canice denied inmates privacy at every level. Within this "cage," everything from bathing to public punishment was exposed for all to witness. This forced stripping away of personal boundaries was deeply humiliating and detrimental to Janice's psychological development. She not only lost a firm sense of the distinction between her private and public selves, but "[t]he fact that [they] were always expected to be submissive, either to the nuns or to the dominant girls was humiliation as well." Janice still possesses an internalized sense of humiliation, which she traces to being considered "a bad person, bad enough to be locked up." But another contributor to this, one that she more recently identified, was having repeatedly witnessed the nuns' "abuse of inmates" and the inmates' consequent "self-abuse." This cycle of abuse, always within sight, further normalized humiliation and submission.

Janice now sees herself as having lacked "a sense of entitlement"—she and her fellow inmates had been without advocates, people who had their best interest in mind, and as such they were unaware that other options could or should have been made available to them. In addition, the rules of silence under which they were forced to operate signalled to them that their voices, their opinions, their questions, and their observations and understandings were of no value. In recent years, Janice has been thinking about invalidation and how her identity was rendered void through institutionalization. Mount Saint Canice represented a cancellation of her. Seeing it in these terms has helped Janice to understand the kind of person she was when she emerged from that environment and what she needs to hang on to in order to move beyond mere survival. "Now," she told me, "it is essential for me to keep hold of my sense of self."

Prior to being institutionalized, Janice's two joys were her bike and her "excursions into the bush," where she would sit and listen to the creek and the birds. "I loved to do this," she told me, "and to explore old house sites. I was allowed to do this as long as I did not move too far from home. We had a lot of land so I was able to roam within our property or that of my great-grandmother's." At that time, Janice's relationship with her great-grandmother and their shared affinity for the natural world was a source of comfort for her. Her great-grandmother always had a wonderful garden and "she was never depressed." Janice remembered one spring taking her great-grandmother, then stiff with arthritis and with failing eyesight, to feel the tips of some emerging bulbs growing wild in the paddock. Feeling this new life emerging brought a thrill to her great-grandmother because she knew that spring was on its way. "I think my love of flowers and my intense relationship with the seasons came from all this somehow. I knew then that they would always be back and this made me feel really good." Knowing that the seasons would change helped Janice as a child when she experienced feelings of gloom or heaviness. However, this hope was lost when she was institutionalized.

There were moments in Mount Saint Canice when Janice would see a bird land on the guttering, as she lay in bed in the early mornings. She would wish she was that bird and that she could fly free. Singing, which she did at Mass, was the only time she felt any freedom while in Mount Saint Canice. In those moments she had a voice:

> I liked the early Mass because I was allowed to sing. I had a beautiful voice when I was young. And I used to like to go in the very early mornings and sing and I was allowed to go to the other side where the nuns had a microphone and an organ and there was a [nun] who gave me some tutoring on death canons ... some harmony.... I really liked the sanctuary of the church. It was quiet, very quiet. And in the mornings when you sang it was a little bit of release.

Apart from that small relief, and the escape of retreating to her imagination each night before sleep, she simply survived from day to day. "It is very disturbing when I look back with the vision I have now," Janice said. "I really didn't know how much damage was done there."

Then and Now

Incarceration at age twelve caused Janice to lose connection with society: "that was huge," she said; "it's almost like I didn't have a language when I got out." Trying to survive alone in the outside world after four years of captivity, with little understanding of how society operated, left Janice vulnerable to influences she would have understood if she had not been locked up. In those lost years, "I could have been learning and hearing and I wouldn't have gotten pregnant I don't think had I not gone to Mount Saint Canice, not at that point anyway."

Janice initially coped with her social deficit by copying the behaviours of those around her. "That," she said, "went on for a long time." While imitation was an effective method of managing in the short term, it only masked underlying problems. Sometimes, for example, Janice was forced to make decisions or act according to her own instincts and tastes and found herself ill-equipped to do so. In one such situation, having been just released from the reformatory and beginning a retail job, she needed to figure out how to dress appropriately for a work situation. Having had no mentoring or instruction in this, she chose what she considered to be a respectable outfit. When a fellow worker admired her new clothing, she quickly replied that her grandmother had chosen it for her. This, Janice felt, would give her choice validity, whereas owning it would have discredited it. Institutionalization had denied Janice a sense of personal authority and created an associated loss of trust in herself. The stigma of being a "bad" girl, which Janice fully believed, was complicated by years of having been denied decision-making authority. "I don't think I knew I had a voice," she said. "I think it was the institution that created this because I certainly had a voice before I was in there."

Her time in Mount Saint Canice also altered Janice's relationship with social spaces. To this day, for instance, she does not like or function well in large places, neither institutions nor larger urban centres. She describes herself as having become quite reclusive and the noise and smell of the city can still cause her to feel anxious and confused at times. "I believe I became institutionalized," she said; "I think I am still a little bit institutionalized." Years of therapy have helped Janice understand how incarceration shaped her in these ways but, despite her inner work, she still carries residual anxiety about being re-institutionalized. She shared a telling anecdote in this regard. After a workout one day, she felt "disoriented" and became concerned about what would happen if she had a stroke and they put her "in a place." Janice's realization in that moment was that she was probably never going to get fully beyond the fear that she could be re-institutionalized. "I don't care if I die," she told me. "I just don't want to be institutionalized."

After Mount Saint Canice it was imperative that Janice not be recognized as "the girl from the Magdalene home." One way to avoid this association was by having "the cleanest house." Keeping a clean home would demonstrate her respectability and camouflage her history: "It showed to others that I was very good ... it was a demonstration of a good person." The nuns' emphasis on cleaning and cleanliness fixed in Janice the view that bad women are dirty and must clean perpetually. Driven by this directive, Janice maintained an image of clean yet felt "very unwell" in the two decades following her incarceration. She was perpetually frightened and out of control with her anxiety, unable to find emotional health or happiness. Nevertheless, she persevered. Janice earned a university degree, lived and worked in various locations in Australia, pursued several intimate relationships, and gave birth to a daughter.

Janice said that Mount Saint Canice became internalized in her as self-destructive compulsions that controlled and tormented her in emotionally and physically harmful relationships, low self-esteem, and deep-rooted social anxiety. In search of peace, Janice eventually left Australia and settled in California. There, she undertook a long-term course of psychological therapy, she began to write creatively,[2] and she has sustained an enduring and committed relationship with her spouse. Here also, Janice has located a sense of home and finds comfort and satisfaction working in her garden. Janice's garden represents an important reconnection with her past. There, she feels at one with her great-grandmother, one of the few people in her life whom she trusted unconditionally and with whom she shared a sense of hope and grounding in the natural world. From the distance of California, Janice has painstakingly renewed connections with her daughter and her grandchildren. As the trust grows within these relationships, she views them as her greatest source of joy.

On the strength of these inroads, Janice returns to Australia regularly to spend time with her family. On one trip, she visited Mount Saint Canice at a point when it was being refurbished for a retirement complex. Upon re-entering her former "prison," she was accompanied by her partner and armed with a camera to document, and hopefully disarm for herself, the source of her nightmares. Going in there alone "would have been too much." As it was, being inside Mount Saint Canice and seeing the long red corridor that she and others had scrubbed on their hands and knees was overwhelming. These painful reminders sparked an anxiety attack that

---

2 Janice writes poetry and short fiction. As p. 46n33 indicates, she has also published versions of her Mount Saint Canice experience.

drove Janice outside, onto the lawn of the institution, to breathe and regain her bearings. This she did and found the courage to re-enter the building. Seeing the chapel and the rooms where she had slept rekindled a deep loneliness. She was also briefly gripped by a fear of being held in that institution as a senior. In that momentary vision, Janice felt concern for the seniors who would live out the rest of their lives "with the ghosts of generations of Magdalenes."

Leaving the country that institutionalized her afforded Janice distance from social stigma and constant physical and social reminders of her incarceration. Yet, even as she gains health and perspective from a distance, her sense of outrage at being imprisoned as a child grows. Janice's mounting anger and indignation, now sometimes simply expressed as "how dare they!," fuelled her desire to tell me her story. When we first spoke, she said, "How dare they jeopardize my growth and future by incarcerating me for no reason other than that a foster home could not be found." Incarceration with the Good Shepherds rendered her a permanent social outcast, if not in the eyes of others, certainly in her own view. There are moments when, even as a woman in her sixties, she feels perceptibly marked by the stigma of incarceration. The sense of isolation and hopelessness of being that "Haggy Slaggy from the Maggie" still visits her sometimes. In this and other ways she considers the harm done to her by the nuns as "almost impossible to calculate and enumerate," and she does not want other children to suffer similarly.

Janice accepts that she will never be fully able to put her experience to rest, so she continues to try to understand it through writing and other means. This work has not been fruitless; in contrast to her sense of herself in the years directly following incarceration, there has been a significant shift in how Janice experiences her life: "I have a need in me now to be quite free," she told me. "That's growing, an ability to get up and think and do exactly what I want, for me. It's only now that I can feel the stirrings of I can do it alone."

Mount Saint Canice was fully operational from 1893 until its forced closure in 1974, when a boiler explosion in the laundry destroyed it, killing eight people. To Janice, it took this massive explosion—and further suffering and loss—to set in motion "the awareness that people are entitled to something more than being stuck in an institution performing unpaid labour." Yet, she wonders how far this awareness extends. Indeed, as the laundry, with the Church's encouragement and support, was reformed into a retirement village built upon the damaged remnants of Mount Saint Canice, it was done with an apparent disregard for the human suffering and loss of life that occurred there under the Church's watch. This negation of the institution's troubled past is evident in the Governor General's commendation for the work of Southern Cross Care Tasmania at the retirement complex's opening. In taking on the restoration of Mount Saint Canice, she said, "they have preserved an invaluable and an inspiring legacy."[3] This 2017 characterization of Mount Saint Canice as an "inspiring legacy" is for Janice, and undoubtedly for other former inmates, a powerfully hurtful and inappropriate whitewashing of their incarceration experiences.

---

3 http://www.saintcanice.com.au/saint_canice_opening.pdf.

CHAPTER FOUR
These Lovely Christian People

As soon as Maureen Sullivan arrived at the Good Shepherd laundry in New Ross, Ireland, she knew something was wrong. This place was not at all like it had been described to her and her mother. A nun who knew Maureen's family told them that Maureen, who was twelve then, would go to a good school in New Ross, where she would receive an education and be safe from her abusive stepfather. But, once there, Maureen was measured for a box designed for her to stand on so that she could reach the laundry equipment. She straightaway found herself working full time in the laundry alongside adult women. Maureen never again saw the schoolbooks and the new pencil case she had brought with her to New Ross. Her name was also taken from her and replaced by Frances.

When I spoke with Maureen for the first time, she told me was that she had recently received an apology from the prime minister, Enda Kenny.[1] This significant apology, from the highest office of Irish government, represented hard-won recognition for her years of suffering in Magdalene laundries. The

1 The then-prime minister of the Republic of Ireland issued this apology in 2013 following the release of the McAleese Report, a study that detailed the suffering women endured in the nun-run institutions from the 1920s.

state had finally acknowledged that they had played a part in forcibly confining generations of girls and women in the laundries. "I am the first Magdalene that ever got it." She continued, "It took me five years."[2] I soon learned from Maureen that in that time she had largely turned over her life to the pursuit of justice for herself and other former Irish Magdalene laundry inmates. During my visit with Maureen in Ireland, her cellphone interrupted us frequently with questions and requests for advocacy from former Magdalene inmates. Her activism on their behalf, she told me, has helped her to channel some of her own hurt and anger into something more productive.

What Maureen lost because of incarceration was enormous, and so, understandably, the resentment she carries is great. But for many years, Maureen could not connect the difficulties she experienced throughout her life to incarceration. Nor then did she fully consider what happened to her as a violation of her basic rights. It was much later—"when you get older that you start thinking back and you see people talking about human rights and things on television and you think now, hold on, how come all them horrible things happened to me? There are so many stories like mine out there." Through other people's stories and protests, Maureen began to relate to the harm that had been done to her, and in other peoples' struggles, she saw parallels to her own difficulties.

One difficulty that still looms large for Maureen is that she was not allowed to attend school for the two years, between 1964 and 1966, that she was in the Good Shepherd laundry. When following that, at age fourteen, she was sent to a Sisters of Mercy laundry in Athy, County Kildare, she received no education there either. Her resulting limitation with reading and writing continue to inhibit and demoralize her in her adult life. She considers it as one of the greater harms to come out of her incarceration experience because it has excluded her from countless work and social opportunities. For her, it is also a legible symbol of where she has been and

2 In this chapter, unless otherwise indicated, all quotations attributed to Maureen Sullivan are taken from a series of interviews between Maureen and Rie Croll, which took place between 2009 and 2017.

a concrete reminder of what has been taken from her.

In describing her early life, Maureen recalled that her schooling began around age five but that it had been frequently disrupted due to sickness. The precise nature of her illness was never explained to her, since none of what was happening to her in her home at that time was ever openly discussed in her family. She attributes this lack of transparency to her stepfather's abuse of her and to the family secrets surrounding that. It was not until much later in her life that she understood the relationship between the abuse, her childhood illnesses, and her incarceration in the laundry:

> I was out sick for a long time because they said I had a bleeding kidney. That's what I was told when I was a child. But I don't know the half of what my stepfather was doing to me because I blanked an awful lot of it out. So, I was sick for a long time. Out for a few months ... in for a month or two. I think that I got about two years of education altogether.

It was Maureen's mother who approached the Good Shepherd nuns about her husband's abuse of her daughter and was told that they had "a lovely school for Maureen," in New Ross. There, "she'll get a great education and then she can come back to Carlow and she can hold her head up high." Maureen believed the nuns, and apparently, so did her mother.

Maureen's memory of her time in the Magdalene laundry and of her home life prior to her incarceration is disjointed. As such, her account contains many splinters of memories that she cannot fit into any continuous timeline. Intensive counselling decades after the laundries has helped Maureen to understand how the trauma she experienced at home was greatly compounded by her captivity. It caused her to compartmentalize and even forget details of her life. In addition, the forced separation from her family, particularly from her grandmother, sent her into shock. As a result, she is still unable to recall many memories from that time.

As a child, Maureen had a very close relationship with her grandmother, one that nourished her. "Oh, she was grand," she told me; "she was everything ... our father, our mother." Her Granny was the centre of her life, the family's anchor:

> And then when I was moved to New Ross ... I think the shock.... I think I was in such shock about what happened to me, and being taken away from my grandmother, and everything went out of my head ... everything just left me.... I went into a state of shock and I couldn't function for a long time. I know that.

Before she was sent to the laundry, Maureen asked the nun assigned to take her there if she could live with her grandmother instead of being sent away. The nun apparently responded, "oh you can't live with *her*." Maureen knew what was implied by the nun's tone: "you can't live with her ... because my Granny had my father out of wedlock. Oh, they were a cruel lot; so cruel. Granny adored us." An unmarried pregnancy, Maureen suspected, made her grandmother morally unfit to parent in the eyes of the Church. Maureen also suspected that her grandmother's pregnancy meant that she too had been committed to a laundry, or a similar institution. There were unspoken hints of that, "uncomfortable responses to the mention of the place."

Once in New Ross, Maureen soon recognized that she was the only child working there. That anomaly became a key point in her later struggle to have the state take responsibility for what happened to her as a child. "This was a hard battle to wage," because she met with a wall of denial; she was repeatedly told that there were no children in the laundry and that, therefore, she could not have been a laundry inmate. The laundry's sister institution, St. Aiden's industrial school, which was physically connected to the laundry by a tunnel, housed girls in an industrial-school setting. There was apparently no record of Maureen's having been there either or, at least, this is what she was told when she first began searching for any record of her incarceration. One thing was clear: the nuns firmly believed that there should be no contact between the morally tainted "fallen women"—the Magdalenes—and the children of St. Aiden's.

Despite the state and the Good Shepherd's claims to the contrary, Maureen was a laundry inmate. She may have slept in the dormitory with the St. Aiden's girls, but she was not allowed to eat or attend school with them. "I slept over at St. Aiden's," said Maureen, "but I would get up at five o'clock every morning and I wasn't brought back over to St. Aiden's until half past seven, eight o'clock at night." Maureen ate with the Magdalenes and went to Mass with them each morning before breakfast. This arrangement was designed to prevent her from speaking with the girls in St. Aiden's, but the reasoning was, for a long time, something about which Maureen could only speculate:

> Maybe they didn't want me talking to the girls over in St. Aiden's or maybe saying to anybody why I was there; what happened with my stepfather. And they probably didn't want me telling things to the other girls. And it would have been handy to put me into the laundry. I would have been another worker for them.

While the timing of Maureen's day was generally designed so that she was gone before the St. Aiden's girls awoke and returned once they were in bed, there was occasional overlap. One time particularly stood out for Maureen, perhaps because this was the first occasion that she had to speak with one of the St. Aiden's children. "There was one girl," she recalled; "she was crying, it was of a Sunday":

> That girl was one who wet the bed and it was raining that day and I had to hold the mattress up at the window so that the mattress would dry. And the girl came up to me crying and it was the first time that I ever got to speak to any of the girls and I said, "are you okay?" and she said, "no, they cut my hair."

> And I said, "O God, did you have lice?" because I thought that's why they did it, because they done the same to me. And she said, "no," she said, "it's because I hit another girl."

The image of this shorn and humiliated girl still grips Maureen. She wonders if this was because it was so rare in New Ross for her to be exposed to the suffering of someone her own age. Regardless, as an adult, this memory has helped her to connect with the vulnerability and isolation that she felt as an institutionalized child.

Maureen was not allowed to speak with the women that she worked alongside in the laundry either. Silence, as in other Good Shepherd institutions, was the rule. Maureen described the monitoring that kept inmates silent and separated from one another. Despite this surveillance, there was one woman, with grey hair and no teeth, who always stared at Maureen:

> And, she used to always say to me ... but her accent was funny ... and I know it was because she had no teeth, but God love her she couldn't speak properly, and she said, "you're a child." "Come here," she'd say, "come here. You're a child, why are you here? You're only a child." A nun heard her speaking to me one day and she came over to her and she thumped her on the side of the head.

While Maureen recognized that this woman was trying to reach out to her, she learned in that moment not to respond, as a way of protecting them both from harm.

Apart from this woman's show of concern, Maureen had no meaningful contact with anyone in the laundry. So, with her separation from the St. Aiden's girls, Maureen was doubly isolated. Silence was a cruelty for a terrified twelve-year-old, but the segregation from all community had even more damaging consequences. Maureen once asked a nun if she could join the girls from the industrial school whom she saw playing outside: "I said, can I play ball with the girls, and the nun just looked me up and down." The look was judgmental, "like why would we let the likes of you associate with them." As a result, while in New Ross, Maureen had no fresh air or exercise, and for two years of her childhood she was forbidden from forging the personal connections that might have offered her some solace or protection.

A further isolating and disorienting feature of Maureen's incarceration was the erasure of her name. It was replaced with a new one as soon as she entered New Ross. This "felt horrible," and, yet, she was expected to respond to it as her own, immediately, on pain of punishment. Unfortunately, Maureen's adaptation to her new name did not come quickly enough to spare her physical abuse:

> If you didn't answer to it, [the nuns] would come down and pull your hair, and punch you or box your ears ... if you didn't answer to that name. You see, they wanted you to catch on to that straight away. And, when they were calling me Frances ... you see, to me, I wasn't Frances. I wasn't used to that. And, I wouldn't answer. And, they'd come down and I'd get a box in the ears, and after a good few boxes, you learned to answer. You know, when your ear is sore and your hair is pulled, and your head is sore, you'll answer.

Maureen's birth name was the last vestige of her family and identity. Its removal broke her down to a nobody. It essentially wiped out her past, something she later realized was the nuns' intention. Learning to respond to her new name was necessary for survival, but it came at the cost of surrendering her former self to the nuns and splintering her identity.

Adding to the estrangement caused by her renaming was being assigned a number. "We all had numbers," Maureen recalled, and "[they were] up over the beds." Looking back, she felt that this system of numbering inmates added to the stripping away of their significance as living beings; it was clear that, to the nuns, they were nameless nobodies who were classified on their ability to perform labour. Much later in her life, Maureen recognized that her mistreatment by the nuns, especially their complete emotional neglect, created psychological damages that, for long afterwards, were beyond her understanding and expression. Those conditions, she told me, "damaged me for so long in my life without understanding what it was that had caused the damage. I didn't know what was wrong with me."

Fragments from Inside

> *Every chance they got, they degraded you.*
>
> (Sullivan, interview, 2009)

Although Maureen was the youngest worker of the thirty or forty inmates in the New Ross laundry at the time, she was still required to work from before the sun came up until tea time, and then afterwards until 8 p.m. Even still, she considered herself fortunate because her laundry job, of feeding the wet sheets into the machine that pressed the moisture from them, was less dangerous than others. Some girls ended up being chronically injured doing their jobs, so Maureen felt "lucky" that she got to keep her job. The work of taking the sheets out on the other side was much harder: "the sheets would come out steaming hot and it burnt your hands." On the occasions that Maureen did do that job, she had to endure the pain of scalded hands: "and you don't get nothing for that, you don't get no cream." The throbbing from that would sometimes wake her up in the night.

Maureen worked Saturdays and Sundays, as well as weekdays. Some mornings, they strapped polishing cloths to her feet and she, along with others, polished the floors before breakfast. On Saturdays, Maureen cleaned the church:

> I scrubbed the floor and polished the floor. And then Sunday I had to do the Rosary beads and the ironing. I started work

> around eight o'clock and I didn't finish until eight o'clock at night because you would be making Rosary beads after work and they called that recreation time. And all of them were sold and they called that our recreation.

The income generated from the sale of the rosaries made by the inmates—and from their laundry labour too—profited the Good Shepherds. Maureen resents that this money did not go to the inmates in any form beyond subsidizing their paltry room and board. "Those fortunate enough to eventually be released from New Ross," she pointed out, "left penniless" and largely unable to cope in the mainstream. Maureen felt that a lack of concern for anything beyond the welfare of their organization characterized the nuns' approach. She felt, in other words, that "they would always put their reputation and their bottom dollar" before any of the girls and women whom they professed to help and care for.

The mistreatment that Maureen experienced while in the nuns' "care" permanently scarred her, but not all her scars resulted from abuses directed at her. Some of what still haunts her comes from the mistreatment that she witnessed: a nun's abuse of one inmate disturbs her decades later. The elderly inmates and those not able to work as well as the others were always treated more harshly by the nuns:

> There was one woman in the Magdalene laundry and she was pretty old—very old—and I used to see the nuns digging the cross on the Rosary beads into her back because she wasn't working quick enough. And so, I'd say they wanted a lot of younger girls in. I'll never forget it because I always remember the cries of that poor woman. I remember her being in so much pain. Poor thing. The poor lonely, lonely broken person. Oh God! And can you imagine how that was on me as a young girl? I was terrified.

This incident was particularly distressing because it epitomized the nuns' deliberate cruelty. Maureen saw that this woman was helpless to defend herself against their bullying, and, while the nuns cared for none of the inmates, those most in need of protection were persecuted the most.

Over time, bits of memories, things that she had not thought of since she was in the laundries, returned to Maureen. Our interviews stirred up even more distressing recollections. Maureen was unsettled by this, because she thought she had "moved beyond the point of flashbacks." But, this was not the case. In one interview she said, "last night, I was back there again":

> I just lay down and I was going to sleep and I was back in that laundry again. And I thought oh God how is all of this coming back? A woman told me that that happened to her and I couldn't understand that. I said, "oh you've got to move on and you've got to let go of it." I don't know if it's as you get older, or.... but I was back there again last night and there's things you remember. Everything starts coming up in your mind what happened. Things that I hadn't thought of before.

The long-term consequences of the laundries were clearly more complex than Maureen imagined, as were her various reactions to incarceration. While over time, for example, she had reflected on the emotional and physical pain that New Ross had caused her, she had not attended to the ways in which the suffering of those around her had affected her. The vicarious effects of those cruelties were and, to an extent, still are unresolved. At the time she was incarcerated, and for many years afterwards, Maureen could not see beyond herself and her own survival. At that point, survival was all she could manage. She knew that what others were enduring had also been awful but she could not dwell on that then.

What Maureen recalls most from being in "survival mode" was that physical punishment and humiliation were to be avoided however she could. This was a knee-jerk reaction. To avoid punishment, she kept her head down—literally—and obeyed. Despite her compliance, she discovered years later that the nuns had described her as defiant. This confused Maureen, as it in no way represented the obedient, frightened child she remembered herself as:

> So, I don't know how they put down on my piece of paper—I'll show it to you—that I was bold and insubordinate. And I don't know how they could put that down because when you see the way that some of the other women were treated, you knew not to do anything out of place.

Maureen learned quickly how to behave in there, by taking a quick reading from the older women whom she worked alongside, those who were beaten down in their demeanour. Her response was to act the same: "you'd have to be completely stupid not to cop on, you get institutionalized very quick." Maureen understood how the other women came to be like this, because it happened to her too. Reflecting on her two years in New Ross, she said, "they broke me there."

As a child, and for a long time afterwards, Maureen was at a loss to fully understand why the nuns' treatment of her felt so cruel. Some obvious examples came to mind, but less understandable ones she described as bodily invasions. The nuns took control of her and other inmates' bodies in a diminishing way. When Maureen got lice in her hair, for example, they cropped it completely off. Although this shearing may have been a practical solution to the problem, it was the nuns' attitude that made it so brutal and violating. When it happened to her, her response was to scream, "maybe because I was shocked":

> I didn't know what was happening. And I'll tell you this and you mightn't understand this, and I didn't for years and years, and it's only now as a grown woman that I am beginning to understand it ... they seemed to get pleasure out of it. That's

> the sickening part of it, they got pleasure out of it. I think it was power and I think there was a bit of sexuality involved as well.

Considering this event in light of other bodily violations she experienced and witnessed at New Ross helped Maureen to later piece together just why it seemed that the nuns' rough handling of her body was sexualized. It was not their overpowering of the inmates' bodies per se, but a combination of leering at and ridiculing their bodies. Maureen recalled, for instance, how uncomfortable it was when she was forced to undress and use the bathroom while the nuns watched. Her twelve-year-old self could not figure out why they did that:

> I tell you, why would they peep at you and be looking at you when you were undressing? I felt awful uncomfortable about that. They were always watching me while I was undressing and looking in at the poor other girls; passing terrible remarks on you, degrading you all the time. Every chance they got they degraded you.

Maureen seldom went to bed at the same time as the girls in St. Aiden's. Usually, they were all asleep when she returned at the end of her day. It was then that the nuns watched her when she went to the bathroom: "they would say undress in there so I don't wake up the other girls and they'd be staring into the bathroom at you and I used to cry and used to feel so uncomfortable."

Part way through her two-year sentence, Maureen's sleeping arrangement was suddenly changed. Late one night, the nuns got her out of her bed in the industrial school and walked her over toward the laundry and put her into another bed. When she woke up in a dormitory the next morning, she recognized around her the women that she worked with in the laundry. This was where she slept from then on:

> I have no idea why I was moved, and you daren't ask. You don't ask questions. There was no point in asking a question, you wouldn't get an answer. They are very, very strange people, with a very strange outlook. Their behaviour and their ways is to me now, very weird. It was like a concentration camp.

The callous treatment of inmates by the nuns has become less understandable to her over time. Once, for a brief period, this treatment was all that she knew and she could not question it, but it has become increasingly difficult for her to understand how human beings could treat other vulnerable human beings the way that they did.

What Maureen recalls feeling most strongly from her time in New Ross is fear and degradation. While her anger and resentment came much later, she was aware that for many of the laundry inmates, who had been there much longer than she had, resentment of the nuns ran deep. Although most of them were "institutionalized," numb with repressed anger and too afraid to rebel, a few did strike out in rage. Some even attempted to escape. Maureen recalled the turmoil that ensued when two laundry inmates ran away:

> I remember a great big commotion going on and one of the nuns sent the guards in. And I remember the Reverend Mother and all the nuns was running around the place. But then we wouldn't be allowed to see what was done to them. We never seen them after that. I'd say they were moved to another place ... another Magdalene.

Maureen could not imagine the consequences for such a grave infraction. The day-to-day punishments were frightening enough. She described women who had committed what she considered to be minor transgressions, on their hands and knees scrubbing the long corridors. "They would be made to scrub all day," Maureen told me; "they would start in the morning, and when we would be going for our meals you could see them still scrubbing the big long corridor. A woman told me one day, 'you better be good, or you'll be punished,' and she pointed to the women scrubbing."

Another telltale sign that an inmate had been punished was her cropped hair. This too was a caution to the rest of the inmates to obey the rules. The hair was not just short: "it was cut right to their head. It was really, really bad." She could always tell when someone had been punished a second time because the hair that had just started to grow back "would be chopped up again." Punishments were given out regularly for not doing what you were told: "if you didn't do certain chores … if you were disobedient three times." One person especially, Mother J, stood out for Maureen as a frightening enforcer of order.

Maureen was also frightened of the nun who once punched her repeatedly in the stomach as she was about to receive a long-anticipated visit from her mother. During Maureen's two years of confinement in New Ross, her only contact with family or the outside world was this one visit from her mother, so this was an especially memorable moment:

> The nun came down to me and she said, "Frances, your mother is coming to visit you." I was brought in back under the tunnel and over into the convent to see my mother and I said—when I got over the tunnel—like a fool, that "I'm going to tell my mum that I'm not going to school." That's when she punched me into the stomach. She punched me right into the stomach a few times. And I was bent over with pain.

Challenging the nun was "a stupid mistake." She said that she should have known by then not to provoke them about anything. She knew that they were not to be defied, because even the more hardened, long-term inmates were afraid to contradict them. But, in that moment, Maureen learned for herself why this was so. Following the assault in the tunnel and just before they entered the room where her mother waited, the nun warned Maureen once more: "if you tell your mother anything like that, you won't be seeing her again." "So, I knew when I went in," she told me, "not to say anything." The nun then sat nearby, controlling their conversation with "dirty looks," while Maureen and her mother spoke. This event added to the shock that she suffered while in the nuns' care. "And we were supposed to think that these nuns were respectable," she said, "but I seen how cruel they were."

Despite remaining silent about the conditions in New Ross, Maureen did not get a second visit from her mother. She never knew if this is because she threatened to speak to her mother about not receiving any schooling or because her mother just did not care to come back. But, the combined circumstances of being punched in the stomach and realizing that no one, not even her mother, would help her, brought Maureen a hopeless recognition that there was nothing she could do to alter her situation. This was the point at which hopelessness became "a condition of suffering." In this unrelieved state, she shut down emotionally and withdrew all expectations. This response was not planned; it just happened because of too much suffering. "I suffered so much in the beginning," she said. "I cried so much I don't think I have any more tears left. I don't let it get to me as much as it used to, but it never leaves you."

It was in this low emotional state that Christmas in New Ross came and went. Maureen described it "as a very terrible time" and a turning point, in that her sense of despair reached a peak during that holiday. Decades later, Maureen was disturbed to learn of the nuns' claim that she had been sent home for Christmas. This was untrue. Because of that Christmas spent in there, she told me, "I get depressed at Christmas still." The generalized depression that Maureen suffers from during the holiday season is not tied to any specific memories; it returns each year at that time and has become one of many predictable after-effects of New Ross.

After New Ross

They just got rid of me.

(Sullivan, interview, 2010)

Maureen began to recognize the Church's capacity for "ruthlessness" for the first time just before she was sent away to the laundries. Her mother was in the hospital in critical condition following the birth of one of her children, when the local parish priest, in his "long frock and black collar," visited their house. He had come to tell Maureen's stepfather that they had found "homes" for Maureen and her two brothers, the children from her mother's first family. As Maureen understands it, it had been the priest's idea to place her family in various institutions. Not knowing any of this in the moment, and caring only for how her mother was doing, Maureen asked the priest if she could go to see her mother in the hospital:

> I said, "I need to talk to her ... if she's going to die because," I said, "my daddy died." And he [the priest] was cold and heartless towards me and it stuck in my mind. And I knew I don't like them. I thought there's something not right here. He threw me aside like I was a piece of dirt.

Fortunately, Maureen's mother did not die, and returned home with her new baby. But, Maureen was sent to New Ross anyway, and her family was permanently splintered by this Church interference. The new family "were brought up seeing the three of us as different. We were the bad ones. Our father had died, and we were sent away and there was something bad about us. They look at us like that today. They still do, we are different."

The conviction that Maureen and her brothers were somehow unworthy of remaining within their family has stuck with her. To be ousted from one's own family, upon the Church's suggestion, was a powerful demonstration of its authority. Maureen emphasized that the Church's reach was so great that it could extend to the heart of her family. The lesser value they applied to Maureen and her brothers was an appraisal that even her mother came to believe. "Even my mother made us feel different," Maureen told me. "I know that she had feelings for us. I know she loved us ... But still, she always made us feel that little bit less than the other family."

After two years in the New Ross laundry, Maureen was sent home. They were beginning to close it down: "that's why I was allowed out. They just got rid of me. They couldn't have cared less if I came back and my stepfather was starting to abuse me again. That didn't matter anymore. They were finished with me." As she was preparing to depart New Ross, Maureen was cautioned by a nun not to tell anyone that she had been there. And once back home in Carlow, another nun said that Maureen was not permitted to return to her former school because no one could know that she had been in the New Ross laundry. The secrecy around where Maureen had been, she realized, was a far cry from the initial promise that she would get a fine education and could return home with her "head up high." On the contrary, the nuns were treating her like an impurity and quarantining her from other children in her community. It was quickly dawning on Maureen that, in the eyes of the Church, she was to blame for her stepfather's abuse, and having been incarcerated in the Good Shepherd laundry further vilified her. As a result, Maureen said, "I was only about two or three days with my mother before I was sent to another laundry."

Maureen described herself as a scapegoat for her stepfather's abuse. She was incarcerated not because the nuns were trying to protect her but because they were trying to protect her stepfather. The Good Shepherds, she said, badly skewed the situation. In their version of things, Maureen was "the sinner," not him, and so it was she who was sent away to a place of "endless punishment." They clearly did not see the picture as she did, that she was a child and "he was doing [her] wrong." It was clear to Maureen that, in their eyes, she did not count: "I was the sinner. I was leading my stepfather astray." Even though, as she added in her defence, "I was only a child and didn't know what was happening and didn't know why he was doing these terrible things to me."

Alongside the growing realization that she had been blamed for her abuse was anger and a sense that she had been betrayed on all fronts. Maureen eventually had to admit to herself that her mother had played a role in her scapegoating. It was decades later, in a conversation with her solicitor, that Maureen got this perspective on her mother's role in her incarceration. He told her that she needed to consider "the edict of the Catholic Church," one that her mother had bought into, which was to forget about the first family and "be grateful that a man married you with three children." "Be good to your husband, was the Church's message," said Maureen; "he is a good man." Her lawyer pointed out that Maureen's mother was probably told to forget about her first family and move on. "That," Maureen told me, "I didn't like! I know my mother should have been a bit stronger and she should have stuck up more for us. I was betrayed, and you find it hard to accept that your mother done it, but you have to. It is silly not to. You best take it all on board and deal with the whole lot of it."

Maureen spoke little of the second laundry she was sent to, but she did point out that by the time she arrived there she was already "broken." After two years of incarceration in Athy, that laundry also began preparing to close. From there, Maureen was sent to do more unpaid work, for the Sisters of Charity in their school for the blind in Merrion. "That's in Dublin," she told me, "and I was made to work there until I asked for my wages, asked why wasn't I getting paid." It had never occurred to Maureen that she should be paid for her labour until her mother came to visit her there and asked Maureen, who was then approaching sixteen, if she was getting paid yet. "So, then I asked," Maureen said, and "my case was packed so quick and I was handed four quid and I was landed at Euston station to be taken home. Back to the abuse again." She figured out then that, once she was no longer useful to the nuns, "they couldn't care less" who was abusing her. "I have no time for them," she told me; "oh my God I feel so bitter towards them. I know I should let go of it. I am trying. I'm really trying."

When Maureen left the school for the blind in Dublin, she returned home to Carlow. She was sixteen then, with no education, no social community, and nowhere else to go. "I had no nothing," she said flatly, "the only place I could work was the laundry." As depressing as that option was, she took a job working in a commercial laundry in Carlow. But, the smells and feelings associated with this work produced awful memories of the laundries in New Ross and Kildare. On top of this, Maureen had only been home a short while before her stepfather began abusing her again. Together, these conditions made remaining in Carlow unbearable, and Maureen knew she had to get out. Having been incarcerated since she was twelve, she was now clearly an outsider at home, with no one to confide in or ask for help.

Maureen's grandmother, who would normally have been a source of support, was getting old and Maureen did not want to upset her by telling her about the abuse. That, Maureen felt, "would kill her." And so, she did what she thought was the kindest thing, she left quietly, without letting her Granny know where she was going, or why. "I just went off," Maureen said, "and she died eventually with a broken heart because we left. We were her three grandchildren and we left." Maureen understands that she could not have stayed in Carlow and that the details of her abuse at home and by the Church would have crushed her grandmother, but she still feels an intense fusion of guilt and anger about being torn from the most important person in her life.

At this desperate point in her life, Maureen left Ireland for England. "I slept on the streets in London for I think it was over a week," she told me, "cause I had no money. I couldn't go and get a decent job." Faced with no other options, Maureen once again took a laundry job. "That was the only thing I knew," she said. Although she would have gladly trained for something different, the odds were stacked against her landing another type of job due to her incarceration history. Every time she approached a potential employer, they would ask her where she went to school and what level of education she achieved. These questions could not be evaded, because they were on the interview forms; "and [she] couldn't fill out an interview form."

Part of Maureen's problem was that she had been told never to say that she was there. From her perspective, "we should have been proud to say that we were there with good Catholic nuns looking after us ... these lovely Christian people ... But, they were so clever. If we were afraid to say that we were there, then we would never tell anyone what happened to us would we? They were very, very clever." This gag order was further complicated by the fact that practically no one, let alone inmates, could ask questions of nuns, or challenge their authority, even when their message was riddled with contradictions. As Maureen put it, "in them days, you didn't ask questions to them people; they were gods, they were up on pedestals. That is why we couldn't say, you're the brides of Christ, we should be proud to say that we were with you. But, they were telling us the opposite."

The woman who managed the commercial laundry in London where Maureen came to work became fond of her and introduced Maureen to her sister. The manager's sister, it turns out, worked with a college in London, and as she and Maureen got to know one another, the sister expressed concern about Maureen's lack of literacy. She offered to help Maureen, and her kindness in this regard felt like a foreign gesture. She said to Maureen, "okay, come on, you can do it. I know you can do it. So, she helped me out [teaching Maureen to read and write]." Through their months of working together, Maureen's trust of her grew and she even became comfortable enough to disclose to her new friend why she was denied a formal education and what had happened to her in the laundries. "And so, I told her my story," Maureen said, "and we just remained friends after that. She's dead now. A lovely woman."

Besides reading, the manager's sister taught Maureen many "different little things," including life skills that she had missed while being institutionalized. Until Maureen met her, for example, she walked with her head down. Her new friend noticed this and helped her to correct it: "she said, 'Maureen, hold your head up.'" But, Maureen confessed, "it took me ages to hold my head up. I felt ashamed. And you always felt downgraded because they treated you so bad." Her friend also encouraged Maureen to buy the council house in London that she had been renting. Such a thing had been unimaginable to Maureen because she had never seen herself as worthy, or of being able to exert such control over her life. "I couldn't believe it," she told me. "I said, oh sure I can't have my own home. How could I have my own house?" But, Maureen took her friend's advice and eventually bought the house.

Flashing Back/Stepping Forward

> *Learning to love myself, at least enough to want to live, took into my 40s.*
>
> (Sullivan, interview, 2013)

Maureen is still unable to summarize what she lost as a result of being sent to the laundries. "They took so much away from me," she told me, and because so much of it is still indescribable to her, she knows that a great deal of it also remains unresolved. The effects of institutionalization keep returning to Maureen as a host of privations in her life, and as unresolved grief and anger. In recent years, Maureen has returned several times to the laundries where she was incarcerated, accompanied by supporters and advocates for her and other Magdalenes. Together, they have searched for lost memories and confirmation of parts of her experience that have been denied by the Church. On one visit, to the site of the former Athy laundry, they stopped at what is now a restaurant located in the former nuns' chapel, once a small private chapel for nuns and inmates. While drinking coffee there, Maureen noticed that the floor tiles were the same ones that she had scrubbed and polished, on her hands and knees, each weekend. Despite this upsetting memory, and the array of negative emotions that came with visiting the place of her former imprisonment, the stress she felt about returning there was nowhere near what she felt when she revisited New Ross. It is not that her experience in Athy was not a bad one, but by the time she got there, she said, “I was institutionalized. You get used to it. You become used to the abuse and you don’t take it as bad.” New Ross, in comparison, took far more from her because it took her innocence. She went there with the childish optimism of a fresh start in a new school, but she was imprisoned instead. This, then, was a far greater shock. By the time she got to the second laundry, she knew what to expect and her will had already been broken.

When Maureen began investigating the details of her incarceration in New Ross, a nun looked her straight in the eye and denied that she had ever been a laundry inmate. The nun told Maureen, “no child in St. Aiden’s ever worked in the laundry. Oh no, no that never happened. Get that out of your head, that never happened.” The nuns flatly denied that such an arrangement existed between the institutions and that the tunnel she passed through each day and night between St. Aiden’s and the laundry had ever existed. They told Maureen that this memory was a false one. Refusing to have her memories negated, Maureen returned with others to New Ross and found the tunnel through which she had travelled:

> I went back down to the Magdalene laundry where I worked, and I could find it. You could have put a blindfold on me and I would have found it, but I couldn’t find where I had slept. And I said it is along the corridor, and the tunnel. And everybody thought I was stark raving mad till this other woman came along that worked there and she said, “I know where you’re talking about” and she said, “that’s all blocked off now.” So, we went around and got us in through the convent and I was able to take them right to the tunnels, right down the corridor, the way I came every morning and went over every evening.

Despite this evidence, Maureen’s solicitor told her that, in the face of the nuns’ denial that she had been a child labourer in the laundry, there was little that they could do to disprove them.

The road leading to this point had been complicated by the Good Shepherds' refusal to acknowledge that Maureen had been working as a child in their laundry operation. They had not officially registered her in their industrial school, where, given her age, she should have been, and they could not afford to publicly admit that they had registered a child with the Magdalene laundry. But, as Maureen's solicitor continued to find evidence that could combat the nuns' ongoing denials, he had an insight that ultimately confirmed the accuracy of Maureen's memories. He "pointed out what nobody had even copped to":

> He said, "you made your confirmation there; you got confirmed. What girl ever in a Magdalene laundry got confirmed?" And I said, "I don't even know what you are talking about." He said, "we'll ring up New Ross," and he rang up New Ross parish church. You see, I went out to the New Ross parish church and made my confirmation with the girls from St. Aiden's. That's how I won my case.

It was on this point, Maureen told me, "I proved that nun wrong."

In addition to confronting the Church on the truth of her incarceration, Maureen has taken her case to the justice system and to the Irish media. By making some of her own story public, she has raised awareness about what happened to generations of girls and women in the laundries. Giving this silent—and silenced—group a public voice has been important; however, through this work, Maureen has also become sensitive to the fact that not all survivors are seeking the same retribution or even justice. Some, she said, just need to be heard so that they can begin repairing themselves; others want compensation. For example, in 2010, Maureen organized a meeting between former inmates and a group of nuns. The incentive was principally a desire for "closure." The women needed answers from the nuns: "they wanted to ask them why were they treated so cruelly. What was the reason for all of this cruelty?" Maureen went into that meeting fully prepared for the nuns to deny her and other inmates' realities. "They'd already done that to my face," she told me. "Nothing," she added, "nothing would shock me about them now—nothing." While this meeting did not produce Maureen's worst-case scenario, which would have been a complete denial of their suffering, it did not come close to acknowledging the harm that had been done to former Magdalenes.

In addition to organizing meetings with Church and state officials, Maureen brought together a group of former inmates so that they could simply meet one another and share their stories. While just being together as a group of survivors was restorative for Maureen, it also made it plain that some were managing in their lives far better than others. Some were "still barely coping nearly five decades later." For example, one woman whom Maureen told me about, whose mother had been in a Magdalene laundry, was clearly still suffering. The intergenerational consequences of this woman's situation were heart wrenching for Maureen to hear:

> She never seen the face of her mother and her mother was buried in an unmarked grave. Her mother had two children ... her brother ... her brother is dead. And this woman, if you were to see her, oh my God you could tell straight away that she never got anyone to help her with her life. This poor woman had nobody to help her. I think she went on to drink as well, and I think she was abused by a lot of men. I think she led a terrible life because of it all. Just to look at her you can tell, and she's a lovely person deep down.

The experience of bearing witness to these stories of despair confirmed Maureen's sense that while they had all suffered deeply under this ruthless regime of incarceration, the abuses that they endured played out differently in each of their lives and in the lives of their families.

In hearing about how these other women had fared following the laundries, I wondered if Maureen had identified a turning point in her life, a moment or an event that helped her to move beyond the state of suffering that she had described living in until she was thirty-five or forty. Until that period, Maureen considered herself "nothing," completely without value. But, at one very low point, shortly following her return to Ireland, when she tried to kill herself, she was taken to the hospital and saved:

> I think after that, when they wouldn't let me out of the hospital until I agreed to go for counselling, I think that was the start of looking up. And it was far from survival, I was just kind of living from day to day, but then when it all come out in the open, then I was more of a survivor because then I could deal with it. All the previous years it was suppressed and you're abusing yourself and letting other people abuse you.

Prior to her suicide attempt, Maureen still felt "institutionalized." She expressed this as carrying "the psychology of a prisoner," a feeling that she had next-to-no power to alter her life direction. But, after trying to end her own life, Maureen decided to live, and this choice to exist was hers. This in a sense was her rebirth, as it marked the beginning of her escape from institutionalization. However, healing was another matter. That process only really began in counselling, when, for the first time, someone heard what had happened to Maureen and believed her. That was another crucial turning point. But "learning to love [her]self, at least enough to want to live, took into [her] 40s."

The longer Maureen stayed away from Ireland, the more painful it became for her to return. Rare visits to see her mother were filled with torment because of their associations with the past. Eventually, Maureen refused to go back altogether. But, one day, out of the blue, she was invited to be part of a healing-touch ceremony associated with the Catholic Church. At first, Maureen outright refused, saying, "I'm not going near the Catholic Church. I want no part of it." With her relationship to religion having been so badly damaged, having anything to do with the Church seemed out of the question.

But, the woman who had contacted Maureen persevered, sensing that this could be an experience that might help Maureen move past the abuses that she had endured in the laundries. While Maureen insisted that she did not want "healing from no Catholic Church," she was also curious about how it could allow for any kind of non-traditional spiritual approaches. This was not the Catholic Church that she knew. It, in fact, seemed so different from her experience that she thought it might be safe to try: "I went to this healing. It was the first time I ever had hands-on healing in my life. Never heard tell of it before. It was all new to me. So, I went for it and whatever happened—that healing, that night—changed my life."

Within two months, Maureen had put her London house on the market and was living back home in Ireland. She said it all moved so quickly that "it was like a dream." She looks back at this "strange" turn of events as something that still makes little sense. In coming home to live, now with a child, to the house where she was born, Maureen broke down; "I *really* broke down," she added. Her surroundings were demoralizing, partly because going home was a return to poverty. Once back in the house where she was born, with no indoor toilet, and having given up her little house in the city, her past all came back to her. At that point, Maureen remembers crying and crying: "I was so sore from crying and my eyes were always swollen."

Around this time, Maureen met a woman who had been in an industrial school and understood Maureen's suffering, because she had lived it herself. She encouraged her to get counselling and even introduced Maureen to the counsellor that she had seen. Maureen went to this counsellor for a year but, as a single parent, reached a point where she simply could not afford to pay for it. "I never went anywhere," Maureen told me, "because I had to pay for this healing, this counselling. But it was good. It was the best thing I ever done."

As Maureen was leaving counselling, her therapist told her about the Fellowship of Isis, a spiritual group which honours the Divine Feminine. She suggested that Maureen might find support in this group and a way to continue healing from the injuries and condemnation that she had experienced as a female within the Catholic system. Maureen pointed out that this faith, based on the goddess Isis, is rooted in the empowerment of women, not in censuring and blaming them. "So, I went to the Fellowship," she told me, "to the Temple, and I went through the ceremony and I tried to learn more about it." The irony of returning to the practice of any form of religion, after being abused in the name of it, is not lost on Maureen. The important difference: she chose this form of spirituality because it resonated strongly with her. "I am a great believer in the Goddess. I am very much into the Goddess Isis," she told me; "it's about the mother of the universe," and, she added, "I think that changed my life too."

When I went to Ireland to interview Maureen, she took me to the Temple of Isis to meet the former archpriestess, Olivia Robertson. Having me experience this place, and this significant person in her life, was more important to her than showing me the laundries where she had been incarcerated; the Temple represented her stronger, recovered self. What she particularly identifies with in this faith "is its underlying conviction that the Church suppressed the feminine years ago." This perspective has helped Maureen understand how women and girls were so undermined within the Catholic Church and how this diminishment was so widely justified. As she summed it up, "The Church took over women's power, and that got sick":

> Now I can see how the Church got away with it. I can see the power that they had. I can see all the wrongdoing and how we were brought up to believe in them. And I think society should have a big guilt trip as well, because people knew what was going on and they didn't do anything about it. They were afraid, or they looked up to them too much.

Following our visit to the Temple, while eating our lunch all together in a country hotel, I noticed that Maureen was becoming quite distracted by incoming texts. She apologized for the interruption, telling us that a woman who had heard of her advocacy work with laundry inmates was visiting Ireland and hoped to meet with her. This woman was considering seeking justice for her incarceration.

As they texted back and forth, Maureen was surprised to learn that the woman was staying in the hotel where we were having our lunch. Some moments later, the woman appeared in the doorway of the restaurant. As Maureen stood to greet her, she began crying and I heard her say quietly, "I know this woman." The woman also began to cry, and they embraced. Maureen later explained that when she lived in England, she and this woman, Mary, were friends and had met regularly at a local pub after work "for a pint and a chat." Both were from Ireland and they had taken comfort in that shared familiarity. Neither one, of course, had told the other that they had fled Ireland to evade their pasts in Magdalene laundries. The nuns' threats and stigmatization had made that part of their lives unsafe to share. So, each had tried to pretend that she was "a different person with a different past."

Observing this unexpected reunion gave me an insight into how being a Magdalene had forced Maureen and others to rewrite and delete large parts of their lives. As these women are now beginning to speak out about their injuries, the Catholic Church has responded by becoming more vigorous in its efforts to bury the past. At the time that I was interviewing Maureen, for example, the Church was tearing down the Athy laundry. "They are getting rid of all these places really quick." This concerned her. With the destruction of those institutions, Maureen felt that important evidence was being lost. "There's a lot to be hid," she told me, "and another thing, the reason why they're tearing them down and building houses, is because there are children buried there. I know, I swear, trust me."

Maureen described a disturbing scene that she witnessed while in New Ross. It happened one night when the pain of her scorched hands woke her: she heard a commotion downstairs—a "fluttering about and a baby crying." She got out of bed to get a cold washcloth to soothe her hands and peered over the staircase to see what was going on. She saw something that shocked her—a nun coming inside holding a shovel:

> I could see the other nun with a blanket all wrapped up, and the blood was down her cream cloak or habit, or whatever it was called ... the Good Shepherds wore cream gowns. And I could hear a baby crying, but all of a sudden there was no more crying and they all went out the back and what was done with what was in that blanket ... I swear it was a baby. And I know to this day that they buried a baby, but they'll only deny it and it will never be proven.

In interviews with police decades later, Maureen described what she had seen. But, she told me, there is nothing they can do about it. They asked her if she saw a baby that night and she told them that she had not, that it had been wrapped in a blanket. This, she was told, was not enough evidence to go on. "Plus," said Maureen, "there are buildings and everything there now, built over that spot. So, they wouldn't be able to do anything about it. But, I believe in my heart that they buried a baby that night."

Other former inmates told Maureen similar stories about babies being buried by nuns. Hearing this deeply upset her, because it confirmed what she had suspected, that what she saw that night was not a one-time occurrence. Undocumented deaths, and accounts of children being buried at these institutions, was something that reporter Mary Raftery publicly revealed in her investigation into the laundries. Yet, when those mass graves were discovered, Maureen said, "there was a shocking lack of concern for the bodies that were taken up." She felt that the Church's responses were, at best, evasive when people were demanding explanations for the presence of unidentified bodies in these mass gravesites. Maureen cannot believe that somehow, between the Church and the state, bodies were permitted "to be cremated straight away." Now, said Maureen, "all the evidence is gone." Yet, when she shared her concerns about the destruction of evidence with the Department of Justice representative, she was brushed aside. She described their dismissal of her perspective as part of a general lack of concern about preserving evidence of crimes and other injustices committed against former Magdalenes.

Maureen's and others' activism eventually helped to effect an admission of Irish state involvement in the Magdalene laundry system. While she sees this as a victory, and a long-awaited first step toward accepting responsibility for what happened to former Magdalenes, she believes that other, and more inclusive, apologies and acknowledgements are needed. For instance, Maureen would like to see a detailed acknowledgement of the abuses that they suffered; she perceives the superficial response to their injuries as part of a larger pattern of Catholic domination of the Irish people. The resulting power imbalance, she feels, has created in the Irish people an ingrained submissiveness that makes it difficult for them to recognize the harm that has been done to them. Consequently, "we can't seem to put two and two together over here in terms of what has happened to us." Maureen thinks that the Irish people are "downtrodden so much in their lives" and find it difficult to "get things together and to put things into proper perspective." "The Irish ethos," she feels, "is to keep a certain lot of people down." Ireland, she added, "is not the nice place that everyone thinks it is."

Because it was "people of the cloth" who incarcerated Maureen, the public perception was that she was guilty and deserving of her punishment, and that they were justified in their actions. And yet, "it shouldn't matter what uniform anybody wears, if somebody does you wrong, you should be able to speak about it ... and be supported." But, because the Church was beyond criticism, Maureen served an adult prison sentence for a crime that was committed against her as a child. Her early attempts to speak out about the harm that had been done to her cast her as a fringe whistle-blower whose story was unbelievable. In addition to being cast in this light, trying to express the truth of what happened to her was further complicated by her own programming by the Church. Maureen's Catholic upbringing had conditioned her to trust that the nuns "would do her no wrong." In fact, she initially went to the New Ross laundry thinking "they were doing [her] right." It took her a long time to absorb the betrayal that she experienced, and it is something that she is still unable to forgive.

For her own sake, Maureen feels that she needs to let go of her anger toward the Church. But, she has not yet been able to fully do so, because, for one thing, the nuns' denial of her education stands as a permanent impasse in her day-to-day life that she is unable to get past. A routine question about something so simple as where she went to school can cause her to abruptly and unexpectedly revisit "a terrible place," and it has the same effect on her every time. The minute she is asked where she completed her schooling "[i]t all comes back into your head. You remember that nun said don't say you were here. So, all you get is flashback. I mean that remains with you for the rest of your life." In addition to flashbacks, the anticipation of this and related questions demand that Maureen be forever on guard; each time someone asks her where she went to school she must decide whether to lie about her past—and bear the guilt and social distancing of dishonesty—or make herself vulnerable to stigma by exposing the truth of her incarceration. Maureen does not view this contradiction as accidental. For her, it all comes back to her earlier description of the nuns' strategy: "If we were afraid to say that we were there, then we would never tell anyone what happened to us would we? They were very, very clever. There was more to them ... there was a lot more to them nuns than anyone would ever know."

In keeping with what Maureen characterizes as an Irish attitude of "forget and move on," her boss was always telling her to forgive the nuns so that she could get past her pain. But, Maureen kept responding, "no, I'm not going to forgive people that stole my education." She perceives her education to be one of the greatest tangible losses to come out of her imprisonment, what she feels "most bitter about." Having heard this from Maureen numerous times, her boss suggested that he and Maureen make an appointment to meet with the head of the Good Shepherd nuns in Ireland. He felt that Maureen might benefit from asking them, for one thing, why she had not been put in a school setting with the children in St. Aiden's. Maureen reluctantly agreed to request a meeting, and she soon found herself sitting face to face with a nun in a hotel lobby in Kilkenny.

At that meeting, Maureen's boss served as a mediator. He told the nun that Maureen needed clarity on some of the details of her incarceration and that she especially wanted to know why she had been denied an education. The nun's response surprised Maureen because it referred to details of Maureen's past, very personal and sensitive details, that Maureen had not shared with her boss. This information could only have come from the Good Shepherds' records, and yet, Maureen was told repeatedly by the nuns that they had no records of her time with them:

> Now don't forget one thing, they were always telling me there was no file on me, that there was nothing on me, that they didn't know why I went there or nothing. I didn't tell my boss about the abuse at home or anything, and she said, "well, you must remember that Maureen was sexually abused in the home by her stepfather ... Maureen could not be allowed to play with the other children." And my boss said, "no, I am sorry"; he said, "hold it a minute, are you telling me that the innocent child is punished for the sins of her stepfather?" And she says, "yes." She said, "the way they looked at is, would you want your daughter playing with the likes of Maureen?" She said, "it was wrong"; she said, "it was very wrong," and she said "Maureen, I am so sorry." She said, "what happened to you should never have happened."

Maureen left that meeting feeling confirmed. Rather than being upset by what the nun said, as her boss was, she saw it as the moment when she could finally stop fighting. The apology that she had so badly needed to hear had finally been delivered. This admission of wrongdoing from someone in a senior position with the Good Shepherds was what she needed to move on with her life. "It didn't matter about their twisted way of thinking," she said, "the evil that they done to me, it didn't matter ... the truth was out at long last." This, she told me, was the first time that anyone had told the truth about her situation. "And," she added, "it was real, so it kind of gave me my life back."

As far as Maureen knows, she is the only former Magdalene to have received an apology from the Good Shepherd nuns. It was not even so important that the apology was issued privately in a hotel lobby, as opposed to in the media, or in a formal document. What mattered was that "the truth was told" and that she could begin to live her life honestly. With that, she said, "I didn't have to hide, cover up and tell lies anymore. The truth was out, my mother was gone, and she couldn't get hurt, now this is my time and that's all I asked for. And that day meant so much to me. That was a wonderful day." Although the nun's apology did not alter Maureen's past, nor undo the suffering she had endured, it did redirect the blame from her to the Church and the state, where it properly belonged. As Maureen pointed out, the Church was not alone in covering up her unlawful incarceration in an adult reformatory. The government, she stressed, refused to acknowledge their role in this too. They refused to treat her case as different from that of other Magdalenes. Even to this day, no one at the governmental level considered her case of child incarceration as exceptional. Not one person whom she petitioned said, "we as an Irish state, and our Irish constitution protects you. Not one of them stood up and said we're dealing with your case differently." They wanted to hide it: "every one of them wanted to cover it up. This country is so corrupt."

The last time Maureen and I spoke, she mentioned that she is still in counselling. The support and insight that it provides is a crucial touchstone. Ever since her time in the New Ross Good Shepherd laundry, she has lived with indescribable hurt, often turned inwards as depression and the persistent sense of being a social outsider. Incarceration, she told me, has damaged everything in her life, even her closest relationships. As an indication of this, Maureen described how her connection with her daughter and her son were deeply harmed by her incarceration, particularly with her daughter, whom she had when she was younger, before any of Maureen's own healing had begun. Because of the frightening and emotionally remote institutional environment she was immersed in as a child, Maureen later found herself unable to trust or to be vulnerable with others, let alone to nurture them or assume a parenting role—she could hardly provide that for herself. In the past, she said, "I could never be too warm a person." However, she added, "I can be a good friend now, I can be a genuine person but too close to somebody I still cannot do." Decades of counselling has helped Maureen to understand and accept this response. And, in recent years, her spiritual practice of endeavouring "to see the divine in everybody" has fortified her re-emerging self. Maureen feels that if she can attempt to do that every day, to "look at the divine in a person, and salute the divine in them," she says, "it gives me great healing and it gives me back my power."

CHAPTER FIVE
Dissociation

We were like human animals in one of the old-style zoos.
(Autumn, interview, 2015)[1]

When Autumn[2] and I met first met face to face, following an extended email conversation, she asked me to meet her outside the former St. Mary's training school, where she had been incarcerated as a young teen in 1961. Once inside the now-renovated community centre, I was taken aback by a large statue of Pinocchio standing in the centre's main entrance area. The tale of the lying puppet child seemed so inadvertently fitting on so many levels, and darkly ironic, given the extent of the deceit that Autumn uncovered in trying to find out more about her incarceration.

1 In this chapter, unless otherwise indicated, all quotations attributed to Autumn are taken from a series of interviews between Autumn and Rie Croll, which took place between 2013 and 2017.

2 Autumn chose this name as a pseudonym to avoid being recognized. She had been ashamed of having been incarcerated and had worked hard to conceal this part of her life from those she knew. She is still concerned that those she loves will find out about her past and will view her as harshly as she once viewed herself.

Autumn wanted me to see this place—the material evidence of her incarceration—and she needed me to bear witness to where her injuries and violations had occurred. Together, we walked the mostly transformed hallways, as Autumn pointed to where the original dorms, dining hall, and isolation rooms had been. The tiny stark isolation rooms remained unaltered, complete with their chipped institutional-yellow paint. Being inside that building and seeing the rooms that had been a source of terror for so many girls was a disturbing experience for me, but I later learned that it had been a healing one for Autumn. Walking through the centre with me, she later told me, brought her strength where once she had been a victim; "bearing hidden secrets with you," she said, "I felt safe."

Our work together on bringing her account forward caused Autumn to "travel back many years to revisit a lot that has been suppressed because of the pain it caused." She recognized in herself a need "to let those demons out once and forever and put them to rest," and yet, returning to these memories was at times tormenting. When she first began telling me her story, Autumn said, "It's been a long time since I walked those halls in my mind ... It's a wonder we didn't go mad!"

Thirteen-year-old Autumn was sentenced by a judge to the St. Mary's Euphrasia Training School in Toronto, Ontario, for being "unmanageable." This school was governed by Our Lady of Charity of the Good Shepherd nuns, who had been operating reformatories on and nearby this site since the establishment of their first laundry reformatory in 1876 (Laycock 1991, 37). Autumn's story reveals some remarkable similarities between the operations of this reformatory training school and the Good Shepherd laundries described in the previous chapters. Her incarceration experience in St. Mary's was likewise one of a harsh regimentation of work and prayer, in silence, based on an overarching conviction that the all-female inmates were immoral and sexually promiscuous.

At the time of the judge's ruling, Autumn was told that she would be incarcerated for six months, but she soon learned that the nuns could, and most often did, modify the court's decision at will. This practice of randomly extending inmates' sentences was so common that other inmates laughed when Autumn told them that she was there for half a year. They told her that anyone who entered St. Mary's stayed for at least a year. And, true to their prediction, Autumn's six-month sentence passed the one-year mark, and there was still no end to her imprisonment. Ultimately, the nuns extended her sentence to a year and a half. This, Autumn blankly stated, "is a significant amount of time to take away from a young person's life."

The nuns' power to manipulate her release date contributed to Autumn's feeling of hopelessness and left her chronically apprehensive about whether her next word or action might prolong her sentence. Under this threat, she felt "stuck in limbo," with no control over the outcome. Autumn now views this undefined end date as a strategy which allowed the nuns to maintain the upper hand by keeping inmates always off balance and "at their mercy." This tactic, she surmised, also had a financial incentive for the Good Shepherds; as soon as she entered St. Mary's, Family Allowance payments no longer went to her family, but were redirected to the nuns.

Autumn repeatedly stressed that she had not committed a crime and never should have been incarcerated. What is clear from the court transcript in which Autumn's sentencing is outlined was that her mother, who had emigrated from Eastern Europe and who communicated through a court translator, considered her daughter "unmanageable" because Autumn's grades were slipping, and she had stayed out late with friends on several occasions. Her mother agreed to have her committed to what the court and social worker told her was a "training school" so that her behaviour could be better controlled. Given her mother's language barrier, it is not clear if she fully understood that training school meant reformatory. Nevertheless, with no objection from her mother, and with apparently no foster homes available, the judge sentenced Autumn under the Training Schools Act.

Autumn wondered if her family's status as working class and non-English-speaking community outsiders provoked the court's decision to incarcerate her in Toronto rather than negotiating a more local and non-punitive arrangement for her. She recalled the sting of being bullied by children who labelled her DP, slang for displaced person. Early on she was made aware that she was not one of them, and her stepfather's tendency to socially isolate the family only exacerbated this outsider status. Whatever the rationale, Autumn viewed her sentence as a betrayal by both her family and the social welfare system, an indication that no one wanted her and that she did not fit in, not at home or elsewhere. "All I ever wanted in those years," she told me, "was a normal family life, to be loved and accepted."

At her hearing, Autumn was asked by the judge if she wished to make a statement in her defence, but she declined, feeling that what she had to say "would not have been understood or believed." She had been taught to obey and serve without question, and any assertiveness from her was punished. Autumn described her home environment as stark and "loveless," saying that the man who was an unofficial stepfather to her and her older sister was utterly "unfatherlike": she portrayed him as physically, mentally, and verbally abusive. He demanded rigid obedience and unending household work from them all, mother and daughters alike. Given these conditions, Autumn sensed what she now knows, that "it was impossible for a thirteen-year-old to speak to the courts and defend herself." She knew that she had no authority to represent her circumstances or to portray the abusive conditions of her home life. She also knew that speaking out about her home life would have brought "payback and retaliation." All told, her life prior to her sentencing had conditioned Autumn to accept that she was "unlovable ... bad at the core" and probably deserving of the state-sanctioned punishment that she received.

Both in and outside her family, Autumn was isolated. She spoke of having no real relationship with her mother, and of her mother's marriage as little more than a financial arrangement. It seemed to Autumn that her mother's singular purpose was preserving the financial support provided by her husband, despite his cruelty to her daughters. In short, Autumn felt that their safety was a lower priority for her mother. "Her understanding of survival," she said, "did not include us." In addition, friendships were discouraged outright. Outside of her attendance at church functions, her stepfather denied Autumn most social contacts. "I didn't have the freedom to come and go as my peers or cousins," she said; "my only freedom ... was school, church, and working in the garden." Autumn could tell that the other children at school led happier and freer lives, and she wanted to be like them. So, with the onset of teenage-hood, she sought out small social connections that she tried to slip past her parents' radar:

> I started associating with the girls from high school—we would go for a Coke and fries and gravy. When I returned home, of course I was in trouble. A few times when [stepfather's name] and my mother were asleep, and they went to bed early, I would sneak out for a few hours of "heaven"; where I could laugh with the girls and slowly come out of my shell.

Autumn came home one night and got caught, which started the process with Family Court.

An excerpt from the court transcript shows Autumn's wariness about exposing her stepfather's cruelty. Knowing it was not safe for her to do so, and wanting to avoid a further escalation of events, she assumed complete responsibility for the trouble at home:

> Court: You think you are being fairly treated at home?
> [Autumn]: I guess so.
> Court: I want you to understand [her name], that this is a place where you can speak out freely without any fear. If there is anything between you and your mother or stepfather that you think is not fair or quite proper, we'd like to hear about it.
> [Autumn]: There is nothing.
> Court: In other words, you are taking all the blame on yourself.
> [Autumn]: Yes.[3]

---

3 Autumn provided me with a copy of the court transcript from this hearing, from which

Autumn wondered what the outcome would have been if, in that moment, she had been taken into the judge's chambers for a one-to-one conversation and had disclosed her stepfather's abuses. She often reflects on how her life course might have been altered had Social Services chosen to investigate her home environment a little more closely and protect her from incarceration.

Disembodied

Autumn initially thought she would be safe at St. Mary's because she was told that nuns ran it, and it was nuns who had taught her from grades 1 through 8. But, when she was taken straight from her court sentencing to a jail cell, where she was held alone overnight, her faith in what was to come began to unravel. As someone who had never been allowed far from home, who had not had sleepovers at other children's homes, and who had never spent a night away from her family, this was a terrifying experience. "How I survived the night before my departure by air to St. Mary's," she said, "is beyond me. Was there not another way to hold a thirteen-year-old before being transferred? I know that I did not sleep a wink. I had never been so frightened in my life.... I still now can see those bars on the cell and window." In the morning, Autumn, accompanied by a social worker, was flown to Toronto.

When Autumn arrived at St. Mary's that night, her suitcase was immediately taken from her for inspection, and she was deloused and directed to bathe under the direct supervision of two nuns. Both her hair and her body had to be washed, an experience she described as "horrific." There was no way for her to hide her naked body from the gaze of these strangers. From this point onward, her body was no longer her own. She recalls being handed pajamas and a housecoat and escorted by a nun to a dormitory, where girls

---

I drew the quotation included here. In order to protect her anonymity, I do not provide a citation for this court appearance.

were already lying in cots in the dark. Rather than turning on the light, the nun led her by flashlight in silence to an empty bed. As she crawled under her blanket, she heard the girl next to her whisper "hello." This was her only welcome to St. Mary's.

The next morning Autumn woke to the sound of a key unlocking the dormitory door, followed by a "clap, clap" of hands from the nun on duty. The girl who had spoken to her in the dark whispered, "do what the other girls are doing and don't talk." All the girls around Autumn dropped to their knees and repeated "Our Father, Hail Mary, and Glory to God" after the nun. Beds were then made and pajamas placed under pillows. That first morning in St. Mary's, Autumn learned that the way to dress and undress was to always keep her body covered. She found this odd. Day after day the girls, "robot-like," would put their housecoats over their heads, take off their pajamas under their housecoats, and then, with housecoat still on, dress in the allocated uniform. This skirt and blouse were worn for a week before being substituted by the nuns for clean ones. If a girl dirtied her clothes before that time, she had to see the week through in dirty clothes.

Whether the inmates needed one or not, Autumn does not recall a bra being part of the uniforms. But she does remember that "hideous bloomers" served as underwear. They were given two pairs each, "and [they] were responsible for washing them." Autumn felt that refusing to provide the inmates with bras was part of a greater denial of their bodies. Consistent with the rule of keeping bodies constantly covered, anything to do with bodily functioning, personal hygiene, and particularly the sexual body was never discussed. "When I entered St. Mary's," Autumn told me, "my cycle stopped. Perhaps it was a blessing, as I don't know what 'protocol' was in place for the girls. Certainly, it was not discussed amongst us. I attributed amenorrhea[4] to the stress of my environment."

After dressing each morning, inmates would line up to go to the bathroom, and quickly wash and brush their teeth. (Autumn recalls that the

4 Amenorrhea is an abnormal absence of menstruation.

bathroom had six to eight sinks and four tubs, but no showers.) "If we were slow or pokey," said Autumn, "the nun would herd us like cattle to hurry on." From there, the girls were expected to form a line to go to Mass. If it was a significant religious day, it was a High Mass; on regular days, a Low Mass. The girls would receive communion and after Mass they again were lined up to head down to the dining room for breakfast. "Down the stairs, up the stairs, we got used to the routine," Autumn recollected.

There was incessant surveillance throughout this and every other part of their days. Inmates were watched through two-way mirrors while in their dorms; they could be seen but never see their watcher. This method of observation worked efficiently for the nuns because, "if there was a scuffle or something of significance going on in the dorm, all they had to do was look in the window and see the action, and the appropriate staffing would rush in." Through archival research a few years ago, Autumn found the original blueprints for St. Mary's. In them she located, among other things, the plan for the two-way mirrors. Seeing that the surveillance strategies had been built into the very architecture of St. Mary's rekindled the distress that Autumn had carried since her incarceration about being chronically and invasively monitored.

Where there were no two-way mirrors, nuns kept watch over the inmates in person. Autumn vividly recalls the nun, "a frightening force," who ruled the dining room with an iron fist. No talking was allowed during meals, she recalled, "we would eat in silence." Silence, in fact, was her overwhelming memory of mealtimes. "Sometimes one would discreetly pass on a piece of toast to another hoping it would not be witnessed. Our heads were mostly kept down as we concentrated on our meal in front of us." If a girl was caught talking or giggling during a meal, she would instantly be removed, and punished. In other areas of daily life too, anything beyond the basic communication that was sometimes required for work was punished. The rule of silence was something that most inmates followed for self-preservation.

Mealtime, like the rest of their days, was uniform in both routine and content. The food was consistently bland and starchy. "[I]nmates' nutritional needs were met with powdered milk and a lot of carbs; carbs became our staple," she said. "I do not recall drinking orange juice or apple juice." The end of each meal was signalled by the "clap, clap" of a nun's hands, which meant they were discharged from the dining room and dispatched to their assigned chores, which ranged from washing floors and polishing them to washing dorms and bathrooms. Autumn estimated that three-quarters of each day at St. Mary's was spent cleaning, ironing, and doing other designated chores, and the rest of the time was for schooling. For the purposes of schooling, the inmates, all of whom were under the age of sixteen, were divided into two groups. Group A did a few hours of morning education and then began work; Group B did morning work and went to the schoolroom in the afternoon. This way, "everyone got a little bit of instruction, as backwards as it was." Apart from Latin, there was little academic content in the St. Mary's curriculum:

> The first priority was religious education, that was the longest class. This would be our guarantee that the Ten Commandments etc. were fully ingrained in our fragile minds. I remember the typing class and since I had started that in grade nine in the outside world, I welcomed that time. I also took a sewing class and remember making skirts for the girls.

Although Autumn was told when she left St. Mary's that she had grade 10 equivalencies, the nuns' educational focus on sewing, crocheting, and cooking left her ill-equipped to handle the grade 11 curriculum.

Working in silence—not education—was the focus of each day. Autumn particularly remembered the endless ironing for the convent, the Church, and the clergy that took up a large portion of each workday. Her overriding memory of this ironing and, more generally, the cleaning she performed, was that it had to be "perfection." She now "hates ironing" because of its association with St. Mary's. If her "cleaning didn't meet the standards of the nuns," she told me, "it would be re-done. I remember washing the floors on my hands and knees, scrubbing is a better descriptive." This scrubbing would be followed by inmate-operated floor polishers, "humming their way back and forth, back and forth, up and down the long halls until that shine was perfect." This way, "all bases were covered in terms of having a very clean institution. Everything had to be perfect."

Training in these domestic areas prepared the St. Mary's girls for little more than homemakers. It left them ill-prepared for the more complex skills of the workforce, and thus for economic self-sufficiency. The sparse education provided put inmates so far behind in the education system that their chances to pursue further education afterwards were limited. The phrase "training school" was a vague description "of a menacing reality." Autumn deeply resented that the training implied by this title prepared the girls to be little more than "maids for the nuns." The work of their institution was prioritized. Even an inmate's genuine illness was met with anger, because illness "meant you were holding up the work that had to be done."

The same nun who guarded over the rows of long tables during meals gave the inmates weekly "instruction" each Friday evening. The girls were rounded up in the gym for this regular reminder that they were "evil and bad." Instruction was an explicit recounting of how they "were worthless creatures that would amount to nothing"; they were irreparable failures:

> We would be lucky if we were able to get a job and would society accept us? No. We had to change our ways; the devil was doing his work. We were corrupt, liars, thieves—every possible derogatory descriptive was thrown at us. We would never make it to heaven; if we were lucky we would be in purgatory for a long time doing penance. Hell was our destination.

These piercing reminders of their failings as human beings reaffirmed what they heard about themselves throughout the week—they were the wayward girls that society wanted nothing to do with. The necessity of severing them from worldly things was also reinforced during instruction. One of the bigger dangers posed by worldly things, they were told, was their association with the sin of pride and, by proxy, vanity. Any packages sent to them from the outside were examined before being distributed. Worldly items such as lipstick and nail polish were removed. Inmates were regularly lectured on the vanity of looking at themselves in a mirror. In accordance with this valuation, Autumn does not recall any mirrors in St. Mary's.

A nun would often use instruction as an opportunity to humiliate and punish anyone who had disobeyed the rules. This happened to a girl who had written a letter to her parents in which she mentioned her friend who had died in a bathtub while at St. Mary's. Autumn could still see the nun holding "that letter in her hand," and the girl "was put into isolation as punishment." This "was an example to all of us of the consequences." What happened on the inside was not to be spoken of outside. Yet, despite the nuns' concerns that details of institutional life would be leaked out or that worldly affairs would be let in, letter writing was mandated.

On the weekends, if inmates did not have a visitor, the time was to be used to write letters to their families. Because they were told they had to, Autumn wrote to her mother and sister, and her godmother, but her letters revealed little of anything beyond mundane descriptions of daily activities. She made no inquiries about what was happening at home. Autumn had learned the hard way not to ask anything about life outside the institution. She had made that mistake in an early letter where she inquired about her friends at home. The letter was confiscated, and Autumn was strapped and then made "the dunce in a corner every night for a week." Following that, "any letters that I wrote were generic and I did not ask about the outside world." Describing what she was currently sewing was safe territory, so she stuck to that and offered little else about her life inside St. Mary's. "My letters were dull," she said, "but at least I did not get centred out during 'instruction' for writing forbidden worldly things. As much as I longed to know what was happening in the world, it was safer to stagnate."

The letters that Autumn received from her sister told her that she and her mother missed Autumn. Given that her mother had sent Autumn "into this nightmare" and never once visited her there, Autumn found this contradiction hard to accept. However, she described the letters from her godmother as "lovely and genuine." Those letters and several visits from her godmother were a lifeline for Autumn. But in-person visits also had to be kept superficial since she could not tell her godmother what was foremost on her mind, her suffering and the conditions she was subjected to in St. Mary's.

Apart from these sporadic contacts, Autumn was alone. The nuns, whom the inmates were ordered to call Mother, offered no respite from the cold institutional existence. "There was no privacy, no care, no love or support in there," said Autumn. It was the nuns' deliberate intention to keep conditions remote and unsympathetic. The nuns, according to Autumn, were present mostly as enforcers. Being locked in her dormitory each night hardened this reality for Autumn. The nuns carried the keys to each of the institution's doors in clusters suspended from their waists, like prison guards. There were "a lot of keys!" she remembered: "it was an instant giveaway when we heard the clang of keys; that meant the nun was close by and be on your best behaviour whatever you may be doing." Most doors were permanently locked so that inmates' whereabouts could be controlled. Even the nuns' quarters, she pointed out, "where they slept after they locked us up for the night," were not accessible. This separation punctuated the prisoner-guard relationship.

The nuns' emotional and physical disconnection from the inmates, the unrelenting surveillance, and a denial of access to anything that might have been emotionally enriching caused a deadening in Autumn. In this punitive environment, expressions of her developing anger were unsafe, so emotional numbness took hold instead:

> I am positive the time I spent there I went through a depression ... My self-esteem was the lowest ... but survival was the name of the game and I was terrified of being punished further. I lived in fear a good part of my time there. Life was

> bleak. My young body, my days, my dreams and plans, my hopes, my psyche, my health did not belong to me. I was under their control, the thumb of the sisters. I had no sense of being at all.

One result of this loss of self was that even the tiniest decision, such as moving without approval, created unease in Autumn, which she characterized as "a scarily ungrounded feeling," connected to having no idea of who she was or who she was becoming. With no firm sense of self to combat the many humiliations directed at her by the nuns, they took hold in Autumn as truths.

The nuns' conviction that, despite the young age of many of the inmates, most had been sexually active prior to their incarceration was damaging and, in many cases, inaccurate. Some children in St. Mary's were nine and ten years old, and Autumn wondered how anyone could have justified putting them in there, let alone treating them as "bad" and "fallen." This stigmatization followed many of these young girls throughout their lives, since it extended beyond the nuns to those in the outside community who knew of St. Mary's and places like it. "I remember," said Autumn, "when I returned home from St. Mary's, I was approached by a classmate who quickly informed me that he knew 'why' I was sent away." Her classmates had presumed that she was pregnant, and he told her so. "I am sure the news travelled quickly throughout my grade eleven class," Autumn said. This stigma, a particularly powerful one in the early 1960s, made an already difficult social re-entry almost unbearable. "How does one deal with that?" asked Autumn.

The nuns shaped the inmates' intake procedure at St. Mary's around a belief in their lack of sexual "purity." Although Autumn had not been sexually active, "the modus operandi," as she put it, for all the girls entering the training school was an internal examination "to ensure they were disease-free and not pregnant." A day or two after her arrival Autumn was horrified at having to undergo the violation of this examination and tried to resist the doctor. However, her struggle was pointless. "I felt cheap and dirty that his hands would touch my private parts," Autumn said. "I will never forget that day." In that moment, Autumn understood that there was nothing over which she had any control in St. Mary's. This intrusion into her body was merely one of numerous legally sanctioned violations she would endure while incarcerated.

Another intrusion was the removal of Autumn's top teeth. She had entered St. Mary's with two broken teeth but, rather than cap or fill them, the nuns took the least expensive route of pulling out all her top teeth and replacing them with inexpensive, ill-fitting dentures—"another horror that [she] had to deal with":

> I recall the terror in me when he decided that all of my top teeth would be extracted. The dentist worked on me at the school.... There was no time for healing. The pain was horrific and I remember my mouth still bleeding with the teeth that I came to hate. If I received any aspirin to dull the pain, I do not know. It felt like forever before my gums healed; removing the dentures at night calmed some of the throbbing.

In recent conversations with other former inmates, Autumn learned that it was the norm at St. Mary's Euphrasia to extract rather than fill teeth. The consensus among those she spoke with was that this was the cheaper route and the nuns were reluctant to part with their money. From Autumn's perspective, the clear message was that the inmates "were worth less than those whose teeth were worthy of preservation." And, the nuns did not think that these unworthy people needed to be provided with the dentistry that would allow them a small measure of self-esteem. This powerful message was thus successfully implanted in Autumn—both physically and psychologically; she felt marked by it for decades. "It is a cruel system," she told me, "that planted the doubt in you and denied you your humanity and dignity."

Removing Autumn's teeth without explanation or her consent left her with a sense of having no jurisdiction over her own body. The false teeth became a recognizable symbol of where she had been, what she had been branded as, and all that she later tried to cover up. She feared that others could read her incarceration and her unworthiness from the dentures. To avoid having people see into her history, she stopped smiling altogether for a while. Autumn showed me an unsmiling black and white photo of herself, taken by her godmother during a visit to St. Mary's. In it, Autumn's eyes look sad and lifeless:

> I remember the dress, it was pretty red cotton, and I wore a cross around my neck. I had curled my hair with bobby pins the night before. After the visit, the dress and cross were put away ... and back to the regular clothing. I was sad in that photo and I didn't smile because of the "teeth." Looking at it today, my heart aches....

Long after Autumn left St. Mary's, she remained self-conscious about her teeth. She knew of no one who had dentures at such a young age and, for decades, Autumn habitually covered her mouth with her hand when she spoke or smiled. But it was not until much later that she fully understood what had been taken from her, that in removing her teeth the nuns had taken a large measure of her self-confidence.

When Autumn was an adult and earning a decent wage, she had the dentures replaced. In contrast to the callous dentist who, without communication, had extracted her teeth, the one who did this work was compassionate. She recalled his inquiring gently about where her dentures had been made, but because she wanted to conceal the fact that she had been incarcerated, Autumn replied that she did not know. The humane approach of this dentist, compared to the one hired by the nuns, was a catalyst for Autumn's insight into the subhuman treatment that she and others had received in St. Mary's. She later discovered that the dentures she had been given by the reformatory dentist were numbered and she wondered if perhaps her current dentist knew where she had been but did not say.

Dissociation

> *There was no going back; there was no spot remover to eradicate the stigma that incarceration held. Many of us felt shamed and outcast from society.*
>
> (Autumn, interview, 2016)

Being abandoned in St. Mary's by those who should have protected them, Autumn said, "only increased our worthlessness." As far as she knew, none of the girls that were with her in the reformatory had committed crimes; none "that warranted imprisonment at least." And yet, they were all cut off from society and herded together under lock and key. "We were like human animals in one of the old-style zoos," Autumn remarked, and "we were lumped together against our will." And with no one to modify the nuns' harsh characterization of them, "it didn't take long to be stripped of [their] self-respect, hope, and trust."

One of the few things Autumn eventually learned from the scant material that had been recorded in her St. Mary's ward files was that just as her original six-month sentence was concluding, the nuns made a notation describing her as "deceitful." The note stated: "appears to appreciate opportunities offered but is easily influenced and deceitful. *Further training is advisable.*" This portrayal shocked Autumn. "Deceitful," she said emphatically. "I think my heart skipped a beat when I read that.... I was hurt." To her, this meant that she was perceived as "dishonest, fraudulent, untrustworthy, devious, a cheater; when," she said, "all I was doing was trying to survive ... I wonder what I did that was deceitful." She considered this portrayal another cruelty among many dispensed by the nuns. This one-word evaluation justified their adding a full year to her six-month sentence. "Isolation from human contact," Autumn reflected, "is no way to rehabilitate. It didn't turn us into model citizens. It does not reform."

Seclusion from society was only one part of the suffering created by incarceration. In addition, Autumn found that the physical regulation of her body was also considerably stressful. Outdoors, for example, was a privilege that was reserved for spring, summer, and early fall. Autumn had no memory of going outside in the colder, or winter, months. "There were no winter jackets or coats. It would have been costly to outfit a hundred plus girls with winter boots, mittens, hats and jackets." There were two areas where St. Mary's inmates were allowed outside, one at the back of the building, where the nuns owned acreage, and the other at the front entrance, where the yard bordered on Lawrence Avenue and was surrounded by a high fence topped with barbed wire. In both areas, Autumn felt caged. "If I wanted to sneak away or find some alone time," she told me, "the barbed wire fencing stood in my way. Not that I toyed with the idea of running, I was too scared; too scared of the unknown, of the world out there that was changing while I stayed dormant. Too scared of getting thrown into isolation."

If some of the girls managed to evade the nuns' watch when they were let out for fresh air, they were strip-searched for contraband upon re-entry. This procedure applied to parlour visitations too; if the nun supervising an inmate's visit was not vigilant, a strip search would be performed before the girl was allowed back into the common areas. Visits from family were also scrutinized, with nuns frequently listening in on their conversations. Autumn remembered one girl telling her that she tried to alert her mother to "the insanity going on in the school"; however, the nun interfered, the visitation was soon over, and the girl was sent to isolation. Autumn frequently heard swearing and crying coming from girls being taken to isolation. She described it as "haunting and upsetting." One girl, who was apparently the nuns' favourite, did the physical work of dragging resistant girls into isolation. "She was not liked at all," said Autumn; "we would stay clear of her."

Isolation could be enforced for anything ranging from speaking or giggling with another girl to attempting to run away. Autumn remembers girls trying to "run for it." "Some made it," she recalled, "some didn't." Those who were caught were thrown into isolation immediately; frequently, they were still bleeding from the barbed wire that cut them when they attempted to scale the fences. Autumn said that she could not have run if she had wanted to. "In reality, where would I go?" she said. "I didn't know the city and was afraid of being caught and punished." Isolation especially terrified Autumn. When she later studied the blueprints of St. Mary's, she found that the single room cells used for inmate isolation were labelled "dissociation rooms." Autumn was aghast at this sanitized description of what had been for her a place of torture. "To us," she said, "it was the 'hole.'"

During Autumn's first year at St. Mary's, she was sent to isolation three times. A feeling of hopelessness engulfed her in there, leaving her with the unshakable sense that she "would never get to leave this place, this hellhole." Perhaps due to the frightening conditions of seclusion, her memory of this time is not precise. Perhaps, as the name of the room ironically suggests, she dissociated from those experiences. Either way, while Autumn could not recall for certain what she had done to warrant isolation, she did know that she was allegedly committed once for "bad" behaviour and twice for illness. She remembers having had boils and suspects that this was the reason for one quarantine. However, the room in which she was confined was not a medical room but a detention room without comforts or amenities and without windows or proper ventilation.

Autumn described these detentions as unforgettable. Whatever the nuns' misgivings about her health, she concluded, "to be locked away in a small holding cell, sick, frightened, and in pain, now seems inhumane." As for being isolated for poor behaviour, it did not take much to end up in the hole, and Autumn is certain that whatever line she had crossed was minor:

> I either got secretively chummy with the girls … and we plotted something stupid and word got out, or I laughed or talked when I should have been quiet.… I was not a violent person and I did not use foul language to the nuns. So many others went ballistic, swearing and kicking when reprimanded. They would not allow the nuns to control them but in the end the nuns and injections won.

The "injections" were administered by medical staff to inmates who were considered out of control. In these cases, girls would be "drugged into a stupor"—a chemically induced dissociation of sorts—and confined to isolation.

Autumn's self-worth was so low while in St. Mary's that she did not even question whether she deserved to be locked up in isolation. That question came to her much later. What she remembers most of isolation was crying continuously in a state of prolonged terror. Other inmates had told her that snakes, which she associated with the devil, came out of the toilet in those cells, so she dreaded using the bathroom while in there. "Would he visit me in this room where no one would hear me or help me?" The nuns had so completely convinced Autumn of her depravity, of the fact that she was "both evil and bad," that a visitation from this incarnation of evil seemed highly possible.

The degrading experience of weekly instruction combined with the ever-present threat of once again being locked in isolation cemented in Autumn the conviction that survival meant becoming a "yes person." This became her survival creed. "No matter what the nuns said, I would agree with them, do what they asked of me even though in my heart, I didn't want to." Survival, or the failure to survive St. Mary's, Autumn realized, was entirely in her hands. One event that epitomized her survival approach was "either Mother Superior's Feast Day or Mother Margaret Rose's feast day." It was a big celebration at St. Mary's and Autumn was asked to lead the procession from the chapel to the church, with all the girls and nuns following behind her. "It was a privilege and not to be taken lightly," she said, but rather than feeling special Autumn was more focused on pleasing the nuns. This was her form of survival.

Autumn understood that each inmate survived in her own way. Some of the girls, for example, were "tough, street wise" and needed to keep fighting to feel alive. She recalled a riot in one of the dorms where "the girls went ballistic" and news of it spread quickly throughout the institution. The next morning at breakfast, the nun on duty harshly reminded the inmates that the consequence of this type of behaviour was isolation. That terrifying thought reinforced the necessity of Autumn's "yes person" strategy. "If there was unsavoury activity happening near me," she said, "I would remove myself as far as possible, so I was not implicated." Autumn obeyed the nuns and complied with anything that was asked of her, "whether it was scrubbing toilets or setting tables," as she was convinced that if she resisted the nuns' demands, she would be "headed straight to hell."

Community, Communication, and Holy Cards

> *Silence was the order of the day whether you were having dinner in the dining room or working on your designated task.*
>
> (Autumn, interview, 2015)

Being a compliant St. Mary's inmate meant an almost total suppression of Autumn's body, voice, and personality. Submission to the institution's rules meant that she and other inmates had little choice but to adopt covert ways of expressing their anger, fear, depression, and despair, and of forging fragments of community. Autumn pointed out that anyone who survived that reformatory environment found their own way to do so, and inmates were not judgmental of one another's coping strategies. Cutting and tattooing were two outlets that expressed their pain and confirmed connections with one another and loved ones. What they were not permitted to speak or act out could be represented symbolically through self-wounding and inking. Even these small gestures, Autumn felt, helped them to cope. With few means available to them, the inmates refitted existing implements to their purpose. "If they didn't have access to ink," said Autumn, "they would use ballpoint pens or pencils. Some of the tattoos and cutting left permanent impressions. Scars bearing initials of someone of significance and carvings of 'Mom' or hearts were common." If the nuns discovered cutting or tattooing among the inmates, the offending girl was sent to isolation and would not be returned to the general population until her scars had healed.

The nuns instructed inmates to never talk to the girls who were cutting and tattooing themselves. And, while Autumn was careful not to blatantly contradict the nuns, she silently empathized with these girls, whom she knew were in emotional pain. She later appreciated that carving and inking their own bodies was a self-directed resistance to losing themselves. Autumn focused on finding her own way through that "hell," foremost by keeping her head down and obeying. While inmates' methods of coping differed dramatically, she believed that each one of them was alone and doing her best. "We were young children," she said, "who needed to be loved, nurtured, and guided; we needed a safety net. Incarceration was not the answer."

When Autumn first arrived at St. Mary's, she recognized a girl from her hometown. When she tried to speak to her, she was quickly cautioned by another inmate that she must not do so or they would both get into trouble. The girl clearly recognized Autumn too but did not try to communicate. It turned out that the girl was close to the end of her sentence and was not prepared to jeopardize her release by speaking with Autumn. Had they chatted, this girl would likely have had her sentence extended. After that first mutual recognition, each time Autumn saw her, the girl "would shake her head indicating 'no.'" On threat of punishment, inmates were expressly ordered not to speak with one another about why they were there, or even mention the outside world. To the extent that the nuns could enforce it, the outside world did not enter St. Mary's through voice, radio, television, or worldly comforts or possessions. "We were not allowed to share any of our personal history," Autumn said, "no talk of our life outside the walls of the school. We were bad girls."

But sometimes, when a new girl arrived, the others "would get snippets of life on the outside." Most of the time, though, Autumn said, trying to get this information "was too risky and the punishments too severe" for inmates to even inquire. As time went on, her loneliness and need for human connection overrode her dread of the isolation room, and Autumn struck up a friendship with another girl. Their contact was hidden and sporadic but, in their loneliness, it was good to "have someone to share [her] fears with." That opportunity "did not present itself very often.... only when [they] were outside the nuns' radar." Autumn's friendship deepened, and they counted on one another's presence, if only in a glance across a room. "We were secret friends," she told me; "we kind of looked out for each other when the opportunity presented itself."

As in other Good Shepherd reformatories, underground communication strategies were passed down between generations of inmates. One approach for relaying messages, for example, was through the strategic re-gifting of the holy cards that the nuns sometimes gave the inmates. At St. Mary's, for example, the inmates received holy cards with their names and the year typed on it on religious holidays such as Mother Superior's Feast Day, Christmas, or Easter. Autumn kept hers inside a prayer book that her godmother had given her. As time passed, she and a few of her fellow inmates exchanged their cards, but before trading them, they discreetly put their home addresses on them in code. They wrote their house number on one card and on the next that they exchanged, they provided their street name. "We would never put the city," Autumn told me, "that went to memory, and in those days, postal codes were not required." In this manner, inmates could exchange addresses undetected, so that once released, contact with one another was possible.

This communication method made it possible for Autumn and her friend to reconnect through letters after their release. In her estranged state following St. Mary's, this reunion provided Autumn with some comfort. She told me that only someone who had been there could fully understand the pain and isolation that imprisonment produced and the secrecy it imposed. She and her friend understood this without having to speak of it; just knowing what they had endured was enough. In this connection, there was some comfort; they could drop the façade they had maintained with others concerning this part of their past.

Many years after her release from St. Mary's, Autumn found several holy cards that remained where she had placed them decades ago, inside her prayer book. Individualized possessions were so scarce in St. Mary's that she held on to what was hers. Among the cards was one dated Christmas 1961; this had been her Christmas gift at the school. Another of the cards had a saint on it, around which she had drawn a rose, and all over the rose's stem, she had drawn thorns. "Thorns on roses," Autumn said, "means that every beautiful thing has a hurt attached to it." The date on the back of this holy card was May 21, 1961, at which point Autumn had been in St. Mary's for only one month. She told me that the hurt she was feeling then "was strong" and her way of expressing that pain, "rather than cutting, or inking, as others were doing, was drawing roses with thorns." With hindsight, it was not lost on Autumn that her response to this damaging environment, much like Rachael's a continent away, had been to embellish fragile roses with pain-inflicting thorns. These drawings were likewise therapeutic for Autumn, as they allowed her flickers of self-expression and fleeting dissociation from her pain.

Pandora's Box

> *I guess we were all caged guinea pigs ... for the nuns, for the government, and the church to experiment with.*
>
> (Autumn, interview, 2014)

Decades after her release, a diagnosis of a serious illness required that Autumn locate her medical history and any other information from the time of her incarceration that could be used to inform her plan of care. Her doctor asked, for example, if she had ever been exposed to toxins. Given the excessive cleaning work she performed, Autumn felt that this was a definite possibility. She wondered if overexposure to the cleaning chemicals used in St. Mary's could have caused her illness. Her research into Canadian reformatories of the era, including residential schools, revealed that the use of DDT powder for inmate delousing was a common practice. For the girls entering St. Mary's, this delousing was followed by a bath in some chemical.

The orchards, like the inmates' bodies, "were most likely sprayed with this toxin too, and anything else that was grown in the gardens or at the convent garden." "I do remember having fevers at the school," she said, "but fevers fighting what, I don't know." In addition to fevers, Autumn described painful boils on her face, those that had led to her isolation, but she did not recall having been seen by a health-care professional for this. Instead, the boils were lanced by the nuns. She later learned that a range of things, including improper nutrition, immune system disorders, and diabetes, could cause boils. "Improper nutrition," she told me, "certainly hits home." But, with no documented evidence, Autumn could only speculate.

While Autumn's research began for personal medical reasons, the focus of her search broadened as she waded more deeply into her past. That mission opened a "Pandora's box." Like Pandora's mythical experience, once Autumn lifted the lid of the proverbial box that was St. Mary's, the evils poured out. One of the greatest ills that she uncovered was the extent to which her and others' suffering had been intentionally deleted from social awareness. This absence of information fuelled Autumn's determination to expose the contradictions she had witnessed, and, unlike Pandora, she was unwilling to close the box that she had opened. She vigorously pursued any and every lead that could shed light on her experience. Frustratingly, online searches about St. Mary's Euphrasia disclosed a ghostly absence of information about the training school, its detainees, and the nuns who ran it. It was as if this chapter of the Good Shepherd mission had not existed.

The invisibility of St. Mary's invalidates the realities of all those who unwillingly inherited the brutal legacy of that place. Like the many others who survived Good Shepherd reform institutions, Autumn felt that the nuns who ran St. Mary's had, at best, whitewashed her experience of imprisonment. They were not forthcoming about the abuses of power that took place in there, and she continues to resent the benevolent and gentle perception of the nuns that they persist in portraying to the public. In contrast to that image, there were "secrets and lies, so many ... that existed in that institution and the Church." Because of this broad contradiction, combined with an absence of information about St. Mary's, it became vital for Autumn that her time in St. Mary's be verified. Launching her own investigation into their record keeping was a step toward taking control of what had once been removed from her and of having her experience acknowledged.

When Autumn came up nearly empty-handed with her online search, she redirected her attention to the still surviving nuns who had worked at St. Mary's. In a written request to meet with the nuns, Autumn included information about her personal situation, that she was facing serious health issues and required their assistance:

> I am writing to you for help.... My doctors asked for my medical history; however, I was unable to go back to certain periods of my life, one being the years 1961 and 1962. Those years would be the time that I became a ward of St. Mary's Euphrasia School. This medical history is not only significant to my future plan of care but crucial that my children and grandchildren be privy to.

Having shared the importance of her situation, Autumn believed that the nuns would be forthcoming with the information she required and release her medical records. Instead, she told me, "they did little more than set up a series of roadblocks."

Autumn's meeting with the nuns was, at best, disappointing. It had been suggested that she might meet with the Mother Superior, but this amounted to a five-minute encounter before she was passed along to several nuns and a spokesperson for the Good Shepherd. "Upon entering the convent," she told me, "Mother Superior was in the lobby and we were introduced. I presented her with a box of chocolates. She proceeded to inform me that she was unable to be present for the tea, as she had to attend to other commitments." The tea that followed amounted to what Autumn described as little more than a public relations attempt to suppress her inquiry.

The nuns' representative "nicely" told her that they did not have the information that she sought. It had taken much courage for Autumn to make this appointment and to keep it, and she had considered her meeting with the Mother Superior a way for the Good Shepherds to finally do something right by her, if only in a small way. And so, the nuns' trivialization of her plight and their ultimate failure to acknowledge her experience felt like a cruel jolt.

Not to be deterred, Autumn followed up her meeting at the convent with an email to the nuns. In it, she asked that the Mother Superior write to her confirming their claim that they did not have her medical or personal records. Her letter triggered a letter of response from the nuns' lawyer, who informed Autumn that the nuns who did remember that time had no recollection of how records were handled or which doctors and dentists may have helped at the school. The lawyer concluded:

> I can certainly appreciate your desire to seek out personal information, but the information is not available, at least not from or through the Sisters. I say this with respect, but I think you have to accept the fact the Sisters cannot provide you with what you are looking for and you should not let it continue to upset you. The Sisters will pray for you.

The letter's final sentence struck a sharp chord in Autumn. The nuns' last words to her, as she was being released from St. Mary's, had also been that they would pray for her. Her response to their second offer of prayer, having had years to digest the implications of all that they had done to her, was intense. "I don't want their prayers," she told me; "they were evil and sadistic. They ruined so many lives ... women who today still cannot turn that page and go forward. Many have tried but their old habits kept dragging them back into that cesspool. They have been condemned." In addition to the second unsolicited and patronizing prayer on her behalf, and all the unacknowledged damage it concealed, Autumn found it quite telling that the nuns responded to her through a lawyer, rather than in person. "That raises an eyebrow," she said, "why would the Sisters need legal representation?"

Autumn interpreted the lawyer's letter as a veiled caution against proceeding with her inquiries. It accomplished its purpose too, because when faced with this demonstration of "how powerful the umbrella is that shields the Sisters," she was deterred from contacting them again. By this point, Autumn did not think that there was more that she could do about getting her medical records and, as she said, "I was worried about having a restraining order from further contacting them, or even a harassment charge."

With the shutting of this door, Autumn turned to the Archdiocese of Toronto, where she learned that institutional records of this nature were "beyond their jurisdiction" and closed to the public for research from 1961 onward. From there, she was directed to the archives of specific religious orders for information about the training schools and reform institutions; however, once again, she came up with nothing. Not to be deterred by being sent in circles, Autumn shifted her focus to the Archives of Ontario. There, her investigation reaped a small reward in the form of some St. Mary's files. These included court transcripts confirming Autumn's admission and release dates, some general information about the administration of the training school, and blueprints detailing the layout of the reformatory at the time of Autumn's incarceration. Meanwhile, an employee she had been in contact with from the Catholic Archdiocese sent Autumn some paper clippings concerning former inmates' lawsuits against St. Mary's, telling her that "he was tired of covering up for them." Considering the growing number of negative public allegations against the Church, he told Autumn, "I am tired of protecting the nuns and the Catholic Church, and the truth has to come out." This response both intrigued Autumn and energized her search. "There was nothing stopping me," she said. "I felt like I was 'on-fire.'"

Among Autumn's provincial archive discoveries was verification that St. Mary's had been privately run by the Sisters of the Good Shepherd.

This was an important detail, because while the Ontario government had partially funded the institution, it clarified that the nuns nevertheless had a mandate to fulfill. One facet of their obligation to their charges, Autumn found out, was to maintain complete and accurate ward files on each of them. "Again," Autumn said, this finding re-confirmed for her what the Ministry staff had told her: the Sisters of the Good Shepherd were responsible for archiving the ward files of St. Mary's inmates and, upon closure of the institution, packing and shipping all their related documents to the province. However, when she approached the nuns, through their lawyer and in her face-to-face meeting, they denied ever having any files pertaining to her time at St. Mary's, and said that her records were and had been the responsibility of the province. Despite the existence of provincial regulations which should have warranted her access to any medical and legal information gathered about her while in the nuns' custody, Autumn continued to come up empty-handed concerning the information that she most needed.

Countless more hours of searching produced the files that Autumn had been seeking. However, this material, which was finally made available to her under Freedom of Information, "solidified" Autumn's "worst fears." The medical report contained within her file was blank; her name had not even been entered in it. The "history," "immunization record," "physical examination," "general impression of physical condition," as well as the "recommendations to the school" sections of the documents were all blank. There was not even a mention of the extensive dental work that had been performed on Autumn. Her discovery that the nuns had failed to uphold even the most basic administrative responsibilities for the lives entrusted to them indicated to Autumn a shocking level of disregard for her and other inmates' worth as human beings. She knew that there had been little expression of care while she was their prisoner, but this final evidence of the nuns' indifference came as a blow.

Despite further searching, this meagre information was all that Autumn could piece together from her time in St. Mary's. As she deals with her third very serious illness, she continues to wonder, as do the specialists who have been treating her, what she could have been exposed to that could have so drastically compromised her immune system. With no health record, Autumn is left to speculate about how her imprisonment, including the stress of it, might have provoked the development of these diseases. The Church and the state's failure to document the lives of children placed in the care of the Sisters of the Good Shepherd has left Autumn and others with gaps that continue to ravage their adult lives.

Afterwards

> *The journey that we were on had no direction, no instruction manual for getting it right. We learned as we went along and did our best to stop our world from spinning out of control. Some of us hit rock bottom, some of us were able to coast, and some became very successful in life afterwards.*
>
> (Autumn, interview, 2014)

One August morning after breakfast, a nun clapped her hands and ordered Autumn to follow her. "It did not cross my mind," she told me, "that I was being released; I figured I would be there until my sixteenth birthday. I understood that the school could not keep me after that." Autumn compliantly followed the nun but, inside, she said, "my gut was twisting." She thought she had done something wrong and was once again headed to isolation. Yet, without a word, the nun proceeded to the front parlour doors and, upon unlocking them, announced that Autumn would be going home that day. This moment held a thrilling realization of freedom for Autumn, followed by a sense of dread. She had no idea what she was being released to or what awaited her in the world that she had not seen for eighteen months. Autumn's release was as unceremonious as her arrival:

> Whatever clothes I had upon admittance were packed for me along with clothes from the school. I had to wait quite a while for someone to drive me to Union Station where I would be boarding the train. I received a small amount of cash, I don't remember how much but it was enough to feed myself while on the train. Once on the train I sat in my seat and watched the miles go by only this time I was not going to be under lock and key.

When Autumn's train left Toronto, heading northward, her "sense of liberty expanded." As the landscape unfolded from urban to rural, she recalled feeling in her chest "the magnificence she had so missed."

Reflecting on her trip home from St. Mary's, Autumn questions the nuns' decision to send a fifteen-year-old alone on a two-day train journey. "What if something happened to me and I never arrived?" she wondered; "what if I was kidnapped or raped? How would the institution respond to that? ... Someone should have accompanied me. Not knowing what to expect, my emotions were all over the map."

Autumn's mother and aunt were at the train station to meet her when she arrived home. She cried when she saw them. "The tears," she clarified, "were a release of pent-up emotion":

> I was finally free, no longer held against my will although uncertain what life would be like. I was happy to see my aunt; however, I felt like my mother was a stranger. It was her words that sentenced me to eighteen months under the thumb of the Sisters of the Good Shepherd. Eighteen months of my life taken away from me.

Autumn arrived home to discover that little had changed in her absence, even though a home visit prior to discharge indicated significant changes. "It only looked good on paper," she told me; "my toxic home environment was not modified to accommodate my arrival." Autumn had hoped that permission would have been granted for her to live with her godmother, who had always been willing to take Autumn, but that did not happen. Apparently, during the home inspection, Autumn's stepfather was adamant that she be returned home. He asserted that Autumn's godmother had no business sticking her nose into his affairs. This might have made sense, Autumn felt, if he had legally adopted her, but she stressed again, "he was my mother's husband and not my father."

With the dawn of the new school year in September, Autumn moved up from grade 10 to grade 11. On her first day back, she wore a red pleated skirt and white bulky sweater. "I distinctly remember it being the school colours," she said. "I remember white sneakers. There was money for a trench coat." However, her faintly hopeful feeling of a fresh start in new clothing did not last long. For one thing, there had been only a brief interval between returning home and starting the new school year and this, Autumn felt, left her with little time to adapt to the outside world. The transition from incarceration was far more complex than she could have anticipated. In addition to the unchanged malfunctioning family situation, she was not prepared for a return to a social situation in which she had been stigmatized by her peers in her absence:

> I had a very limited opportunity to try to fit in. Whispers about "the girl who got sent to the reformatory" to "she was pregnant and is now back." Being locked away from society with no rehabilitation strategies in place, no tools to help one fit in.

With no support and no follow-up, Autumn was dropped back into her stepfather's hard-bound rules and his insistence on keeping her socially isolated. She was allowed no contact with any of her former friends, no outings on school nights, and all extracurricular activities were forbidden. For a soon-to-be sixteen-year-old who was trying to enter a now foreign social environment, these restrictions further impaired a rapidly declining situation. Her academic deficit, thanks to the Good Shepherd nuns, was the final blow to her chances of a successful re-entry. Autumn recalled vividly that "school was a disaster":

> French was part of my curriculum and of course I was behind my peers. I remember being asked to read in front of the class and will never forget the words "je suis" ... the start of a sentence that I pronounced incorrectly and the kids all laughed. I wanted to die.

During the winter, Autumn wrote to her friend from St. Mary's. Their ensuing correspondence revealed that they were both equally marginalized and unhappy at home and school, and they both found themselves to be behind a year in their school curriculum.

As the semester wore on, Autumn discovered that no amount of studying could fill in the curriculum that she had lost while in St. Mary's. There was so much to learn, she told me, she would have been better off repeating grade 10. Despite her best efforts, her grades continued to slip:

> The end of the school year was around the corner and I knew I would not be going into grade twelve. I got a summer job at the dry cleaners pressing shirts for a low wage. Report cards were supposed to arrive in the mail. I was paid in cash in a brown envelope; [stepfather] would take his share and leave me little. That amount of money I put away. Instinct told me that it was impossible for me to continue living under [stepfather's] roof.

When her report card arrived in July, Autumn's stepfather was furious at discovering that she had failed her year. Without telling him anything, Autumn packed up the few things she owned and told her mother that she was leaving. For a little while, Autumn managed to support herself with a job pressing shirts, but keeping herself fed was a challenge. It was a particularly hot summer that year, and the long hours of ironing with no air conditioning grimly reminded her of St. Mary's. It was not long before these depressing conditions closed in on Autumn, and she and a friend hatched a plan to head back to Toronto, this time in search of a better job and "a better life."

Autumn emerged from St. Mary's feeling much altered: "they took my teeth and eighteen months of my life and then threw me back to the wolves with no safety net in place." She told me that a piece of her life had been flatly destroyed by this period of incarceration and much of the rest of her life miserably altered by it. In searching through the "wreckage" of that time, she has been unable to locate anything of value from that experience. "Did St. Mary's make me a better human?" she asked. "[T]he answer is no." Instead, Autumn characterized St. Mary's as a time when she was a "slave child" to the nuns. From her perspective, many "broken" children and teens were sent to the nuns after society had presumably given up on them, but instead of working to reverse this condemnation, they denounced and reduced them further still.

By chance, Autumn eventually found herself living in a part of Toronto that made it impossible for her to avoid travelling past St. Mary's on occasion. As a passenger driving by the school, she would steal a peek at the building. "My eyes didn't linger long," she said, "for fear I would give myself away. How sad. As for the school, it was behind me. I would never again cross those steps leading to the horrors I experienced." But, some fifty years later, Autumn did return to St. Mary's, looking for answers and hoping to make peace with herself. "Peace," she said, "and confirmation that I should never have been in that institution." She described herself back then as "a broken young teen who did not deserve the treatment she was subjected to." This perception of herself, as vulnerable in the face of unjust treatment, was validated in a reunion of former St. Mary's inmates, courageously organized by Autumn.

In September of 2013, Autumn brought together some of the women who, as children, suffered greatly under the "care" of the Sisters of the Good Shepherd. She hoped that this group of former inmates might support one another through a sharing of their stories. She wanted to know too whether any of them had been able to gain access to their medical files and institutional histories. While Autumn was disappointed to learn that others had been similarly frustrated in their attempts to gain access to their personal information, the reunion did result in a powerful exchange that helped Autumn better understand the destructive effects of incarceration on them all. Cross-referencing the details of their imprisonment with one another was restorative because it validated abuses which authorities had covered up, whitewashed, and outright denied.

The two-day reunion allowed Autumn and the other women to speak unguardedly, some for the first time, about being in St. Mary's Euphrasia. In their exchanges, Autumn saw intimately how others, like herself, had been deeply harmed by the nuns' characterization of them as bad and unfixable. She "sympathized and identified" intensely with each of them as they shared their distressing accounts, but it was not easy for her to do. For, as she told me at the time, "I feel that I visualized too many memories of the school and I am enraged." She described feeling an unshakable heaviness, which she portrayed as having picked up too many rocks in her heart. "I usually put the rocks back," she remarked, "but today I simply couldn't." Their experiences of the place, Autumn said, "made [her] reflect back to how tragically [their] time at the school has affected so many of [them]." None of the women had trouble recounting the pain that they suffered while incarcerated and their accompanying anger, but it was the sometimes-terrible ways that their lives unfolded afterwards that made their stories so particularly difficult to tell, and for Autumn to bear. For many of them, an inability to get past St. Mary's left them trapped in patterns of self and systemic abuses:

> From our early years to the time spent at the school and afterwards, some chose only to kick ass. They experienced poor

> self-esteem and problems with trust, especially physical intimacy. In many cases, they went through a period of post-traumatic stress disorder that included flashbacks and nightmares. Many felt guilt, some abused alcohol and/or drugs, and some prostituted themselves for years after. It was their coping mechanism. It was their way to dull the pain. Others turned to a life of crime—some spent time in penitentiaries.

All of them were, in some way or another, "still dealing with the aftereffects—fifty years later."

Being part of this collective process of remembering helped Autumn realize just how important the exchange of stories was for all the women who had been institutionalized in St. Mary's. Comparing their experiences reassured them that they were not alone in having been "condemned." Each of them had been convinced by the nuns that they deserved the disgrace that followed them and that they were unworthy of better treatment. And yet, Autumn feels strongly that none of the inmates merited the kinds of punishment they received, no matter what their histories entailed. As these women gradually began to realize this for themselves, most stopped blaming themselves and began looking at the cruelties that the Roman Catholic Church heaped onto their already troubled lives. Accordingly, many of the women whom Autumn met with that weekend expressed an interest in suing the Church for damages. While this is not Autumn's intent, she feels adamant that "the Church and the sisters need to recognize and apologize to the women and their families for the wrong that has been done." Frankly though, her confidence that the nuns will "own up to what transpired" is slim. She pointed to the Catholic Church's long history of "sheltering those who have abused the innocent," as support for her position. Autumn fears that the Church's acknowledgement of the damages that they caused might never happen or, if it does, will never reach those most affected. She pointed out that "many of the former inmates from St. Mary's Euphrasia are getting on in age," and some, she added, "have killed themselves."

Although Autumn no longer considers her incarceration something to be ashamed of, seeing her time in St. Mary's as beyond her control has been a complicated process. "To be honest," she told me, "I was ashamed that I had been taken before the courts and sent away to a reformatory ... I was ashamed of being in jail, of being bad, of having no teeth.... ashamed of what people would think. How could I be a good mother, wife, or friend when I was put behind bars?" The fact that the weight of the law and the Church had been behind the decision to incarcerate Autumn further confirmed that her imprisonment was deserved. Despite eventually being able to release herself from self-contempt, she is not yet convinced that others could hear about her time in St. Mary's without judging her. Her husband has heard only scant details of St. Mary's, and she has still not told her adult children or her closest friends. Hiding her past has protected her but it has also made her feel dishonest and has placed those she loves always at a slight remove. In the case of her children, this secret has become an unspoken legacy for the next generation to bear.

The weekend that Autumn spent with other survivors of St. Mary's has helped her to see how they suffered similarly. Likewise, it has helped her to view herself and her fellow inmates more compassionately. "We were born into a harsh life with an unlucky star to guide us," she said. She knows now that each woman coped in whichever ways she could. Autumn recognizes that, in comparison to the others, she is in some ways fortunate. Through therapy, she told me, "I have been able to release the demons that haunted me for so long." The grim and extensive work of opening her concealed past has helped Autumn to finally feel secure in the knowledge that she "can never be hurt or punished by the nuns again." She is no longer privately driven by the nuns' negative valuations of her worth or their perfectionistic cleaning standards. "I no longer wash the floors on my hands and knees," she told me. "In my home," she added laughingly, "the dust bunnies like to visit."

CHAPTER SIX
Enduring Legacies

> *[I]t is from those who have suffered the sentence of history—subjugation, domination, diaspora, displacement, that we learn our most enduring lessons for living and thinking.*
>
> (Bhabha 1994, 172)

In the summer of 2016, when an article about my Good Shepherd laundry/reformatory research appeared in newspapers and online magazines across Canada,[1] on Twitter, and in international Magdalene Survivor groups' websites, the broad effects of the pain suffered by this group was brought home to me once more. On the one hand, this flash media coverage produced welcome inquiries and responses from former Magdalenes and their family members, but on the other hand, it illuminated the extent to which many still suffer in isolation. Several women contacted me, asking about the scope of my book, while others inquired if I knew of the Good Shepherd laundries where they or their loved ones were once detained. Most said

1 http://www.macleans.ca/news/canada/researcher-probes-canadian-links-to-abuse-at-magdalene-laundries/.

simply that they wanted me to know that they had read the article and appreciated that the laundries were finally being talked about outside Ireland; a few said they would like me to mention their story in some way or add the presence of a specific laundry to my manuscript. Three of these email conversations grew into short telephone interviews, parts of which I include below. These most recent conversations pick up refrains common to the accounts in the previous chapters. What consistently emerged were concerns about public refusal to acknowledge what happened within the Good Shepherd reformatories, the lack of transparency about the girls and women who were held in these institutions—and the conditions of their confinement—and frustration that Magdalene experiences of incarceration were largely absent from public awareness outside Ireland. Two of these interviews add the perspective of intergenerational impacts, a key area for future study.

Clara,[2] for example, whose mother was in a Halifax, Nova Scotia, laundry, said that prior to reading the newspaper article about my work, she had no idea that Magdalene laundries had existed in Canada. Until that moment, she had felt completely alone with her mother's story. Similarly, Karen Riggs, who in a recent genealogical search of her family discovered that her mother's sister was absent from their family home in the 1921 Canadian census, learned that she had been living in the Good Shepherd Refuge for Fallen Women in Toronto that year. Despite her own research efforts, Karen has been able to learn almost nothing about this institution, why her aunt was detained there, or for how long. This void has left her frustrated, with many unanswered questions.

For Kate Mary Reid, who was institutionalized in an Auckland, New Zealand, Good Shepherd laundry, the article profiling my research at first stirred anger. Once again, she was rendered invisible; "Ireland was mentioned and Australia and Canada, but there was no mention of New Zealand,

2 Clara is a pseudonym.

it was if it never happened here."[3] Kate, like Karen and Clara, had only ever heard of Irish laundries. This incarceration of Magdalene women was simply not publicly acknowledged where they lived. And, between a lack of documented proof and the Church's denying researchers' access to the limited archival material that exists, their experiences are almost entirely deleted from the written record. Kate commented that when she tried to find out more about the Good Shepherd Convent in New Zealand, she found nothing: "There were no cases, there was no mention of it, it was like this didn't happen." This void of information about the reformatory in which she had been incarcerated was profoundly unsettling to her, and in probing further she wondered too about all the other unmentioned girls who had been there with her: "I thought, this place didn't exist, and it made me angry. Because these people robbed me. It's the invisible thing. This happened in New Zealand. And yet if you don't mention it then it doesn't exist."

For many years, Kate participated in this collective silence. Like so many others, the combination of trauma and imposed shame caused her to bury most of her memories of her incarceration. But, during a family genealogy search, those memories resurfaced unbeckoned with the accidental discovery of a photograph of the Good Shepherd reformatory where she had been held. This visual prompt caused a return of splintered memories from that time, memories she had until then buried. More memories have returned since, but while Kate can now recall parts of her experience in broad strokes, she still has trouble remembering many details. In our conversation, she mentioned several times feeling disturbed that so many of her memories from that time remained inaccessible to her. "It scares me what I don't remember," she told me.

Kate had been sent to the Home of the Good Shepherd in January of 1964, as soon as she turned fourteen, and left just prior to her sixteenth birthday. She told me that running away from home after her eldest brother

3 All quotations attributed to Kate Reid are taken from an interview between Kate and Rie Croll, which took place in July 2017.

raped her was the catalyst for her being sent to a reformatory. Her grandmother, whom she cared for deeply, had also just died and, in search of support, she ran away to look for her father. "Nobody even asked me why I ran away," she said. Because Kate had not yet turned fourteen, she was first sent to a girls' reformatory, where she was held until her fourteenth birthday. She was told that the preferred place for her was with the Good Shepherds, but they would not take her until she was fourteen and legally old enough to work. "At thirteen," Kate said, "they would have had to continue my education, but once you've turned fourteen you can work."

Rather than receiving an education at the Home of the Good Shepherd, Kate worked endlessly in the laundry alongside older women. She remembers the repetitiveness of that work, of feeding wet sheets through the rollers and ironing shirts with big presses. Her description of the routine matches others' accounts completely. She would get up very early in the morning, she told me, go to chapel, have breakfast, and go straight to the laundry. "It was always so dark," she said, "I remember that, and spending hours and hours just washing these dirty bloody sheets." During the day she did not see the school-aged girls who also lived there. This memory stood out for Kate because "they got to attend school," while she did not. "I wanted to be with them," she said, "because I loved learning." Much to her regret, this is where Kate's education stopped, and it was not until many years later that she was able to resume it. In the intervening years, it was too difficult to return to school because she was "in survival mode," just trying to keep going. "It's only been in the last 15, 20 years," she said, "that I have been able to think about that," her "love for learning." This she does through reading, research (which she is particularly fond of), and writing.

One of the first topics Kate discussed with me was seeing a clinical psychologist for the past nine years, trying to work through complex post-traumatic stress disorder. Much of her counselling focused on searching for the "missing piece" that would help to explain the roots of her pain and dysfunction. When Kate told her psychologist about the photo of the Good Shepherd convent that she accidently unearthed and the concomitant laundry memories that resurfaced with it, her psychologist felt strongly that this was the missing piece in their search for insight. Before this, Kate had never spoken to her psychologist about the laundry because those memories were sparse, and she still felt ashamed of having been sent there. As she put it, "I was in a naughty girls' home, because I was a runaway. I never discussed it." When, at her next counselling session, the psychologist asked Kate to talk about the photo of the Good Shepherd building, Kate found herself unable to do so. She did not "know how to get inside that building." She had closed off those memories. However, when Kate had the image of the building enlarged, she recognized an alleyway between the dormitory on the one side and the laundry on the other side, and that detail caused a flood of memories to return. Later, when Kate returned to Auckland and found the institution where she had been incarcerated, its effect on her was powerful: "I couldn't even stand there; I had to look away for shame."

During our conversation, Kate related how haunted she felt by the continual presence of nuns in the Home of the Good Shepherd. She described them as "everywhere" and "always watching." She recalled not being permitted to even look at another person, let alone to communicate with them. "You weren't allowed to even have eye-to-eye contact," she recalled. "I still struggle with eye contact. I still can't do it. People all the time say to me, bring your head up, Kate." Inmates were watched while they worked, as they ate, and while they showered. And, "[y]ou were always shamed about your body," she said. Kate viewed the nuns as "creepily sexualized" about inmate bodies, especially as they watched the girls showering.

In addition to feeling chronically watched, Kate described two other constants: "the sound of bells going all the time" and "always being hungry." Another lingering image is of the keys and strap that each nun wore suspended from her waist. "They used to strap you," she recalled; "it was always strap against skin. Brutal." Kate described some of these beatings as coming from Sister C, who, "when she got mad she almost turned blue." It was Sister C and another "hard-faced one" who beat Kate the most. "It is something that will never go away," she added. "I was hit a lot and I think that took away my self-confidence." Kate described the environment as "violent." Her existence depended on reading the nuns as they walked toward her:

> You had to because you didn't know whether you were going to get hit or not. They were never nice. There was never a nice moment. The abuse was so numbing. It was so devaluing, it's like you have no value, you are invisible. You were nothing, you know? You are there because you are bad and because you have to do this penance. You are working this off because you are bad.

Kate sometimes remembers "a room somewhere, when I was in trouble, and I'd get hit and put in that room. It was a tiny room like a cupboard or something. It was small. Terrifying. But to not remember the details, it's really bothering me." During these years, Kate's mother never knew, for instance, that after her daughter was hit, she was sometimes locked in isolation. As in other Good Shepherd reformatories, writing letters to home was strongly encouraged, but "they [the nuns] were reading the letters," she told me, and "they were never sent." Her mother visited her twice in the two years that she was there, and during both visits a nun stood beside them censoring the conversation. "And we had to look happy," said Kate; "we weren't allowed to say anything because mom wasn't allowed to know what went on in there."

The memory of "scrubbing and scrubbing" also stuck with Kate. Cleaning was the focus of her weekdays as well as her weekends. "There was no recreation, no down time," she said. "It was a never-ending world of work. You could never do anything right. There was no letup. It was slavery really, when I look at it." And as other former inmates have described, this work was performed in silence. "You weren't even allowed to talk in the dining room," she explained further. "We weren't allowed to talk at nighttime. When did we talk?" she wondered aloud.

Kate recalls "funny little things" about her time with the Good Shepherds that pop up randomly. For instance, she might seemingly out of nowhere be thinking of herself as a "dirty rotten little slut" and wonder, "where on earth does that come from?" In the case of this memory, Kate later recalled that one nun used to say that to her and told her she was in there "to be purified." Long after incarceration she also remembered that they pulled her teeth out. "Like I didn't go to a dentist or anything ... it was always about cutting corners." Another recent memory is "almost dream-like." She found herself wondering, "Why was I called Tanya? And when was I called Tanya?" Kate could not be certain if the nuns gave her a new name, because she just could not nail down the memory. But she does know that it had a haunting familiarity and that the inmates were assigned new names. When Kate saw the picture of the laundry where she had been held, one of her first thoughts was that she had spent two years with those girls and did not know a single one of them, not a single name:

> We weren't to form relationships. I thought it was really clever by the way, that they gave us different names and we're not going to know who these people are when we get on the outside. I think the nuns were flipping clever to give us new names. That meant that we could never, ever find out who these people are. There is no way of knowing. Nobody would have known me as Kathleen.

Both inside and long afterwards, Kate was "in survival mode." One of her survival strategies was running. What she strongly remembers about her time in the laundry is running or trying to run. "I got punished for that," she said. "I just had to get away from there." She described removing window screws in the hope of climbing out of a window, and at one point she climbed up a chimney trying to escape. That impulse to escape continued long after she left. It was one of the long-term effects that incarceration had on her, and the urge to run to safety has remained with her.

Whenever anger arose in her later relationships, for example, it frightened her and she would run away. "When I had children," she told me, "I was always in a hyper panic state of protecting them. But I always ran. My kids used to say to me, 'mom, you're a great mom, but the one thing we hold against you is that you were always running; we were always packing up and going. Always.'" When Kate's children were young, she was so afraid for their safety that, at night, she would sometimes sleep in the hallway outside their bedrooms "so that nobody could hurt them, and to know that they were safe." This was because, in her words, "I knew how easily their safety could disappear." Throughout the years that Kate was raising her children, the focus of her life was about "planning to run away to be safe." Lately, she has stayed put—for about five years now; this is the first time she has remained in one place since she was a teenager.

Kate eventually staged a protest in the reformatory that ended in her release. She recounted what she could recall of her final hours there. She remembers telling the girls in the dormitory, "I am not going in that room tonight." While each night it was the nuns' practice to lock the girls in their dormitories, that night Kate sat on the stairs: "I don't care what they do to me anymore, I just don't care, I'm not moving from here." As she sat there, the other girls gradually joined her. Even when the nuns threatened them with the strap, "we had determined that no matter what they did we were not going to move. No matter how much they hurt us we were not going to move." The nuns supposedly knew that Kate had instigated this revolt, so they tried to separate her from the rest. When at one point she had to use the bathroom, they locked her in there, and, Kate said, that is how it ended. She was pulled out of the bathroom by a nun, taken into her office, and "slapped around." The nun told her that she was "a bad egg and that one bad apple spoils the whole bunch and that I will never ever be loved. Nobody could ever love somebody as evil as me." Kate was then given coins for a bus and "pushed out the front door." At age fifteen, "standing in the middle of nowhere, out in the bush," as she described it, she wondered "where do I go?" It was a frightening moment. "But," she said, "I hid it. I hid it for so long because I thought I was bad. I stopped crying in there. It wasn't till I was about 19 that I actually cried again, I was so shut down." When Kate got out, there was nothing for her. She did not "know how to direct [her] life," and, she added, "I came out of there feeling so lost."

Kate told me that she has had wonderful opportunities in her life but, because of the Good Shepherd's indoctrination, when she gets to a point of success, it always feels undeserved. She also feels that she does not deserve to be loved, and a chronic sense of hopelessness has led her to try and take her life many times. Her past experiences have also compromised her capacity to react. When people walk away from her, "you just shut those feelings down you know? And it's not normal." Some of those Kate has worked for over the years have told her, "it's like you're here but you're not really here." Others have asked why she does not communicate while she works. She has also been told, "it's like you are in another world." Kate did not understand her social responses until recently. "I lost so many jobs," she told me, "and you know I am a good worker, but I don't communicate when I am working. The forced silence has affected me all my life. And I never knew it."

Incarceration had painted Kate as a bad girl, even within her own family. But Kate maintained that she was not always seen that way. "Before I went in there I was a marching girl," she told me. "I had high self-esteem, everybody was knocking on my door. I was confident. But since the laundry I have always felt less-than. I never got that side of it back." After she got out, "there was nothing for [her]." Not even her former relationships with her mother and siblings were restored; there was little chance for that, as her mother did not want her to return home. Kate spoke of working through layers of pain in therapy and found that at the very bottom of her self-evaluation was a sense of having "no value"; "I am invisible," she told me. In reflecting on the impact of her incarceration, Kate noted, "I have worked hard all my life but I have never since incarceration felt any worth. And because it was taken from me, I want an acknowledgement that this was taken from me. I want an acknowledgment that what they did to me was horrific. It changed me so much."

Kate is saddened by her memories from this part of her past. "I feel sad as each new memory comes up. When I got away from there I always felt bad … If I knew I had done something, if I knew I had done something wrong, I could think yah, that was wrong, I really deserved to go in and be changed. But I don't know what I did wrong. I was just called bad. I was not a bad girl. I was a good girl. I really was." Kate knows that she is not the only one who lives with this burden. "There are all of these other voices that have been alone in the wilderness too." Because of this, Kate will do "whatever it takes to help other women to get here"; by "here," Kate means where she is now, no longer ashamed. "I had no control over this," she added. "I did not do anything worthy of this treatment, of having my life robbed from me."

Clara, who like Kate contacted me following the press coverage on my research, shares Kate's sadness about the many women who were silenced and harmfully altered by their experiences in the Good Shepherd's reform system. Her own mother went a lifetime without fully acknowledging what happened to her in a Halifax Good Shepherd laundry. When Clara read the article about my research on the laundries in a Nova Scotia newspaper, she was keen to speak with me about what she knew of her mother's experience. She told me that reading the article validated both her and her mother's experiences. Clara had grown up with what she called her mother's "idiosyncrasies" and knew about the terrible burden of shame carried by her mother as a result of incarceration. But until recently, Clara did not fully appreciate the basis of those idiosyncrasies.

Clara has been unable to find any information pertaining to her mother's incarceration, although she does know that she was incarcerated in 1930 and 1931, when she was fifteen; "I don't know if she was there a year before her father died, or a couple of years before but he died when she was in there, and he died when she was fifteen."[4] While wanting her mother's

4 All quotations attributed to Clara are taken from an interview between Clara and Rie Croll, which took place in July 2017.

story mentioned here, Clara nevertheless requested anonymity in order to protect her mother's identity. She said that although her mother was no longer alive, her sense of shame over her incarceration had been so great that she would have been distraught if anyone had found out about it. Even Clara had not learned until she was twenty-one about her mother's "being sent off to live with the nuns," and it was her aunt who told her, not her mother. Clara's aunt depicted the nuns' treatment of her mother as "terrible"; she told Clara that she was shocked by what Clara's mother had endured. When Clara later questioned her mother about being sent off to the nuns, her mother became deeply agitated. She "lost it," Clara said, "she was crying and sobbing, it was awful. Oh, what I stirred up! Oh, my gosh, it was terrible." Not only was Clara's mother distressed that Clara had found out about "this terrible, terrible secret," but the memories of that time were obviously still raw for her mother. "Not surprisingly," Clara added, because of having been locked up, "she had lots of issues."

Eventually, Clara's mother shared a few details of what her life had been like in the Good Shepherd's laundry, including working conditions: "She said the work was morning, noon, and night, and she never saw the light of day." She described what to Clara sounded "like something one would read in a Dickens novel." After arriving at the reformatory, the first thing that the nuns did was to rename her Cecilia, and told her that, because this was a cloistered Order, she was not allowed to speak. One detail that Clara found particularly distressing was that her mother, who was apparently so little, was given something to stand on in order to reach the laundry equipment.

Clara never did fully understand why her mother, a native of Sydney, Nova Scotia, was sent to the laundry in Halifax. All that she could gather was that her grandmother took her mother to a priest "to see if he would send her there and the priest wouldn't hear of it." However, her mother seemed determined to have her daughter sent away, and eventually she was committed by a judge. Clara was puzzled by the period of incarceration that her mother was given, which her mother described as "indeterminate or indefinite," and she wondered how that could be right. When I told her that it was a practice described by other former inmates, Clara was astounded.

In trying to piece together why her mother ended up incarcerated, Clara wondered if it was truancy from school. "I remember talking about that with her," she told me. Her mother had grown up in a poor family of ten children, and the family's poverty meant that she often had holes in the soles of her shoes, which was a point of humiliation for her mother. She told Clara that when they knelt to say morning prayers in school, the boy who was seated behind her would stick his pencil through the hole in her shoe. This treatment, in addition to whatever else was going on in her life, mortified her, and she began skipping school. This developed into a larger problem, when a truant officer arrived at her home to accompany her to school. "So," said Clara, "I am sure she was difficult to handle."

Clara also wondered whether her mother's incarceration had something to do with sexual abuse. Although her mother was extremely private about it, she did tell Clara that she had been sexually abused by somebody as a child. Her mother relayed a story, perhaps in relation to this abuse, about how one day, while she sat on the doorstep, a man walked by and "made some comment or whistled or something like that." In response to this man's overture, Clara said, her grandmother "beat and beat" her mother. Clara therefore wondered if her grandmother was afraid that her daughter might become sexually promiscuous. She also described the conditions in her mother's home as "difficult," before being sent to the Good Shepherds. Prior to her incarceration, her mother's father was sick with the cancer that soon killed him and, during the period of Clara's mother's incarceration, her mother was left with raising the other nine children on her own.

What Clara learned about the Home of the Good Shepherd from her mother was little, beyond a few anecdotes. One was the story of how her mother was released. Her mother told Clara that she had been incarcerated with older women, so she knew that if she did not get out, "she'd be spending the rest of her life there." So, one day after her mother "had been there for a couple of years at least," the inmates were lined up and heading to a meal, when her mother spontaneously created a scene. She told Clara that there was a window ledge, and when she saw it she knew what to do. "It just came over her," Clara told me; "she knew she had to do something, and she just created a real ruckus." Her mother stood on the ledge and yelled, "I am leaving here dead or alive." She "went on like this for a while," and shortly afterwards, she got out. Clara's sister-in-law also told her that the nuns beat her mother and that she was sometimes "locked in a closet." Clara was particularly upset by those details: "I can't even begin to imagine what that would be like for anybody, let alone a child."

After learning about those parts of her mother's experience, Clara felt "much, much more understanding of her and her idiosyncrasies." One of those quirks, for example, was her mother's estranged relationship with Catholicism. "It was funny in a way," she said, "because mom would tell me, 'go to Mass,' but she wouldn't be going herself. And all of her siblings were very devout, but mom wasn't like that." What also stood out for Clara in her mother's behaviour was how frequently she stressed the importance of getting an education; she found it peculiar that her mother would repeatedly say, "if she had her day to do over again, she would have been a lawyer; because, boy, if you were a lawyer, she'd say, the things you could do, because you would know what the laws were." Clara often wondered what those "things" might be that her mother would have done as a lawyer.

When Clara was younger, she used to ask her mother how far she went in school, and her mother would consistently answer, "I have the equivalent of grade ten." Clara found it odd, however, that she never told her where she went to school. Based on what her mother later told her about the Good Shepherds, and her age during her incarceration, Clara suspects that she received little, if any, education there. The only mention her mother made of anything related to an education in the laundry involved an external inspection of the Good Shepherd Monastery. One day, her mother was taken out of the laundry and put in a room with a typewriter and told to sit there and pretend to type, while an official who was performing an inspection of the monastery did his rounds. According to her mother, "he came and he just sort of looked and he walked by, so he would think that she was learning how to be a typist or whatever." Clara also learned that her mother's work in the laundry was unpaid, and yet she told Clara that the laundry did business for the Church "as well as everybody else's laundry, including rich people in Halifax." It was clear to Clara that the institution was making a profit from her mother's unpaid labour.

Until she read the article about my research, Clara had never even heard of the laundries in Canada. That, she told me, was first the time she had heard about anything relating to her mother's incarceration. Over the course of years, she had heard "that they had these places in Ireland ... and thought, oh my gosh, that's the same as what [her mother] lived through," but Clara had "never, ever heard of anything like this in Nova Scotia in the twentieth century. [She] had never heard anybody talk about it in Nova Scotia." She added, "Talking to you about my mother's experiences in the Home of the Good Shepherd is cathartic."

Karen Riggs, who is also experiencing the second-generational effects of an incarcerated family member, contacted me shortly following the press release about my research. Karen, who lives in Arizona, shared the little she knows about her aunt Ethel, sent to a Good Shepherd refuge in Toronto, Canada, in the early 1920s. Growing up, Karen did not even know about this aunt until, on a visit home from college, she found an old picture of her mother with an aunt she recognized and a woman unknown to her. When she asked her mother who this third woman was, her mother "just kind of snorted and said that's your aunt Ethel." That was all her mother ever said about her estranged sister. Karen can only speculate about why Ethel was committed to the Good Shepherd reformatory, although she suspects that the family's extreme poverty and perhaps some minor acting out on her aunt's part had something to do with it. Karen was told that her mother had been sent away to live with an uncle because the family was too poor to support her. Nevertheless, Karen wonders why two of the family's three daughters, the oldest and the youngest, were sent away, while the middle sister and her two brothers were kept on the farm, to work, or why, at Ethel's wedding in 1927, her middle sister and her father were present, but not her other sister and mother, suggesting "a lot of family secrets."

Karen has not yet figured out why her family was silent about Ethel, but while doing genealogical searches she discovered in the 1921 Canadian census records that Ethel was not listed as living at the family residence on their farm in Essex, Ontario. This absence was curious to Karen, since her aunt would have only been fifteen at the time. Upon further searching, she located Ethel registered as an "inmate" at Our Lady of Charity Monastery in Parkdale, Toronto. This census indicated that there were 183 inmates, 53 nuns, and 1 boarder living there. There are no living relatives who can provide information about Ethel, and Karen has been unable to find out how long, or why, her aunt was incarcerated. She wrote to the Order, feeling hopeful that they would reply to her query, as their website promised a response within forty-eight hours, but they did not reply. If they had responded, Karen would have liked to have found out, among other things, how long her aunt was held there. It has been difficult for her to piece together a fuller sense of this reformatory and she has discovered for herself what Carolyn Whitzman (2003, 297) observed about it: "There is little known about the lives of people institutionalized in the Magdalen Asylum for Fallen Women."

A little information is, however, available. In Toronto, the Good Shepherd Refuge for Fallen Women, as it was called in 1885, received government grants toward its operations, which meant that it was subject to provincial inspections. For this reason, government records of these inspections reveal little more than the vital statistics of the institution in the year of its inspection. Still, this early report reveals that the Refuge kept girls and women as principally engaged in laundry work.[5] Although the inspector makes no comment about who the women and girls were that were held there, he notes the general conditions of the Refuge as "perfectly clean and in good order" (69). This finding is not surprising since, according

5 Ontario. Sessional Papers, Volume 6; Volume 17, Part 6. 1885.

to the inmates that I have interviewed, they spent most of each day and night cleaning. Charles Mulvany's 1884 history of Toronto published a year prior to this 1885 inspection, provides a glimpse of the social perception of the women who were housed there; the women and girls were "the most unhealthy of their sex," adding that they are "those who so truly merit the name of unfortunate" (67).

Moving ahead to 1911 and ten years before Karen's aunt Ethel's incarceration, we learn that the city of Toronto had just begun inspecting private charities to which they were contributing funds. It appears that the Monastery of Our Lady of Charity, as it was now called, was not only receiving provincial government subsidies but financial support from the city. Whitzman (2003, 150) also sheds light on the reformatory's operations in her description of Ethel Abel, a resident of Parkdale, who during the early 1900s, "recalled sending laundry out to the Magdalen Asylum on West Lodge." In addition to the city and provincial grants received, this affirms that the nuns continued to subsidize their reformatory with a commercial laundry business. The 1911 city inspection also produced the following description:

> [It] housed 134 "delinquent females and feeble minded girls and women" who were there to be "reformed, or as explained by the sisters in charge, converted and protected." There was also an industrial school for 29 girls aged 12 to 18, who were admitted on three year "terms" by parents, friends, police, or sometimes inspectors of prisons. There, the girls learned sewing, cooking, and housework. (205)

Based on this report, the length of the younger inmates' sentences for the Monastery of Our Lady of Charity appear to have been three years. This changed within the decade. In 1919, the mandatory length of stay under the Ontario Female Refuges Act became limited to two years less a day (Sangster 2001, 116). According to an article in the *Globe and Mail*, this change in law came following the death of Alice Halloran, while attempting to escape from the House of the Good Shepherd, the same reformatory in which Ethel was interned. An inquiry into Halloran's death resulted in the law's amendment governing both the duration of inmates' sentences to such "industrial refuges" and who had the authority to authorize committals. Honourable W. D. McPherson, the provincial secretary, altered the existing law so that only magistrates could sentence females to these institutions; parents and guardians would no longer be able to place them there as they had done in the past (*Globe and Mail*, 1919). One can presume, therefore, if protocol were followed, that Ethel's sentence would have been no more than two years after having been committed to the House of the Good Shepherd by a magistrate.

While such information began to answer Karen's questions, she also wanted to know what her aunt did while she was an inmate. Was Ethel really taught sewing, cooking, and housework, as the inspector's report suggested? Small details in the census raised Karen's suspicions and caused her to mistrust the written record. For one thing, the nuns declared on the census that Ethel's age was sixteen and her ancestry Irish. Both, Karen pointed out, are "incorrect." Her aunt's vital documents show that Ethel was born in January of 1906, meaning she was fifteen in 1921. Karen also has a complete record of her mother's family tree "published by an historian," and her family "goes back to France with no deviations whatsoever." The fact that the nuns misrepresented her aunt's age in the census has caused Karen to wonder if this discrepancy was a deliberate attempt to evade existing child labour laws which, by 1919, required adolescents aged fourteen to sixteen, with only some exceptions, to attend school full time.[6] Karen also wondered if her aunt ever received any education while she was incarcerated, since so many of the stories she had heard, like those recounted in the previous chapters, tell repeatedly of girls having been denied their education in favour of using them as laundry labourers.

6 Government of Ontario, Ontario Statutes of 1919, The Adolescent School Attendance Act, 1919, s. 3(1), 413.

Once Karen uncovered that Ethel had been sent to the Monastery of Our Lady of Charity, she searched for other evidence of her existence, eventually finding that she married in 1927 and killed herself in 1955 at age forty-nine. Ethel's cause of death is something that Karen deduced by reading between the lines of her aunt's life. Again, her uncovered version of events appears to contradict the official one. Ethel's death certificate stated that she "slipped on a rock," and died. "The Catholics are good at cover-ups," Karen said. By not mentioning the suicide, this allowed her to be buried in a Catholic cemetery near her husband. "Suicides," she added, "cannot be buried in consecrated ground. I'm pretty sure it's suicide as she went down to the Detroit River, on the Windsor side, after dark and alone. That would not be normal behaviour for a housewife in the nineteen fifties."

The Refuge for Fallen Women where Ethel was incarcerated was later relocated within the same neighbourhood and renamed, once more, while still being operated by the Good Shepherds. In its final form, it functioned, without the commercial laundry, as the St. Mary's Euphrasia training school for girls, where Autumn was incarcerated exactly forty years later. Before beginning her search for information about her aunt, Karen had never heard about the Magdalene laundries. Her research, she told me, is frustrating because most of what she is finding about these institutions is coming out of Ireland. More work is thus needed to shed light on and clarify the inner workings of these unheard of or forgotten institutions in all the nations where they existed and where as yet no contemporary inquiries have taken place.

CONCLUSION

[F]ew people are completely unchanged or unscathed by the experience. At the very least, prison is painful, and incarcerated persons often suffer long-term consequences from having been subjected to pain, deprivation, and extremely atypical patterns and norms of living and interacting with others.

(Haney 2002, 79)

Institutionalization within the Good Shepherd regime left those I interviewed in a state of persistent distress. Neither they nor those close to them who knew about their incarcerations were fully able to put this distress behind them. The staying power of the pain incarceration caused is clearly legible in their stories. While this pain will in all likelihood persist, the public perception of these girls and women is finally changing. The climate of shame and secrecy that once inhibited the mere mention of this form of institutionalization has been improved. A far-flung change in public attitudes is in part due to the numerous public forums, inquests, reports, and apologies that have exposed transnational systemic abuses and cruelties in state- and church-supported prison and quasi-prison-like institutions and contributed over the decades to the phenomenon of "deinstitutionalization."

Apologies for state-supported abuses and cruelties have become so commonplace that, Roy Brooks (1999, 3) contends, we have entered the "Age of Apology." Brooks maintains that this apology phenomenon is more complicated than simple "contrition chic"; today's apologies, he says, are comprised of "guilt and mourning, atonement and national revival" which, in turn, raises the "moral threshold" of the society (3). Given that most human injustices "are directly related to conscious political choice" (4), it is vital that responsibility is assumed by those who made those choices so that those who suffered their consequences may be released from stigma and blame. A small but mounting awareness of the laundries has grown out of the inquiries and apologies directly related to the Magdalene laundries. From this direction has come a willingness to look beyond victim-blaming to focus instead on the social/cultural conditions that created and then ignored the unwarranted confinement of generations of girls and women.

Despite shifting attitudes and indications that, in spirit at least, many nations are willing to assume some responsibility for state-legislated confinement and injuries to these women, some critics feel that advances in this direction are tenuous. A July 4, 2017, article by *Irish Examiner* reporter Conall Ó Fátharta, for example, describes the perspective of critics who view the important 2013 state apology to Magdalenes by Irish prime minister Enda Kenny as lacking integrity. In the wake of that official apology, which included the state's recognition of its role in inmates' suffering, the Department of Justice has nevertheless argued before the UN Committee against Torture that there was no "legal advice or factual evidence" to support claims of "systematic torture or ill-treatment" of a criminal nature in the Magdalene laundries.

Internationally, Ireland led the way with its apology for the injustices suffered by former Magdalene inmates. Yet the Justice for Magdalenes Research Group views the state's new claims of a lack of evidence in documenting the nature of the laundries as devaluing that apology through "continuing dignity violations" (Ó Fátharta 2017). The state's violations, according to the group's report, included the routine incarceration of girls and women who were forced to work "unpaid for months, years, and even decades in humiliating and degrading conditions." The state's recent position, says the group, is "highly troubling ... not only because it is an obstacle to Magdalene survivors' access to justice but also because it creates significant problems from an educational and preventive point of view."

As earlier noted, there have been many roadblocks to uncovering information about these institutional captivities of the past, primarily owing to the Church's and the state's refusal to assume responsibility. However, guidance and personal insight into this history has recently been offered by those who lived through the Magdalene laundry experience and, by bringing their stories forward, risked further hurt. Such women, as the previous chapters have shown, offer abundant evidence of what it was like in these institutions, a reality which the powerful Church and state have continued to deny. Thanks to their willingness to bare their private lives to the public and, as such, place themselves under the lens of public scrutiny and criticism, they contributed immeasurably, in documenting for the public record, the details of a history that was made almost invisible. And, in so doing, their accounts address the humanity and inhumanity as well as adding substance and much more meaning to the extant documented official forms and records that have never been made available.

In examining their accounts, it is abundantly clear that contradictions exist between the Good Shepherds' official statements and what actually went on inside their institutions. The Order claims, for example, that the institutional caretakers approached each person "with the same care of Jesus, the Good Shepherd." They say too that they were "guided by the principle that 'One person is of more value than a world'" (Good Shepherd Sisters n.d.). In sharp and compelling contrast, former inmates report having been chronically discredited and degraded by the nuns, who told them repeatedly that they were bad, dirty, and unlovable. As such, they were denied contact with one another and, upon leaving, they continued to be silenced. Their sentences were extended at will, and they were subject to unrelenting and unpaid labour. They were offered at best a substandard education or denied an education altogether. Their institutional worlds meant hunger for some, lack of nutrition for most, and punishment by their overseers in the form of assault, degradation and humiliation, and solitary confinement. What went on was kept a secret, for family members were never allowed past the front parlour to see what lay beyond. Visits by family members and officials were carefully monitored, and letters home examined and censored by nuns for content. Inmates were expressly told what they could and could not say to their families. For all intents and purposes, the laundries operated as "total institutions" (Goffman 1961, 12).

As more and more of these stories are told, their many similarities create a consistent picture of what former inmates remember and describe as abuse, "slavery," and neglect. Yet so much of what they suffered is unquantifiable, such as intense insecurities and fears, which later derailed them in their personal and work lives. In hearing their accounts, it becomes increasingly difficult to comprehend how the staff of the Good Shepherd institutions could rationalize that they were working for the good of the inmates. The conditions in these institutions were also compounded by state neglect, including a failure to thoroughly inspect work and school conditions and to be accountable in ensuring a thorough documentation of inmates' medical and institutional histories when in custody, and afterwards. The Good Shepherds' claims of doing good resonates with Indigenous residential school experiences in Canada and Australia (Swain and Hillel 2010, 3), as another religious mission of protection and assimilation that embodied brutal forms of institutionalization and were sustained, as long as they were, by Church insulation from state inspections.

The unresolved distress of those I interviewed also entails the interfamilial and intergenerational impact of incarceration. Many were indirectly affected as individuals, families, and communities, who also remained silent about this history. At one level, these stories are about how, as a society, we label others; who we label; and, how shame and guilt are used to control and level people. The women whose stories fill the previous chapters have spent their entire lives trying to come to terms with these questions and, although permanently scarred, they are indeed true survivors, human beings who, in sharing their stories, help to lift the veil of silence for others.

It is significant that the last laundry closed just over twenty years ago. These institutions were repeatedly characterized by those with whom I spoke as Dickensian. So why now that they have all been closed does it remain important to document these remnants from a Victorian (and earlier) past, and why must their internal history be made known? Like Kate and other Good Shepherd inmates have emphasized, the disappearance of the physical evidence of their incarceration—where they had been locked away as bad girls—represents a denial of their lives. In my view, as a cultural sociologist, we can only gain a full picture of what went on inside if we speak to those who were placed in these institutions. The women who shared their stories said that they found comfort in knowing that someone was now writing about and giving a voice to experiences that they and/or their loved ones had borne alone for most, if not all, of their lives. They were relieved that at least their voices might survive, even though the physical proof of their incarceration has all but disappeared and been forgotten. As Kate said in frustration after seeing a photo of the laundry in which she had been incarcerated, "I saw the picture of the building and it said, 'unidentified building'—it's a government building for crying out loud, how can it be unidentified? They're hoping that it's going to die out with my generation." Quite ironically, the same architecture had now been turned into "a lovely classy retirement village."

The sense of shame the Good Shepherds intended inmates to carry had been a means of silencing them. So too was the denial of self-reflection that the nuns instilled in their charges, and indeed operated under themselves. The absence of mirrors in these Good Shepherd institutions stands as a metaphor for this renunciation of self-reflection. Dogma, work, and prayer, not inner reflection, formed the supposed route to salvation. Consequently, for all who passed through those institutions, the consistent outcome was self-estrangement, a condition that made recovery and self-understanding a long and complex process. The stigmatization that went along with their indoctrination, as bad girls and fallen women, served only to keep them quiet until some regained the fortitude to make their voices heard. Due to a public inability or unwillingness to recognize the unjust conditions under which they had been held, the voices of a daring few are what is left to represent all of those who have been shut down by the combined forces of the Good Shepherds and the state. These accounts pave the way for the acknowledgment of their and others' experiences of suffering and toil in what are now known as religious sweat shops. The troubled memories they carry, as a result, speak to us of the importance of attending to past cruelties and require proper inquiries by each of the nations who permitted the laundries to take hold, as a lawful and acceptable form of girls' and women's incarceration.

REFERENCES

Agnew, Paddy. 2014. "Reputation of Church 'Placed above Children's Best Interests.'" *The Irish Times*, February 5, 2014.

Agresta, Michael. 2012. "The Redemption of Sinead O'Connor." *The Atlantic* 10 (3). https://www.theatlantic.com/entertainment/archive/2012/10/the-redemption-of-sinead-oconnor/263020/.

Berger, Peter. 1967. *Invitation to Sociology: A Humanistic Perspective*. New York, NY: Doubleday & Company.

Bessant, Judith Cameron. 2013. "History and Australian Indigenous Child Welfare Policies." *Policy Studies* 34 (3): 310–25.

Bhabha, Homi. 1994. *The Location of Culture*. New York, NY: Routledge.

Bordo, Susan. (1993) 2004. *Unbearable Weight: Feminism, Western Culture and the Body*. 11th ed. Berkeley, CA: University of California Press.

Brooks, Roy L., ed. 1999. *When Sorry Isn't Enough: The Controversy over Apologies and Reparations for Human Injustice*. New York University Press.

Cahill, Bette L. 2006. *Butterbox Babies: Illegal Adoptions, Mysterious Deaths, Survivors—The True Story of the Ideal Maternity Home*. Rev. ed. Halifax: Fernwood Books.

Campbell, Victoria. 2013. "The Duplessis Orphans at the Canadian Museum for Human Rights: Healing through Representation." *Peace and*

Conflict: Journal of Peace Psychology 19 (4): 373–77.

CBC News. 2013. "Mount Cashel Abuse Settlement Sets Stage for More Suits." May 24, 2013. http://www.cbc.ca/news/canada/newfoundland-labrador/mount-cashel-abuse-settlement-sets-stage-for-more-suits-1.1311548.

Clear, Caitriona. 1987. *Nuns in Nineteenth Century Ireland*. Dublin: Gill and Macmillan.

Conference and Instruction of the Venerable Mother Mary of Saint Euphrasia Pelletier Foundress of the Generalate of the Congregation of the Good Shepherd of Angers. 1907. London, UK: Convent of the Good Shepherd.

Costello Wecker, Erin. 2015. "Reclaiming Magdalenism or Washing Away Sin: Magdalen Laundries and the Rhetorics of Feminine Silence." *Women's Studies* 44:264–79.

Crowe, Catriona. 2017. "Valuable Addition to History of Magdalene Laundries Uses 'Private' Records." Review of *The Monasteries, Magdalen Asylums and Reformatory Schools of Our Lady of Charity in Ireland, 1853–1973*, by Jacinta Prunty. *The Irish Times*, September 2, 2017.

Cullingford, Elizabeth Butler. 2006. "Our Nuns Are Not a Nation: Politicizing the Convent in Irish Literature and Film." *Éire-Ireland* 41 (1&2): 9–39.

Cuthbert, Denise, and Marian Quartly. 2013. "Forced Child Removal and the Politics of National Apologies in Australia." *American Indian Quarterly* 37 (1/2): 178–202.

Denzin, Norman K. 1991. *Images of Postmodern Society: Social Theory and Contemporary Cinema*. Newbury Park, CA: Sage.

Douglas, Mary. 2002. *Purity and Danger*. New York, NY: Routledge.

Erikson, Kai. 1991. "Notes on Trauma and Community." *American Imago* 48 (4): 455–72.

Fenety, G. E. 1895. *Acts of the General Assembly of His Majesty's Province of New Brunswick*. Fredericton.

Finnegan, Frances. 2004. *Do Penance or Perish: Magdalen Asylums in Ireland*. Oxford, UK: Oxford University Press.

Foucault, Michel. 1997. *Discipline and Punish: The Birth of the Prison*. New York, NY: Vintage Books.

Franklin, James. 2013. "Convent Slave Laundries? Magdalen Asylums in Australia." *Journal of the Australian Catholic Historical Society* 34:70–90.

Globe and Mail. 1919. "Limit Time of Sentence: Females Cannot Be Given Longer than Two Years in Refuges." April 12, 1919, 16.

Goffman, Erving. 1961. *Asylums: Essays on the Social Situation of Mental Patients and Other Inmates*. New York, NY: Anchor Books.

Good Shepherd Sisters. n.d. www.goodshepherdsisters.org.

Gramsci, Antonio. 1971. *Selections from the Prison Notebooks of Antonio Gramsci*. Translated and edited by Quintin Hoare and Geoffrey Nowell Smith. New York: International Publishers.

Guide for the Religious Called Sisters of Mercy Parts I and II. 1866. London, UK: Robson and Son.

Haney, Craig. 2002. "The Psychological Impact of Incarceration: Implications for Post-Prison Adjustment." Unpublished paper, Prison to Home Conference, US Department of Health and Human Services.

Human Rights and Equal Opportunity Commission. 1997. *Bringing Them Home: Report of the National Inquiry into the Separation of Aboriginal and Torres Strait Islander Children from Their Families*. Sydney: HREOC.

Iacovetta, Franca. 1999. "Gossip, Contest, and Power in the Making of Suburban Bad Girls: Toronto, 1945–60." *The Canadian Historical Review* 80 (4): 585–623.

"In Full: Enda Kenny's State Apology to the Magdalene Women." 2013. *The journal.ie*. <www.thejournal.ie/full-text-enda-kenny-magdalene-apology-801132-Feb2013/>.

Isin, Engin F., and Kim Rygiel. 2007. "Abject Spaces: Frontiers, Zones, Camps." In *The Logics of Biopower and the War on Terror: Living, Dying, Surviving*. Edited by Elizabeth Dauphinee and Christina Masters, 181–203. London, UK: Palgrave Macmillan.

Jabri, Vivienne. 2013. *The Postcolonial Subject: Claiming Politics/Governing Others in Late Modernity*. New York, NY: Routledge.

James, Diana. 2013. "Inside: 'Life in Children's Homes and Institutions.'" *reCollections: A Journal of Museums and Collections* 8 (2): 1–6.

Johnson, Brian D. 1997. "Joni's Secret: Mother and Child Reunion." *Maclean's* April 21, 1997, 49–52.

Johnston, Chris. 2013. "The Slaves of Magdalene." *The Sydney Morning Herald*, December 21, 2013.

Kilty, Jennifer M., Maritza Felices-Luna, and Sheryl C. Fabian, eds. 2014. *Demarginalizing Voices: Commitment, Emotion, and Action in Qualitative Research*. Vancouver: UBC Press.

Konstantinidis, Janice. 2013. "Life in 'The Mag.'" *Journal of the Australian Catholic Historical Society* 34:93–104.

Laycock, Margaret. 1991. *Parkdale in Pictures: Its Development to 1889*. Toronto Public Library Board Local History Handbooks: no. 7. D. Friesen & Sons Ltd.

Lorde, Audre. 1984. "Age, Race, Class and Sex: Women Defining Difference." In *Sister Outsider: Essays and Speeches*, 114–23. Freedom, CA: Crossing Press.

Luddy, M. 2001. "Moral Rescue and Unmarried Mothers in Ireland in the 1920s." *Women's Studies* 30:797–817.

Luddy, Maria. 2007. *Prostitution and Irish Society 1800–1940*. Cambridge, UK: Cambridge University Press.

Mahood, Linda. 1990. *The Magdalenes: Prostitution in the Nineteenth Century*. London, UK: Routledge.

Maynes, Mary Jo, Jennifer L. Pierce, and Barbara Laslett. 2008. *Telling Stories: The Use of Personal Narratives in the Social Sciences and History*. Ithaca, NY: Cornell University Press.

McAleese Report. 2013. "Report of the Inter-Departmental Committee to Establish the Facts of State Involvement with the Magdalen Laundries." Department of Justice and Equality.

McCarthy, Rebecca Lea. 2010. *Origins of the Magdalene Laundries: An Analytical History*. Jefferson, NC: McFarland and Company.

McKenna, Yvonne. 2006. "Embodied Ideals and Realities: Irish Nuns and

Irish Womanhood, 1930's–1960's." *Eire-Ireland* 41 (1&2): 40–63.

McMahon, Maeve. 1992. *The Persistent Prison? Rethinking Decarceration and Penal Reform*. Toronto: University of Toronto Press.

Mulvany, Charles Pelham. 1884. *Toronto: Past and Present. A Handbook of the City*. Toronto, ON: W. E. Caiger.

Myers, Tamara, and Joan Sangster. 2001. "Retorts, Runaways and Riots: Patterns of Resistance in Canadian Reform Schools for Girls, 1930–60." *Journal of Social History* 34 (3): 669–97.

National Museum Australia. 2011. *Inside: Life in Children's Homes and Institutions*. nma.gov.au/blogs/inside/.

Nicholls, Tracey. 2012. "Concerning Violence against Women: A Fanonian Analysis of Colonizing the Female Body." *e-cadernos ces*, 16. http://journals.openedition.org/eces/1047#ftn4.

Nytagodien, Ridwan Laher, and Arthur G. Neal. 2004. "Collective Trauma, Apologies, and the Politics of Memory." *Journal of Human Rights* 3 (4): 465–75.

Ó Fátharta, Conall. 2017. "Magdalene Laundry Victims Focus on State Liability." *Irish Examiner*, July 4, 2017. http://www.irishexaminer.com/ireland/magdalene-laundry-victims-focus-on-state-liability-453980.html.

Ó Fátharta, Conall. 2013. "A Moral Obligation." *Irish Examiner*, July 19, 2013. http://www.irishexaminer.com/viewpoints/analysis/a-moral-obligation-237286.html.

O'Sullivan, Eoin, and Ian O'Donnell. 2007. "Coercive Confinement in the Republic of Ireland: The Waning of a Culture of Control." *Punishment and Society* 1 (9): 27–48.

Pickard, Megan. 2011. "Interlacings of Mary Magdalene and Prostitution in Victorian Britain." MA thesis, University of Guelph. Archives Canada Heritage Branch Ottawa.

Polletta, Francesca, Pang Ching, Bobby Chen, Beth Gharrity Gardner, and Alice Motes. 2011. "The Sociology of Storytelling." *Annual Review of Sociology* 37:109–30.

Prunty, Jacinta. 2017. *The Monasteries, Magdalen Asylums and Reformatory Schools of Our Lady of Charity in Ireland, 1853–1973.* Dublin: Columba Press.

Raftery, Mary. 2003. "Restoring Dignity to Magdalens." *The Irish Times*, August 21, 2003.

Randall, Margaret. 2015. "Oral History and Memory: A Personal Journey." *Kamchatka*, no. 6 (December): 293–303.

Royal Commission of Inquiry into the Response of the Newfoundland Criminal Justice System to Complaints. 1991. St. John's, NL: Office of the Queen's Printer.

Ryan Report. 2009. *Report of the Commission to Inquire into Child Abuse*. Department of Health and Children.

Saint John Daily Sun. 1896. "The Laundrymen and the Sisters of the Good Shepherd." April 8, 1896.

Sangster, Joan. 2002. *Girl Trouble: Female Delinquency in English Canada*. Toronto: Between the Lines.

Sangster, Joan. 2001. *Regulating Girls and Women: Sexuality, Family, and the Law in Ontario, 1920–1960*. Don Mills: Oxford University Press.

Sisters of Our Lady of Charity of the Good Shepherd. 1890. *The Rule of St. Augustin and the Constitutions for the Religious of the Congregation of Our Lady of Charity of the Good Shepherd of Angers*. Toronto, ON: St. Basius Seminary.

Smith, James. 2007a. *Ireland's Magdalen Laundries and the Nation's Architecture of Containment*. Indiana: University of Notre Dame Press.

Smith, James. 2007b. "The Magdalene Sisters: Evidence, Testimony . . . Action?" *Signs: Journal of Women in Culture and Society* 32 (2): 431–58.

Spivak, Gayatri. 2007. "The New Subaltern: A Silent Interview." In *The Cultural Studies Reader*, edited by Simon During, 229–40. 3rd ed. New York: Routledge.

Spivak, Gayatri. 1996. *The Spivak Reader*. Edited by Donna Landry and Gerald MacLean. New York: Routledge.

Splane, Richard B. 1965. *Social Welfare in Ontario 1791–1893: A Study of*

Public Welfare Administration. University of Toronto Press.

State Children's Council. 1944. *Annual Report of the Children's Welfare and Public Relief Board*, 88.

Swain, Shurlee, and Margot Hillel. 2010. *Child, Nation, Race and Empire: Child Rescue Discourse, England, Canada and Australia, 1850–1915.* Manchester University Press.

"Timeline of Ireland's Catholic Abuse Scandals." 2009. *Independent*, May 20, 2009. https://www.independent.co.uk/news/world/europe/timeline-of-irelands-catholic-abuse-scandals-1688363.html.

Titley, Brian. 2017. *Into Silence and Servitude: How American Girls Became Nuns, 1945–1965.* Kingston, ON: McGill-Queen's University Press.

Titley, Brian. 2006. "Heil Mary: Magdalene Asylums and Moral Regulation in Ireland." *History of Education* 35 (2): 1–15.

Truth and Reconciliation Commission of Canada. 2015. *Honouring the Truth, Reconciling for the Future: Summary of the Final Report of the Truth and Reconciliation Commission of Canada*. www.trc.ca Library and Archives Canada Cataloguing in Publication.

Valin, Claire. 1950. "A Survey of a Shut-In Population of Dependent Girls." MA thesis, University of Ottawa.

Whitzman, Carolyn. 2003. "The Dreams Attached to Places: From Suburb, to Slum, to Urban Village in a Toronto Neighbourhood, 1875–2002." PhD diss., McMaster University.

INDEX